PRESIDENTIAL ELECTIONS AND MAJORITY RULE

PRESIDENTIAL ELECTIONS AND MAJORITY RULE

*THE RISE, DEMISE, AND POTENTIAL
RESTORATION OF THE JEFFERSONIAN
ELECTORAL COLLEGE*

EDWARD B. FOLEY

OXFORD
UNIVERSITY PRESS

OXFORD
UNIVERSITY PRESS

Oxford University Press is a department of the University of Oxford. It furthers the University's objective of excellence in research, scholarship, and education by publishing worldwide. Oxford is a registered trade mark of Oxford University Press in the UK and certain other countries.

Published in the United States of America by Oxford University Press
198 Madison Avenue, New York, NY 10016, United States of America.

Library of Congress Cataloging-in-Publication Data
Names: Foley, Edward B., author.
Title: Presidential elections and majority rule : the rise, demise, and potential restoration of the Jeffersonian electoral college / Edward B. Foley.
Description: New York, NY : Oxford University Press, 2020.
Identifiers: LCCN 2019015756 | ISBN 9780190060152 (hardback) |
ISBN 9780197582060 (paperback) |
ISBN 9780190060169 (updf) | ISBN 9780190060176 (epub)
Subjects: LCSH: Presidents—United States—Elections. | Election law—United States. | Electoral college—United States. | BISAC: LAW / Legal History. | HISTORY / Americas (North, Central, South, West Indies). | POLITICAL SCIENCE / Government / Comparative.
Classification: LCC KF4910 .F65 2020 | DDC 324.6/3—dc23
LC record available at https://lccn.loc.gov/2019015756

1 3 5 7 9 8 6 4 2

Paperback printed by Marquis, Canada

For Max and Robbie,
with love and admiration,
and in hope for their future

CONTENTS

PREFACE

———— ∞ ————

THIS BOOK ORIGINATED in the classroom. The second unit of the Election Law course, as I teach it, concerns how candidates get on the ballot and the relationship between primary and general elections. Over the last decade or so, as part of our discussion of this topic, my students and I have focused on presidential elections and whether America's existing system for winnowing the field of many contenders, before the primaries begin, to a single winner in November is a sensible process. Because a couple of the court cases we read concern independent presidential candidates, like John Anderson in 1980 and Ralph Nader in 2000, who have sought the right to be on the general election ballot in November after the party primaries have reduced the field to two major-party nominees, we have considered especially what should be the relationship between the initial narrowing of the primary process and the subsequent addition of third-party and independent candidates. Does America, we ask, use a rational method for choosing its commander-in-chief?

Increasingly concerned that the answer to this question is "no," and in anticipation of the 2016 election before it began, I took my interest in this topic out of the classroom and into the library. Fortunate to be invited to a symposium on the law of presidential elections, held at Fordham Law School, I explored methods for managing the role that independent and minor-party candidates can play, even after the two major parties have settled on their nominees. When I began this research, Michael Bloomberg was seriously contemplating an independent bid and easily could have been a major factor in the race. Indeed, precisely because he could not run without tipping the race in a direction he did not prefer, he ultimately declined to enter the contest. His decision made it seem as if the system had escaped from having to cope that year with a three-way race that it was ill equipped to handle.

Then came the results of the 2016 general election. While most everyone else was focused on the fact that Donald Trump won the Electoral College with almost 3 million fewer votes nationally than Hillary Clinton, I was struck by an entirely different statistic: 107 of Trump's Electoral College votes, about one-third of the 304 he received, came from states in which Trump won less than 50 percent of the popular vote. Trump could not reach the 270-vote threshold necessary for an Electoral College victory without at least some of these sub–50 percent states. Although Bloomberg had decided not to run, it turned out that additional candidates besides Trump and Clinton played a role in the race. My concern was not proving whether Trump or Clinton would have won if these other candidates had not been on the ballot. Rather, what worried me was that the 2016 election demonstrated that America's system for electing presidents is incapable of including independent and third-party candidates on the November general election ballot without the significant risk that their presence will alter which major-party candidate prevails. Moreover, as 2016 also showed, this significant risk exists even when each of the extra candidates receives only a very small percentage of the vote (below 5 percent).

Given this troubling assessment of what happened in 2016, it seemed necessary to revisit the initial research I had undertaken for the Fordham symposium and to analyze the issue more systematically. Starting with the goal of finding a policy solution in the political science literature on alternative voting systems, the project quickly took a historical turn. Knowing that the Twelfth Amendment (the part of the Constitution establishing the Electoral College system that operates today) requires that a candidate win a majority of Electoral College votes in order to be president, I was curious what the authors of the Twelfth Amendment would have thought of the sub–50 percent wins that Trump used to achieve his Electoral College majority. I had no idea what I would find.

I was absolutely amazed to discover how deeply and extensively the authors of the Twelfth Amendment thought about implementing a fundamental commitment to majority rule in the specific context of electing the chief executive of a federated republic. In the course of conducting this research, I also realized just how important it is to recognize that the Electoral College in the Twelfth Amendment rests on an entirely different animating philosophy than the Electoral College that was the product of the Constitutional Convention in 1787. This innovative vision was fully articulated and thoroughly deliberated in the debates that led to the adoption of the Twelfth Amendment. Yet knowledge of this innovation has largely disappeared.

Having unexpectedly discovered the rich philosophical discourse underlying the Twelfth Amendment, I also wanted to understand why and how America's knowledge of this crucial component of its constitutional system essentially vanished. That disappearance is another historical story, one that takes place over the course of the nineteenth and twentieth centuries. Figuring out this story required considerable additional research and led to more unexpected discoveries, like the largely unrecognized significance of the 1844 election, or how Lincoln's victory in 1860 should be understood as the Twelfth Amendment working as intended, not as an errant outcome. It became the purpose of this book to convey the totality of the history relevant for understanding how America has a system that can produce an Electoral College majority based on sub–50 percent victories in pivotal states.

This book is the second in which I have turned to history in order to address a contemporary policy problem. The first book, *Ballot Battles*, used history to develop the basis for an institutional reform to reduce the taint of partisanship affecting the decisions made in recounts and other vote-counting disputes. This second book uses the history of the Twelfth Amendment's animating philosophy and subsequent ignorance of that philosophy to point the way to how it can be revived—and how this revitalization can solve the problem of sub–50 percent victories in pivotal states that produce presidents who are elected with the support of only a minority, rather than a majority, of voters.

I am immensely grateful to Oxford University Press, and especially David McBride, for encouraging and nurturing both of these history-based books. I am thankful, too, for all of Holly Mitchell's very helpful editorial assistance at Oxford. Many friends and colleagues, at Ohio State and elsewhere, provided extensive and insightful comments on various previous drafts: Paul Beck, Les Benedict, Robert Bennett, R. B. Bernstein, Richard Briffault, Josh Douglas, Michael Flamm, Anthony Gaughan, Jonathan Gienapp, Mark Graber, Rick Hasen, Vlad Kogan, Ann Kornhauser, Larry Lessig, Michael Morley, Derek Muller, Drew Penrose, Rick Pildes, Rob Richie, Lori Ringhand, Nancy Rogers, Peter Shane, Dave Stebenne, Charles Stewart, Dan Tokaji, Franita Tolson, Chris Walker, and Chuck Zelden. I am deeply indebted to them all. Two of these readers deserve special thanks: my great friend Steve Huefner and my wonderful wife, Miranda Cox, supplied essentially line-by-line edits and suggestions on a near-final draft, all of which improved the exposition of the book's ideas and collectively make for a much better text.

Down the stretch, I had a great group of student research assistants helping get the manuscript, especially its notes, into shape: Frank Bumb, Kaela King, Zach Leciejewski, Sophia Mills, Sean Patchin, Jacob Schermer, and Connor Strait. Cathy Thompson, Allyson Hennelly, and especially Brenda Robinson contributed excellent administrative support, including careful proofreading, and so much more: readers will see a lot of numbers in this book, and this team painstakingly verified the accuracy of all these numbers. Brenda and Allyson also employed their word-processing wizardry to format all the tables to make them as reader-friendly as possible. Daphne Meimaridis, who administers the election law program at Ohio State, supported this book project in various ways, including helping to organize several events on this topic, and did so with her usual skill and good cheer.

I appreciate that Politico Magazine provided the opportunity to write an essay summarizing basic themes of the book. Margy Slattery was a superb editor there, and conversations with her helped to hone key points. Susan Johnson, as a friend and productivity consultant, continues to give me regular and wise advice. As with *Ballot Battles*, I could not have kept the writing and revision of this book on track were it not for Susan's exceptionally helpful guidance. Every author should be so fortunate to have Susan, or someone just like her, to function as a coach from start to finish of the marathon that writing a book inevitably is.

Also like *Ballot Battles*, although even more so, this book owes an intellectual debt to Alex Keyssar and his work. Alex has been writing his own definitive study of the history of efforts to reform or replace the Electoral College, and he has been generous to share not only the drafts of his chapters as they become available, but also his time and insights as we have conversed about our overlapping projects. He, too, has provided extensive and exceptionally valuable feedback on earlier drafts of this book. The degree to which this book builds upon, and is inspired by, Alex's work should be readily apparent to readers.

Above all, Matt Cooper has my unending gratitude for his essential role in this book's creation. As a law librarian, Matt found much of the historical materials that form the basis of the book. Others in the fantastic law library at Ohio State were also involved. Paul Gatz, in particular, played a critical role in collecting and analyzing statutory materials at an early stage of the project, and he undoubtedly would have been an equal partner along with Matt in completing the project had illness not taken him away from the law school lately. Still, Paul's great work is very much reflected in what is written here. Kaylie Vermillion, as the library's circulation manager, kept track of all the books necessary for this project—no easy task, especially given the way I work with books during the writing process.

As great and essential as the library as a whole has been, Matt's involvement with this book has been extra special. He and I have worked on it together, all the way through from beginning to end. We planned what sources to seek out, how to go about collecting them (although in truth Matt did most of that), how to understand what we discovered (especially the significance of specific pieces of historical data in relationship to the overall context of what we were finding), and verifying the accuracy of all the materials ultimately relied upon. This book would not exist without Matt. He knows it, and every reader should as well.

Introduction

THE ELECTORAL COLLEGE system that governs presidential elections today was designed for competitive races between the candidates of two opposing political parties. Think of Jefferson versus Adams in 1800. Or Eisenhower versus Stevenson twice in the 1950s. Or Obama's two campaigns, first against McCain in 2008, and then against Romney in 2012.

But despite its two-party design, the Electoral College system as it currently operates permits the presence of third-party and independent candidates. Teddy Roosevelt in 1912. Ross Perot in 1992. Ralph Nader in 2000.

Although allowing more than two candidates, the existing system cannot handle them well—at least not while keeping true to its goal of electing presidents based on the principle of majority rule. Fortunately, it has not often produced presidents in contravention of majority rule. Unfortunately, however, it has done so several times and may do so again with increasing frequency.

How the Electoral College process ended up capable of violating its own commitment to majority rule, how the process may be reformed to restore fidelity to majority rule, and how this reform may be achieved without need of a constitutional amendment, are the stories this book tells.

The Problem

Imagine a three-way presidential race between Tinker, Evers, and Chance. Suppose Tinker gets 43 percent of the vote, Evers 42 percent, and Chance 15 percent. Should Tinker win the White House on that basis?

Suppose further that in a second round of voting, with Chance eliminated, Evers pulls ahead with 52 percent, and Tinker comes up short with only 48 percent. In other words, the first-round support for Chance splits two-to-one in favor of Evers. In this case, is Evers more deserving to win the presidency than Tinker?

Many would think so. After all, Evers wins more votes than Tinker when the two face off against each other in a one-on-one matchup. Evers also secures majority support among the electorate, after the weakest of the three candidates (in terms of being the first choice of voters) is removed from the race. Indeed, Evers's majority over Tinker, 52–48, is a substantial 4-point spread. It would seem odd to let Tinker win in this situation, knowing that a majority of voters decisively prefer Evers over Tinker.

The Electoral College, as it currently operates, lets exactly that happen. The Constitution's provisions concerning the Electoral College permit states to choose the method by which they appoint their presidential electors. Although it was not this way in the beginning, most states now use a system of "plurality winner-take-all" by which the candidate with the most popular votes, even if not a majority, receives all of a state's electoral votes. At present, only Maine and Nebraska deviate from this statewide winner-take-all system, instead using a district-based alternative to appoint some of their presidential electors. (More details in Chapter 7.)

With plurality winner-take-all, Tinker could win an Electoral College landslide even though a majority of voters would prefer Evers to be president. Suppose that in all the key swing states, the three-way split between Tinker, Evers, and Chance mirrors the overall national three-way split: 43 percent for Tinker, 42 percent for Evers, and 15 percent for Chance. With this result in Florida, for example, Tinker would get all of Florida's 29 electoral votes, despite the fact that Floridians prefer Evers over Tinker 52–48—as would be shown by the kind of head-to-head runoff just described.

The same would be true for Pennsylvania's 20 electoral votes: Tinker would get them all, based on his 43–42 plurality "win" over Evers, even though Evers would beat Tinker 52–48 in a runoff. And so on for all the other swing states—Ohio with its 18 electoral votes, North Carolina with 15, Arizona with 11, Wisconsin with 10—where Tinker has a plurality of 43 percent because of the three-way split. By racking up these plurality victories, Tinker dominates Evers in the Electoral College, whereas the reverse would be true if all of these swing states had used runoffs. Evers would defeat Tinker 52–48 in all these same swing states, if the states required a runoff to determine which candidate gets the benefit of winner-take-all. Thus, the outcome in the Electoral College depends entirely on whether or not states use plurality winner-take-all.

This situation is not merely theoretical. As this book is being edited in 2019, it is entirely conceivable that the presidential election in 2020 will boil down to a three-way race between incumbent Donald Trump running for re-election, the Democratic Party's nominee (whoever that turns out to be), and some third candidate—perhaps, for example, former Ohio governor John Kasich—running as an independent.[1] Trump could be the plurality winner with 43 percent of the vote, with the Democratic nominee receiving 42 percent and Kasich 15 percent.[2] Yet if there were a runoff between Trump and the Democrat, it easily could be that the Democrat gets 52 percent and Trump only 48 percent, because Kasich supporters break two-to-one in favor of the Democrat.[3] Assuming as with the hypothetical example that this pattern essentially repeats itself in swing state after swing state, then under plurality winner-take-all Trump would prevail in the Electoral College, even though a majority of voters in each of these swing states prefers the Democrat.

But the roles could be reversed: the Democrat receiving 43 percent, Trump receiving 42 percent, and Kasich supporters in a runoff breaking two-to-one in favor of Trump rather than the Democrat. Now the Democrat would be the mere plurality winner who triumphs in the Electoral College despite the fact that the majority of voters prefer Trump to the Democrat in a head-to-head runoff.

One should view this outcome as problematic, whether it happens to favor Trump or the Democrat. There is a fundamental procedural choice between (1) requiring the winner of a presidential election to receive majority support from the voters, even if doing so entails the need for a runoff procedure; and (2) letting a mere plurality winner become president, even if a majority of voters prefers another candidate. This procedural choice should be based on a long-term, nonpartisan view about what is best for American democracy. It should not be made simply to achieve a partisan victory in the next election.

This book will explore the complexities that underlie this superficially straightforward choice. As between a mere plurality winner and a genuinely majority-preferred candidate, what nonpartisan analysis would not want the majority-preferred candidate to prevail? But it turns out that it can be a challenge to identify the one true majority-preferred candidate in a three-way race, or indeed in any race with more than two candidates. Still, even after exploring these complexities, this book will return to the basic idea that identifying a majority-preferred candidate is generally better—more consistent with the idea of popular sovereignty underlying democracy—than letting a mere plurality winner prevail.

To be clear, a third candidate does not always affect the outcome between the first two. If Chance's supporters preferred Tinker to Evers, then eliminating Chance from the race would simply increase Tinker's margin over Evers and make Tinker the majority-preferred candidate. For example, assume Chance's supporters split in the same two-to-one ratio, but this time in favor of Tinker rather than Evers. Then, Tinker would end up with 53 percent, rather than the initial 43 percent, and Evers would still trail with 47 percent, instead of the initial 42 percent. The failure to use a runoff in this situation, while causing Tinker officially to remain only a plurality winner (below 50 percent), does not change which candidate ultimately gets to hold office as a result of the election.

Some third-party presidential candidates have been inconsequential in this way. For example, in 1968 George Wallace won 13.53 percent of the popular vote nationally. Richard Nixon was the plurality winner with 43.42 percent, and Hubert Humphrey was close behind with 42.72 percent. Wallace would have made the difference if his supporters had preferred Humphrey to Nixon. But political scientists analyzing voter preferences in the race have concluded that in a runoff Wallace supporters would have preferred Nixon to Humphrey. This analysis, moreover, applies not merely with respect to the national popular vote but also with respect to the key states that determined Nixon's victory in the Electoral College. Thus, Wallace's presence in the race ultimately was not a factor in causing Nixon to win the presidency in 1968.[4]

But over the course of US history, the presence of other third-party candidates *has* determined which of the two major-party candidates won the Electoral College. For example, it is widely known that the 2000 presidential election ultimately turned on whether George Bush or Al Gore won Florida.[5] Although the legal controversies that year focused on problems in the mechanics of how voters cast their ballots—in particular, whether "punch card" voting machines produced "hanging chads" that the technology improperly failed to count as votes—there is little doubt that none of those problems would have mattered if Bush and Gore had been the only two candidates on the ballot.

Ralph Nader's presence on the ballot, in particular, had the effect of causing Gore to lose to Bush. Nader won almost 100,000 votes in Florida that year—97,488, to be precise. With Bush's officially certified margin of victory over Gore at 537, and most Nader supporters viewing Gore as preferable to Bush, it is straightforward to conclude that Gore would have pulled comfortably ahead of Bush if Nader had been eliminated from the race.[6] (None of the other candidates on the ballot that year would have affected this conclusion.) Thus 2000 is a year in which, as between the two main candidates, the one whom the majority of voters preferred lost, while the one whom the majority of voters wanted to lose was declared the winner. This point is true not only nationally but in the pivotal state, Florida, that decided the race in the Electoral College.

It is debatable whether 2016 was another version of this story, with the Libertarian candidate Gary Johnson playing a similar role to Ralph Nader's in 2000. It is also possible that Gary Johnson was more like George Wallace in 1968, ultimately inconsequential in determining which major-party candidate prevailed in the Electoral College—in this instance, either Donald Trump or Hillary Clinton. Our detailed analysis, and thus ultimate appraisal, of how the Electoral College operated in 2016 must wait until Chapter 6. But even the possibility that Gary Johnson might have been the decisive factor in whether Trump or Clinton won the Electoral College, and thus became president, should be disturbing.

The powers of the presidency today are so immense, and so much greater than originally conceived, that the prospect of presidential elections turning on an "accident" of how a third candidate affects which main competitor prevails is far more horrifying now than it was in the nineteenth century. And an accident is exactly how Americans thought of this problem when it first occurred, in 1844, as we shall explore in Chapter 4. Whether or not this same kind of accident happened in 2016, as it surely did in 2000, the uncomfortable but undeniable truth is that it could happen again. In 2020 John Kasich, or another third candidate, easily could reprise the role of Ralph Nader, determining whether Trump or the Democrat wins the next election. Even more to the point, and what would make it an accident, is the prospect that in this scenario Kasich (like Nader) would be causing one candidate to win despite a majority of voters—both nationally and in the pivotal states for purposes of the Electoral College—actually preferring the other major-party candidate.

The Project

How did the United States end up with an electoral system that permits this kind of perverse result? It certainly was not by design. As this book will elaborate, the architects of the Electoral College that America still uses fervently wanted the winner to be the candidate who had support from the majority of the electorate in the states that formed the candidate's Electoral College victory. They clearly cared about majority rule. They insisted that to be president a candidate must win a majority, and not merely a plurality, of Electoral College votes. Moreover, they adopted a kind of runoff in the event that no candidate wins an Electoral College majority. The runoff calls for a special procedure in the House of Representatives, in which each state's delegation has a single vote (in other words, one vote per state regardless of how many representatives a state sends to Congress). Demonstrating just how strongly they felt about majority rule, the architects of the Electoral

College required that to win this runoff a candidate receive the votes of a majority of all states, not merely a plurality of all states, or even a majority of states casting votes in a situation where some states abstain or otherwise fail to vote.

But the system has not always operated as intended. Instead, its majoritarian premises and expectations have eroded during the past two centuries, since the current constitutional provisions on the Electoral College were drafted in 1803 and ratified the following year in time for the next presidential election.[7] Nor is this erosion the first malfunctioning of the Electoral College. The initial version of the system, adopted as part of the original Constitution in the Philadelphia Convention of 1787, backfired catastrophically in 1800. The 1803 fix, the product of extensive and erudite deliberations in Congress, was supposed to assure the Electoral College's consistency with the fundamental republican ideal of majority rule. Yet it has not worked out that way.

This book tells the underappreciated story of the Electoral College's majoritarian foundations. The Electoral College of 1803—*our* Electoral College, because it is the one that still governs us—was designed to yield winners in the mold of Thomas Jefferson's majoritarian mandate in 1800 (and the anticipated confirmation of that majoritarian mandate in his 1804 re-election). The book then demonstrates how, despite this design, in subsequent operation the Electoral College has deviated from its animating Jeffersonian vision. The book, however, explains that the majoritarian ideal of the Jeffersonian Electoral College is not lost forever. Rather, the book shows how, through changes in state laws and without need for a constitutional amendment, it is possible to reform the Electoral College so that it performs according to its original majoritarian expectations. The book discusses why this reform would be both desirable and feasible—indeed, desirable compared to some enthusiastically proposed alternatives in large part because it is far more feasible.

A restoration of the Jeffersonian vision underlying the Electoral College of 1803, it must be acknowledged at the outset, would not make presidential elections turn on identifying the majority winner of the national popular vote. The Jeffersonian vision, as will become clear in Part One of this book, seeks to identify a distinctive kind of majority winner suitable for a federal republic: a compound majority in which a majority vote in the Electoral College itself is achieved by securing a majority of the popular vote in the states that create the Electoral College majority. To return to the hypothetical example with which this book began: according to the Jeffersonian vision, the issue is not whether Evers would beat Tinker in a unified national runoff if Chance were eliminated from the race. Instead, the issue is whether Evers would beat Tinker in a head-to-head race in enough states to achieve an Electoral College majority if Chance were removed from consideration in each of those states.[8]

Now, one might ask, if majority rule is the goal, why bother with the complexity of the Jeffersonian vision and its compound form of majoritarianism? Why not, instead, adopt a simple national runoff? After all, many other countries—including France most prominently (as a major Western democracy with a presidential rather than parliamentary system)—use a simple national runoff to guarantee that the winners of their presidential elections have majority support from the electorate.[9]

The answer is that a simple national runoff would require a constitutional amendment. History, however, has demonstrated the monumental difficulty of eliminating, or even modifying, the Electoral College by means of constitutional amendment—at least since the Jeffersonian alteration of 1803.[10] For the foreseeable future, as a practical matter, America is stuck with the same constitutional provisions that established the Jeffersonian Electoral College in 1803.

Yet at present America follows the constitutional rules of the Jeffersonian Electoral College while abandoning its underlying majoritarian philosophy and expectations. The result is a situation far worse than the operation of the 1803 Electoral College in accord with its original Jeffersonian vision. The compound conception of majority rule that forms the basis of the Jeffersonian vision remains suitable for the United States, which fundamentally is still a federal republic. Until America is able to eliminate the Electoral College entirely, the next best thing—and a thoroughly worthy and achievable goal—is to restore the 1803 Electoral College (our existing Electoral College) to its original Jeffersonian premises.

Part One

The Rise of the Jeffersonian Electoral College

I

The Electoral College of 1787

THE ELECTORAL COLLEGE that governs presidential elections today is not the Electoral College included in the original Constitution of 1787. This important fact is mostly overlooked. Still, one should not completely ignore what happened in 1787 with the creation of the Electoral College. It serves as the backdrop for the redesign of the Electoral College by Congress in 1803. To understand what Congress did that year, and why, it is necessary first to know what Congress was reacting to and replacing.[1]

The key distinction between the initial Electoral College of 1787 and the subsequent Electoral College of 1803, above all else, is the archetypal winning candidate who animates each system. In 1787 the archetype was George Washington; being the consensus choice of all Americans, he was above the fray of partisan politics.[2] In 1803 the archetype was Thomas Jefferson, who as the standard-bearer of one political party fighting ferociously against the opposing party was hardly a consensus choice, but rather was more deserving than his opponent because he, rather than his opponent, was able to secure a federal form of majoritarian support by amassing majority support of the electorate in enough states. Just as the authors of the 1787 Electoral College were looking forward to Washington's victory under the system they had just built, so too were the architects of the 1803 Electoral College looking forward to Jefferson's unambiguously triumphal victory the following year under their redesigned system.[3]

The feature of the first Electoral College most specifically designed to produce a consensual winner was the requirement that each elector cast two votes for president, of equal weight and for different candidates, with at least one of the two votes cast for a candidate from a state other than the elector's home state. The exact language of the original Constitution was that "the electors shall . . . vote by ballot for two persons, of whom one at least shall not be an inhabitant of the same state as themselves." The intent of this provision was to cause electors to identify a second candidate, with the choice based on the elector's conception of the national interest rather than any parochial concerns. If the elector's first-choice candidate was from the elector's home state, then the second-choice candidate must be from elsewhere. By making second-choice votes entirely undifferentiated from first-choice votes (both counted exactly the same), the Philadelphia delegates hoped that a clear consensual candidate might rise to the top from receiving a large number of second-choice votes combined with a smattering of first-choice votes.[4]

Even as the delegates designed this two-vote system to induce a consensual winner, they were careful to include a majority-rule requirement as part of picking the winner. It was not enough that a candidate receive the largest number of equally weighted first-choice and second-choice votes. Instead, to win the presidency in the 1787 Electoral College, a candidate must *both* win more votes than any other candidate (counting first-choice or second-choice equally, since the system did not differentiate between the two) *and* the candidate's total number of votes must amount to a majority of electors. In the exact words of the original Constitution: "The person having the greatest number of votes shall be the President, if such number be a majority of the whole number of electors appointed."[5]

The original Constitution contained a runoff mechanism in the event that no candidate received votes from a majority of electors.[6] The runoff was limited to the candidates with the five highest numbers of electoral votes. These names were to go to the House of Representatives. With "the representation of each state" having one vote, the House selected a winner from among these candidates. But to win in the House, a candidate had to receive votes from "a majority of all the states." (A similar runoff was to occur in the House if two or more candidates in the initial round were tied for the largest number of electoral votes, each with a majority as was possible given that each elector cast two votes. The only difference is that in this case the House runoff was limited solely to those tied candidates.) The Philadelphia delegates expected that after Washington's retirement the runoff mechanism would be used quite frequently, as the fledgling nation might lack candidates of sufficient national stature to emerge as a consensus second choice among a majority of electors, who were required by the Constitution to cast their votes in separate meetings of the electors appointed in each state, rather than in a single nationwide convention of all electors. In this respect, the delegates anticipated that the Electoral College would function rather more often as a kind of nominating mechanism, sending five names to the House, where the actual election would take place with consideration confined to these five candidates.[7]

Although the 1787 Electoral College mechanism was assembled in haste at the end of the Constitutional Convention (a point to which we shall return in Chapter 3, when comparing the 1787 deliberations to those in 1803), its elements of majority rule were far from happenstance. The delegates specifically considered—but overwhelmingly rejected— a proposal to abandon the requirement that a candidate receive votes from a majority of electors in order to avoid a runoff. The proposal, initially advocated by both Madison and Hamilton, responded to the fact that the first draft of the Electoral College process would have had the Senate, rather than the House, choose the president when no candidate won votes from a majority of electors. Madison and Hamilton, among other delegates, objected to giving this power to the Senate because senators were not directly elected by citizens, but instead appointed by state legislatures. They thought that presidential elections should be more reflective of popular will than a choice made by an "aristocratic" Senate. Wishing to reduce the chances of a runoff reaching the Senate, they sought to eliminate the requirement that a candidate obtain support from a majority, rather than a mere plurality, of electors.[8]

The Convention rejected two versions of this proposal by successive votes of 9–2 and 8–3. One version would have let any plurality of electoral votes suffice to win the presidency. The other version would have required a candidate to win votes from at least one-third of electors in order to avoid a runoff in the Senate.[9]

The issue became moot when Roger Sherman proposed that the runoff occur in the House, rather than the Senate, but with each state's delegation in the House having a single vote to mimic the equal voting power of each state in the Senate. Sherman's solution immediately received widespread support, passing 10–1 in the Convention.[10] Madison himself signaled his acceptance of the runoff, now that it was in the House instead of the Senate. He offered an amendment to Sherman's proposal to require that a majority of all states, not merely a majority of participating states, be necessary to win a runoff in the House. Madison explained that if too many states abstained in the runoff, a majority of participating states might not reflect genuine majority support of the states or the citizenry and thus would be an insufficient basis upon which to elect a president. The Convention readily accepted Madison's amendment, thereby confirming its commitment to the principle of majority rule in presidential elections.[11]

To be sure, the commitment to majority rule reflected in the Electoral College of 1787 was not a simple majority vote of the entire American electorate. The Philadelphia Convention contemplated that idea but rejected it as impractical for the kind of federal republic that the new Constitution was creating. Roger Sherman, for one, objected to the idea on the ground that there would be too many candidates, with the consequence that the electorate regularly would fail to "give a majority of votes to any one man."[12]

Consequently, the Philadelphia Convention established the Electoral College as a device for obtaining a distinctive form of majority vote suitable for a federal system. The Convention gave each state the power to choose the method for appointing the state's electors. The delegates anticipated that the states would use this power to reflect their own particular interests.[13] Madison reflected this basic view when, looking back years later, he spoke of "the advantage possessed by the [larger states] in selecting the Candidates from the people," in contrast to the countervailing balance in favor of the smaller states if and when a runoff reached the House.[14] Madison's conception of this equilibrium would not be possible without thinking of the electors as acting on behalf of their states when casting their Electoral College votes.

Thus, in 1787 the Philadelphia delegates expected that a state's electors would reflect the will of the majority in that state. By also requiring a presidential candidate to obtain approval from a majority of electors, the delegates envisioned that they were creating a compound form of majority rule: a winning presidential candidate must obtain a majority-of-majorities. An Electoral College majority, forged from majority support within enough states to secure votes from a majority of electors, could be considered a special federated majority. Whereas simple majority rule made sense for a simple republic, this compound or federated majority rule was appropriate for the kind of federal republic that the United States was becoming under the new Constitution.[15]

As much as the Philadelphia delegates clearly preferred majority rule to permitting mere plurality winners, their embrace of majority rule was nonetheless uneasy. Above all, as is well known to any reader of the *Federalist Papers*, the authors of the Constitution abhorred control of government by any faction. In their eyes, a faction could be either a minority or majority of the populace. The key feature of a faction is that it advances its own narrow self-interest instead of the overall public interest. Moreover, a tyrannical faction could be a tyranny of the majority, oppressive of minority rights, as much as a tyranny of a minority, subjugating the majority.[16]

As part of their effort to thwart any form of government control by faction, the authors of the Constitution designed the 1787 Electoral College not only to embrace majority rule in its distinctive federated form, but also to include its two-vote feature in the hope of producing a winning candidate with widespread support, who would not be beholden to any faction but instead would govern in the overall public interest.[17] The system worked initially, insofar as George Washington was the clear consensus choice to be the first president, as the delegates had anticipated. But, with Washington's retirement after two terms, the system broke down in 1796 and then in 1800 failed spectacularly.

2

The First Four Elections

BY THE TIME the Eighth Congress met in 1803 to redesign the Electoral College, its members had direct and detailed knowledge of the four presidential elections that had taken place under the 1787 version of the system. That familiarity is equivalent to our own first-hand experience with the four presidential elections of 2004, 2008, 2012, and 2016. Although living through and learning from four presidential elections is hardly the same as an in-depth historical analysis of all 58 presidential elections since the Constitution was created, the initial quartet of elections was enough to give the Eighth Congress a strong sense of how the 1787 Electoral College operated, as well as firm views on which elements should be retained and which required amendment.

This experience, most significantly, conditioned members of the Eighth Congress to believe that states would exercise their power to appoint presidential electors in a way that reflected the prevailing political perspective within each state. In particular, once intense two-party competition emerged during the elections of 1796 and 1800, politicians from both parties understood that state legislatures would select methods of appointing electors that would enable the dominant party in each state to promote its own presidential candidate.

The Very First Election

For the first presidential election, although it was foreordained that George Washington would win—he indeed unanimously received one vote from every elector—the states still needed to adopt implementing procedures to effectuate this choice.[1] Because the Constitution gave the states the power to choose the method of appointing their electors, the initial task for each state was to select a method of appointment. Only 10 of the original 13 states participated in that first vote of the Electoral College. Rhode Island and North Carolina had not ratified the new Constitution in time. In New York, the two chambers of the state legislature disagreed over the specific procedure that it would use to appoint the state's electors: the smaller state senate wanted separate balloting in the two chambers, with the need for both chambers to concur in an elector's appointment, while the larger state assembly wanted a single ballot of both chambers convening together as one combined body.[2] Because New York's two legislative chambers could not resolve this disagreement, the state failed to appoint any electors for this first operation of the Electoral College system.

Of the 10 states that did participate, three had their legislatures appoint their electors directly, thereby accomplishing what New York could not: Connecticut, South Carolina, and Georgia.[3] A fourth state, New Jersey, exercised a variation on this theme. It enacted a law that authorized the state's governor and privy council, which functioned as the upper chamber of the state's legislature, to name the state's electors.[4] Thus in these four states, the state's own government retained control over the appointment of the state's electors. Nonetheless, according to the fundamental principle of republican government upon which these states were founded in the American Revolution, the governments of those four states reflected the will of the citizenry in each state. Insofar as this fundamental republican principle held true, the presidential electors in those states would reflect—albeit indirectly through the mechanism of their governmental appointment—the sentiment of the citizenry in those states.

The six other participating states let their citizens vote for who should serve as presidential electors. Two of these six, Virginia and Delaware, adopted district-based systems in which the voters of each district would choose one of the state's electors. Virginia, the most populous state, had 12 electors, and Delaware, the least populous, had three. In each district, the person receiving the most votes would be appointed the elector for that district.[5] Although this district-based voting permitted

plurality winners in each district, it did not permit a statewide plurality
to appoint all the electors of a state. Instead, if one political faction was
dominant in one region of a state, while a different political faction
dominated another region, then the two factions would split control
over appointment of the state's electors, with each faction controlling
appointment of some but not all the electors.

Massachusetts adopted a hybrid system in which the voters of each
congressional district would cast ballots for candidates to serve as presidential elector from that district, and the names of the two candidates
receiving the largest number of votes in each district would be sent to
the state's legislature, which would then choose one of those two to
be the elector for that district.[6] This hybrid system, essentially an automatic legislative runoff between the top two candidates in each district, was a way of guaranteeing that no candidate would be appointed
elector for a district based on a mere plurality of votes from the district. Because the winning candidate would need to receive a majority
vote in the legislature (with the two legislative chambers sitting as a
single body for this purpose), this system necessarily was a form of majority rule. Massachusetts, among all the original states, was especially
committed to majority rule by virtue of its 1780 constitution, drafted
primarily by John Adams.[7] Massachusetts required majority—and not
merely plurality—votes for other elective offices, including governor.[8]
Its initial method for appointing presidential electors was consistent
with the state's overall majority-rule philosophy. (The state's two other
presidential electors, not allocated to congressional districts, were appointed "at large" by majority votes of the state's legislature and hence
also reflective of the state's philosophical preference for majority, rather
than plurality, rule.)

New Hampshire, like Massachusetts, also insisted upon majority
rule for the appointment of its presidential electors, but it did so in
a different—and more straightforward—way. In an entirely statewide
system, without any form of districting, New Hampshire let all the
voters of the state cast ballots for all five of the state's electors.[9] But for
a candidate to become an elector, the state law required that the candidate receive votes from a majority of voters. Otherwise, for each of
the five electors not chosen by a majority of voters, the state legislature
would receive the names of the two candidates who had obtained the

highest number of votes. From these names, the legislature would fill the vacant elector positions.[10] As it happened, the New Hampshire legislature needed to conduct this runoff procedure for all five electors, choosing among 10 names that it received based on their popular-vote totals, because no candidate obtained popular votes from a majority of the electorate.[11]

For the first presidential election, only Pennsylvania and Maryland adopted a statewide popular vote without any form of majority-rule requirement as the method for appointing the state's presidential electors. Maryland's version of this system was distinctive insofar as it required five of the state's eight electors to be inhabitants of the western portion of the state and the other three to be residents of the state's eastern shore.[12] But there is no indication that either Pennsylvania or Maryland omitted a majority-rule requirement because of a deliberate and considered preference for plurality-winner elections. In both states (as in others at the time), politics already had produced a basic division between two groups: supporters of the new Constitution, known as Federalists; and opponents, called anti-Federalists.[13] With politics cleaved in this way, the popular vote for presidential electors would be between two choices: a slate of Federalist candidates and a competing slate of anti-Federalists. Because there were only two slates, whichever slate prevailed would reflect support from the majority of the voters in the state. There was no practical possibility of a third slate of candidates that would cause the winning slate, either Federalist or anti-Federalist, to have the support of a mere plurality in the state. Also, as it turned out, in both states the Federalist slate of electors received overwhelming majority support from the voters, resoundingly defeating their anti-Federalist opponents.[14]

Thus despite the variety of methods chosen for appointing electors, the states conformed to the expectation that the votes cast by each state's electors would represent the will of the majority in that state.

Washington's Re-Election in 1792

As the new nation prepared for its second presidential election, sharp partisan divisions began to emerge among members of Washington's cabinet and their respective allies in Congress. Hamilton and Adams were on one side, bearing the Federalist mantle. Madison and Jefferson led the opposition, calling themselves Republicans. Washington, however, remained above the partisan fray and was the clear consensual choice for a second term.[15]

To conduct this second election in accordance with the 1787 constitutional rules, the states needed to revisit the issue of what method they should employ to appoint their electors.[16] The overwhelming preference among the states this time was direct appointment by the state's legislature. Nine of the now 15 states used this method, including the four states that had adopted it for the first election (Connecticut, South Carolina, Georgia, and, in its own special form, New Jersey).[17] Four states that had not participated in the first election also chose legislative appointment: the two late-ratifying states of Rhode Island and North Carolina, the newly admitted state of Vermont, and New York, which managed to choose a procedure this time.[18] Also, Delaware switched from its previous districting system to direct legislative appointment.[19]

Virginia, however, retained its districting system, and the new state of Kentucky also adopted this approach. Pennsylvania and Maryland both retained the statewide popular-vote systems that they had employed four years earlier. Again, these two states lacked a majority-rule requirement, but again this omission did not reflect a deliberate and considered preference for plurality, rather than majority, voting. There continued to be no third-party alternative to the two main opposing groups, and in both states the Federalists maintained their overwhelming dominance.[20]

Massachusetts and New Hampshire continued to insist explicitly on majority rule for the appointment of their electors, although both states experimented with the particular form this majority-rule requirement would take. Massachusetts modified its initial system by no longer making a legislative runoff automatic in all cases. Instead, if a candidate won a majority of votes in a district, that candidate would become an elector for that district without need for a legislative runoff. But for any elector position not filled by a majority of the popular vote in a district, then as before the legislature by its own majority vote would appoint the elector from that district.[21] In actuality, the Massachusetts legislature needed to exercise its runoff power for 11 of the state's 16 electors.[22]

New Hampshire switched from a legislative to a popular runoff. As in the first presidential election, New Hampshire conducted a state-wide popular vote for all of its electors (now six) and declared a candidate victorious without need for a runoff if the candidate received votes from a majority of voters. But if a runoff were necessary due to one or more of the state's elector positions remaining vacant because there was no candidate with a popular-vote majority to fill that position, then this time the runoff would be in the form of a second popular vote. The two candidates with the highest popular-vote totals in the initial round of balloting would vie for each vacant elector position in this second round of popular voting.[23] In 1792, New Hampshire needed this second round of popular voting to appoint all six of its electors.[24] Given that the second round was limited to two candidates for each vacant position, this popular runoff guaranteed that all six electors would be appointed as a result of receiving votes from a majority of voters.

Again, despite the variety of appointment methods, the choice of each state's electors reflected the will of a majority in that state.

The Partisan Contest of 1796

With George Washington retiring after two terms, the partisan conflict between Federalists and Republicans broke wide open in what became the nation's first actual competitive fight to win the presidency.[25] A key part of the partisan competition concerned what methods states would use to appoint their electors.

Three states switched their method of appointment. Georgia moved from legislative appointment to a statewide popular vote.[26] Maryland and North Carolina adopted district-based systems, Maryland switching from a statewide popular vote and North Carolina from legislative appointment.[27]

The new state of Tennessee adopted its own unique system for appointing electors. The state's legislature would vote to choose three persons from each of three districts, and then the three selected individuals would appoint the elector for that district.[28] Because the legislature would use majority rule for its own role in this multistage process, then insofar as the legislature reflected the majority of the state's electorate, this system was essentially majoritarian in character.

It certainly did not permit all of the state's electors to be chosen based on a mere plurality of the state's popular vote.

New Hampshire continued to tinker with its method of assuring majority rule. Having experimented with a popular runoff in 1792, the state switched back to the same kind of legislative runoff that it had used for the very first election, to be employed if the statewide popular vote failed to fill all of the state's elector positions with majority-vote winners.[29] Once again, in 1796 New Hampshire needed to use its runoff procedure, this time to fill one of the state's six elector positions (five candidates having achieved a majority in the popular vote).[30]

The remaining states retained the same systems that they had four years earlier. Consequently, counting Tennessee, eight states used a version of legislative appointment (the others being Connecticut, Rhode Island, Vermont, New York, New Jersey, Delaware, and South Carolina). Four states used district-based popular voting without any form of runoff procedure: Maryland, Virginia, North Carolina, and Kentucky. Only two states, Pennsylvania and Georgia, employed a statewide popular vote without a runoff. But again, as a practical matter the lack of a runoff, whether in a district or statewide election, did not permit a mere plurality to prevail insofar as the electoral contest in these states (as elsewhere at the time) was simply a two-way race between Federalists and Republicans.[31]

Like New Hampshire, Massachusetts retained its insistence that an elector receive a majority vote in order to avoid a runoff. Continuing to marry this majority requirement to its district-based system, Massachusetts needed a legislative runoff to fill seven of its elector seats. Another seven candidates did receive majority votes in their districts and became electors on that basis. The state's final two electors were directly appointed at large by the legislature, as had been specified by state law before the 1792 election.[32]

The upshot of these various appointment methods was a close result in the Electoral College. John Adams, the Federalist choice for president, received 71 electoral votes. Thomas Jefferson, the Republican choice, received 68. As there were 138 electors, 71 was one more than the minimum majority (70), and that was enough to make Adams the winner.[33]

The Debacle of 1800

Four years later there was a rematch between Adams and Jefferson, and the partisan competition between Federalists and Republicans had become much more intense. Republican anger escalated especially over the Alien and Sedition Acts, which Adams and the Federalists had supported as part of the so-called quasi-war against France. Jefferson and Madison drafted the Kentucky and Virginia Resolutions denouncing this Federalist suppression of dissent as unconstitutional and fundamentally antithetical to the principle of popular sovereignty, upon which the independence of the United States from Britain was founded. In short, the Republicans thought the very essence of America was at stake in the election of 1800.[34]

With this escalation of partisan competition, there was even more rewriting of the rules that states used to appoint their presidential electors than there had been in 1796. Four states abandoned popular voting for electors in favor of direct legislative appointment. Two of these were Massachusetts and New Hampshire, where Federalists controlled the state legislatures. Another was Georgia, where the Republicans prevailed. The fourth was Pennsylvania, in which the two parties split control of the bicameral legislature (the Federalists dominant in the state senate, and the Republicans in the House). This split control necessitated an agreement whereby the two parties would divide the state's 15 electors between them, with the Republicans getting eight and the Federalists seven.[35]

Rhode Island switched in the opposite direction, moving from legislative appointment to a statewide popular vote.[36] Virginia also adopted a statewide popular vote, jettisoning its previous district-based system. Republicans in Virginia, including Madison, feared that Federalists would win in several districts, and with the race between Adams and Jefferson promising to be again very close, just a few electoral votes could make the difference. Because Republicans dominated statewide in Virginia, they could assure themselves of winning all the state's 21 elector positions—by far the largest prize nationally—if they moved to at-large statewide voting for all these positions. Otherwise, Republicans risked losing some of Virginia's electoral votes to their Federalist adversaries.[37]

As a consequence of these various machinations, in 1800, 11 states used legislative appointment: the four that newly switched to this system, plus Connecticut, Vermont, New York, New Jersey, Delaware, South Carolina, and (in its own special way) Tennessee. Three states still retained their previous district-based systems: Maryland, North Carolina, and Kentucky. Only two states used statewide popular votes: Rhode Island and Virginia, which were both employing this method for the first time.[38]

The Adams–Jefferson rematch ended up being close, although not as tight as their 1796 race. This time, however, it was Jefferson who received more electoral votes: 73 for Jefferson, and 65 for Adams. Jefferson's 73 votes was also a majority of the 138 electors.[39]

But there was a huge problem.

Jefferson's running mate, Aaron Burr, also received 73 electoral votes, as a consequence of the 1787 Electoral College system giving each elector two votes to cast. Although Republicans clearly intended Jefferson to get the presidency, with Burr serving as vice president, there was no way for the 73 Republican electors to differentiate their two votes in this way. All of their votes for Jefferson and Burr counted equally, according to the design of the 1787 system, which had hoped to produce consensus winners along the lines of George Washington. (Under the 1787 Constitution, the vice presidency went to whichever candidate received the second most votes overall, not the running mate of the winning presidential candidate.)

Burr was not a consensus choice for president. He received not a single vote from a Federalist elector. Of the 65 Federalist electors, 64 gave their second vote to Charles Pinckney, who was Adams's running mate as the Federalist choice for vice president. The remaining Federalist elector gave his second vote to John Jay as a way of avoiding a tie between Adams and Pinckney. In a political miscalculation of monumental proportions, however, the Republicans failed to throw away a single vote for Burr, and the consequence was his tie with Jefferson.[40]

Under the rules of the 1787 system, a tie was to be broken by the special House of Representatives procedure in which each state had one vote and a majority of all states was required. The problem, however, was that the outgoing House, not the incoming one, would have to break the tie. The outgoing House was controlled by Federalists, who had an incentive to leave the tie unbroken, so that there would be a vacancy. In this situation, the lame-duck Congress could designate a Federalist to serve as acting president for as long as the 1800 election remained unresolved.[41]

The Republicans viewed this possible Federalist ploy as theft of the presidency, which was rightfully Jefferson's. They were even prepared to risk outright civil war to prevent this theft, and Republican governors in Virginia and Pennsylvania began military maneuvers in the event that force might become necessary.[42] The crisis easily could have been averted if Burr had removed himself from consideration for the presidency, stepping aside in favor of Jefferson. But Burr was a self-serving and ambitious man, and he hoped that he might convince Federalists in the House that he was a better choice than Jefferson from their partisan perspective.[43]

Burr's arch-rival, Hamilton, quashed this idea. As much as Hamilton disliked Jefferson, he despised Burr more. Jefferson had horrible policies, according to Hamilton's thinking, but Burr was entirely untrustworthy. Eventually, enough Federalists in the House acquiesced to let Jefferson become president. But it was a nerve-racking and ugly episode, and without Hamilton's intervention on behalf of Jefferson (among other efforts necessary to convince reluctant Federalists), it could have ended in disaster.[44]

From the perspective of Jefferson and his supporters, the faulty Electoral College machinery was clearly in need of major retooling. There should never again be a risk that the minority party might be able to steal the presidency from a majority winner. But from their vantage point, one aspect of the system had worked properly. That was the power of the states to choose their locally preferred method for appointing electors. In the world of two-party competition that had emerged, this power enabled the majority party in each state to prevail.

Whether it was Virginia choosing a statewide popular vote or New York retaining legislative appointment, each state's method of appointment effectuated the presidential choice that the majority of the state's voters wanted. New York's legislature had become controlled by the Jeffersonian party as a result of recent elections in the state, and so appointed electors in accordance with this fresh partisan preference expressed by the majority of the state's voters. In both of these states, the majority choice for president was Jefferson. And being two of the most populous states, they gave Jefferson 33 of his 73 electoral votes, thereby being decisive in giving him rather than Adams an Electoral College majority—and thus his claim to the presidency.

3

The Electoral College of 1803

WHEN AMERICANS THINK about the authors of the Electoral College, they are apt to picture the delegates to the Constitutional Convention that met in Philadelphia during the summer of 1787, including such famous Founding Fathers as James Madison, Alexander Hamilton, and Ben Franklin. But in actuality they should be thinking about the members of the Eighth Congress, which met in the autumn of 1803, and included among its leading thinkers Senator John Taylor of Virginia and Representative George Campbell of Tennessee. Although these figures are entirely eclipsed in historical prominence by the statesmen who crafted the original Constitution 16 years earlier, they were no lightweights and merit our consideration. Taylor, for example, was a leading constitutional scholar of his day and author of *An Inquiry into the Principles and Policy of the Government of the United States*, among his many major books.[1]

Moreover, the members of Congress who deliberated over the Electoral College in 1803 gave far more extensive and well-developed thought to the design of the system they were adopting than the delegates to the Constitutional Convention of 1787 did in creating the original Electoral College. Madison himself acknowledged late in life that the Founders' consideration of presidential elections in Philadelphia during the summer of 1787 was rushed and sloppy. The delegates had left this topic to the end of the convention. After weeks of hard work in stifling hot conditions, and wanting to get home, they hastily assembled the initial version of the Electoral College. In Madison's own words, "as the final arrangement of [the Electoral College] took place in the latter stage of the Session, it was not exempt from a degree of the hurrying influence produced by fatigue & impatience in all such bodies."[2]

By contrast, in 1803 Congress spent hours and hours, over the course of many weeks, debating the new version of the Electoral College. The debate, moreover, was detailed and rigorous, reflecting the experience of the first four presidential elections that had already occurred. During the dozen years between the Constitution's adoption and the 1800 election, as well as in the next two years since then, Congress already had begun to consider changes to the 1787 system. The 1803 deliberations built upon those earlier discussions.[3]

The 1803 debate also reconsidered first principles of government for the United States, including the philosophical foundations of republicanism and federalism, in light of the nation's initial electoral experience. Anyone who doubts the depth, scope, and seriousness of the congressional debate in 1803 concerning the redesign of the Electoral College needs only to read the many pages of the Annals of Congress for that year devoted to the topic. Comparing that extensive and erudite congressional record with the skimpy discussion of presidential elections among the delegates to the Constitutional Convention of 1787—well, frankly, there is no comparison. Simply put, if one wants to understand the thinking behind the Electoral College as it now exists, one must focus on the lengthy and sophisticated debate in Congress during the autumn of 1803.[4]

The Circumstances of the Debate

The Eighth Congress was thoroughly dominated by Republicans, even more so than the Seventh, which had come in on Jefferson's coattails as part of the "revolution of 1800." Whereas Federalists still controlled the Senate at the beginning of the Seventh Congress in 1801 (as a consequence of senators having six-year terms), by the opening session of the Eighth the Republicans held more than a two-to-one advantage in both the Senate and the House: 24–9 in the Senate (73 percent), and 96–38 in the House (72 percent).[5]

This degree of dominance meant that in both chambers of Congress the Republicans could clear the two-thirds hurdle for amending the

Electoral College provisions of the Constitution without needing any Federalist votes. The Seventh Congress had considered various proposals to amend the Electoral College after the system had so badly malfunctioned in the 1800 election, but with the two houses of Congress then controlled by opposing parties, those proposals went nowhere. Now in 1803, with the next presidential election on the horizon, the Republicans could redesign the Electoral College system however they wished.[6]

Their immediate aim was securing the smooth re-election of Jefferson. The incumbent was increasingly popular, especially after the successful conclusion of the Louisiana Purchase in the summer of 1803.[7] Thus, when the Eighth Congress met in the fall of that year to take up the task of amending the Electoral College, Republicans did not fear that Jefferson would lack majority support of the citizenry. Instead, the challenge was to redesign the Electoral College in a way that would assure the translation of that popular majority into an Electoral College victory. For one thing, it was necessary to avoid the possibility of another Electoral College tie between Jefferson and his new running mate (who for sure would not be Burr again).[8] But even more than that, it was imperative to make sure that Federalists could not use the electors' second vote to cause someone other than Jefferson to get the most electoral votes. This unwanted outcome could happen if Federalist electors strategically gave one of their two votes to Jefferson's running mate, since these votes would be added to the Republican votes that Jefferson's running mate received. In combination, the total votes for the running mate could be more than all the Republican electoral votes for Jefferson.[9]

The Republicans' desire to redesign the Electoral College to assure Jefferson's victory in 1804 was not just a crass short-term motive to retain a partisan advantage over their Federalist opponents. Even after Jefferson eventually prevailed in the fraught 1800 election, Republicans continued to believe that the very survival of the Republic was at stake. After all, in 1803 Federalists from New England seriously contemplated secession from the Union, in part because of their hostility to the Louisiana Purchase.[10] Republicans thus feared for the future if Federalists recaptured the presidency in 1804.

The idea of a consensus president, capable of bridging the partisan divide, was long dead. Either the Republicans or the Federalists necessarily would prevail over their adversaries. In a two-party world, moreover, one must be the majority, and the other the minority. As between the two, Republicans fervently believed it should be the majority, not the minority, party that controls the presidency. The fact that they were the majority party at the time made this belief convenient. But it also happened to be the core of their political philosophy: in a republic with an electorate split between a majority and minority party, and thus incapable of achieving the nonpartisan consensus that the 1787 Convention in Philadelphia had sought, the essential republican principle of popular sovereignty required that the majority, rather than the minority, exercise the power of government. While respectful of "equal rights" that "the minority possess," as Jefferson himself proclaimed in his inaugural address, he and his party were adamant that "the will of the majority is in all cases to prevail." Republicanism, in their view, certainly did not require giving over control of the federal chief executive to the minority party.[11]

Thus, as the Eighth Congress deliberated over the redesign of the Electoral College in 1803, the Republicans' overarching objective was to achieve the core republican commitment to majority rule. But the Republicans did not want to replace the Electoral College with a popular vote of the entire national electorate voting as a single body. The Republicans were also committed to the basic idea that the United States was a federal republic, with the essential separate identities of the states preserved within the federal structure. The Republicans, in other words, were federalist in their political philosophy, even though of course they were not Federalist in party identity.[12]

Adhering to federalism required Republicans in 1803 to retain the idea, embedded in the Electoral College of 1787, that majority rule in a federal system entails a compound majority-of-majorities. Republicanism, as a philosophy, demands majority rule at the state level. A federal majority is then formed from an overall majority of these subsidiary state-level majorities.[13] Indeed, once this idea of compound majority was stripped of the 1787 naivete that it would be consensus-reflecting, the Republicans of 1803 became much more committed to this federalist form of majoritarianism than the Philadelphia Convention delegates had ever been.

The Jeffersonian conception of federalism tolerated wide variation in the practice of republican government at the state level. States were entitled to define their own eligible electorates in very different ways. Property qualifications for voting could vary from state to state. Slavery precluded an entire part of the populace from republican self-government, as did the disenfranchisement of women.[14] Jeffersonian republicanism was not, and must not be confused with, a twenty-first-century understanding of democracy predicated on equal voting rights for all adults. Nonetheless, as the Jeffersonians themselves conceived it, republican government existed in both Massachusetts and Virginia at the time, and also in New Hampshire, New York, and North Carolina, despite their regional differences. Whatever the local definition of the eligible electorate, Jeffersonians believed that majority rule should operate to guarantee republican self-government by that locally eligible electorate. With respect to a federation of republics, Jeffersonians believed that the same commitment to self-government required the aggregation of the locally determined majorities into an overall federal majority. Their vision of federalism also caused them to give states seats in the House of Representatives, and hence also in the Electoral College, based on a state's overall population and not the state's eligible electorate. (Their population-based system of federalism was of course glaringly compromised by the "three-fifths" clause, which counted all "free persons" at 100 percent for purposes of a state's federal representation—including all disenfranchised "free" women—but only 60 percent of euphemistically "other" persons, meaning slaves.) Thus, 51 percent of voters in one state would not necessarily have the same weight in the federal aggregate as 51 percent of voters in another state. This federal form of majoritarianism is certainly not the only conception available in democratic theory, but that truth makes it no less of a commitment to majority rule on its own terms. Instead, it is what majority rule entails given the specific postulates of republicanism and federalism that the Jeffersonians started with.[15]

The Republicans of 1803 also recognized that they were not the majority party in every state. The Federalists remained the majority party in several New England states.[16] This status did not entitle these New

England states to secede, as some ultra-Federalists then thought. Doing so would contradict the idea of a federal union. Nor did it entitle the New England states to block the election of a Republican president, if these New England states were a minority in the federal union overall. As long as Republicans were the majority party in most states, as they were in 1803, they were entitled in their view to control the presidency of the federal union. Looking ahead to 1804, Republicans knew that they could lose all the electoral votes of the New England states and still have an Electoral College majority if they won the electoral votes from the remaining states.

Thus, in 1803 the Republicans saw no reason to eliminate the provision that a candidate can become president by winning a majority of Electoral College votes, without needing to invoke the special runoff procedure in the House. They certainly saw the necessity of eliminating the provision of the 1787 Electoral College that gave two undifferentiated votes to each elector. But if electors were required to vote separately for president and vice president, with each elector having just one vote for each office, then a presidential candidate receiving a majority of electoral votes would have achieved the kind of compound majority-of-majorities that earned the candidate the office of chief executive in a federal union.

Republicans in 1803 also saw no need to change the provision that permitted each state to choose its own method of appointing electors. Observing what had occurred in the first four elections, including most especially in 1800 when the partisan competition between Republicans and Federalists had intensified, and projecting that this partisan competition would intensify even further in years ahead (or at least remain unabated), the Jeffersonians in Congress understood that the majority party in each state could control the method of appointing electors. Indeed, in 1800 Jefferson's home state of Virginia had taken the lead in switching its method of appointing electors (from a districting system to a statewide popular vote) so that Jefferson would get the full benefit of being the state's majority-preferred candidate. Jefferson himself had foreseen the benefit of this move and had justified it as a way to effectuate the will of the majority in the state.[17] As long as the appointment of a state's electors reflected the preferences of the majority party in a state, a majority of Electoral College votes would amount to a compound majority-of-majorities appropriate to prevail in a federal republic.

To be sure, some states might continue to employ districting systems to appoint their electors, as three states had chosen to do in 1800. But this arrangement would mean only that the majority party in a state would be willing to share the state's electoral votes with the minority party. It most certainly would not permit the minority party to control all of the state's electoral votes. (As long as only two parties fielded candidates in each district, the majority party statewide would win some if not most of those districts and thus not be shut out of the state's electoral votes entirely.)

In the world of two-party competition between Republicans and Federalists, none of the methods of appointing electors that the states had employed thus far—or could be expected to employ in future elections—would enable the minority party in the state to award all of the state's electoral votes to the minority party's presidential candidate. Direct legislative appointment of electors, the method used by most states in 1800 (and by more states than in the three previous elections), enabled the majority party in a state to award all of the state's electoral votes to the majority party's presidential candidates, if the majority party controlled the state's legislature (as it should if it genuinely was the state's majority party). This, again, is exactly what had happened in New York that year, after the Jeffersonians won control of the legislature there.

A statewide popular vote, like Virginia employed in 1800, would produce electors preferred by the majority party in the state—and would do so even without the kind of runoffs that New Hampshire had employed, as long as the competition to be electors was between only Republican and Federalist candidates. Virginia certainly had not switched its method of appointing electors in 1800 in order to let the minority party in the state control all of the state's electoral votes. Just the opposite, in fact. The move was a way to maximize majority rule in the casting of the state's electoral votes.

When the congressional Republicans in 1803 decided to retain the provision that gave each state the power to choose the method of appointing its own electors, they did so based on the belief that this provision would facilitate majority rule at the state level in the operation of the Electoral College process. As one leading Republican explained:

> The Electors are the organs, who, acting from a certain and unquestioned knowledge of the choice of the people, by whom they themselves were appointed, and under immediate responsibility to them, select and announce those particular citizens, and affix to them by their votes an evidence of the degree of public confidence which is bestowed upon them.[18]

The Republicans also knew that some states might go so far as to guarantee majority rule at the state level, as New Hampshire and Massachusetts had with their various forms of runoffs if candidates to be electors lacked majority support in the popular vote. But even in those states without runoffs, the Jeffersonians in Congress expected the appointment of a state's electors to be consistent with majority rule in that state. After the partisan contestation of 1800, which demonstrated how the whole outcome could hinge on one or two pivotal states, they assumed that no state would permit the minority party in a state to cast all of the state's Electoral College votes. Indeed, they could not fathom such a possibility, as it would defy the logic of the partisan competition that had emerged. Consequently, when the Jeffersonians in 1803 also confirmed that winning a majority of Electoral College votes would entitle the winner to the presidency, they had every reason to believe that an Electoral College majority properly would constitute the kind of compound majority-of-majorities called for in a federal version of a republic.

What the Republicans themselves said in Congress when they explained their Electoral College redesign illustrates this understanding.

The House Initiates Deliberations

In the House of Representatives, where the debates began on what would become the Twelfth Amendment to the Constitution, John Clopton of Virginia took the lead in making the case for the amendment's core feature: the designation of separate ballots by the electors for president and vice president, or what the legislators called simply the "designation" principle.[19] Clopton, an attorney educated at the College of Philadelphia (later University of Pennsylvania) and an officer in the Revolutionary War,[20] squarely rested his defense of the designation principle on the ground that it fixed the flaw that caused the original Electoral College mechanism to thwart the will of the majority.

Clopton started with the basic premise that "in a Government constituted as our Government is, wherein all the constituted authorities are the agents of the people, the suffrages given for the election of those agents ought ever to be a complete expression of the public will."[21] It followed from this premise that an electoral procedure should work to identify as the winners "those persons in whom the Electors intend to place confidence as their agents, in the particular offices for which the elections are made." Here Clopton is using the term "Electors" generically, to mean voters, not specifically to refer only to presidential electors. If an electoral procedure does not work in this way and produces a winner other than what the electorate intended, it acts "contrary to" its essential purpose: "When one person is intended for an office and another person actually obtains it, such election, if indeed it can properly be called an election, is not conformable to the will of those by whom it was made."[22]

Moreover, Clopton specifically and expressly understood that, for an election to function properly according to this criterion, it must yield a winner whom the majority of the voters wanted to elect: "An election, therefore, which may, from the mode of holding it, terminate ultimately in the appointment of a different person to an office, than the one originally intended for by a majority of the Electors, cannot be said to be such complete expression of the public will." At this point, Clopton was still using the term "Electors" generically, although he was about to transition from the general principle of majority rule to its particular application in the context of presidential elections. It would be entirely antithetical to the purpose of any election procedure, Copton asserted, for it to produce a winner "completely at variance with the will of the majority" who employ that procedure. This problem he saw as the heart of the matter.

Clopton gave an example of how this malfunction could occur under the 1787 Electoral College procedures. Imagine two candidates, A and B, as the two clear preferences for president, with C and D the two candidates for vice president. Suppose that the electors split their presidential preference 95 to 81, so that A receives 95 votes, a "clear decided majority" of the 176 electors, and B gets the remaining 81. (Clopton's example was contemporaneously realistic, as there indeed were 176 electors then, and by limiting his example to four candidates, two for each office, he was assuming the world of two-party competition as it then existed.) Suppose that the electors who want A for president carefully waste some of their second votes, so that C does not have as many as A, thereby avoiding the problem that had occurred with Burr in 1800. Assume C receives 75 votes from the 95 electors supporting A for president. Suppose, however, that 25 of the electors supporting B, A's presidential opponent, also vote for C, even though D is B's running mate. These 25 electors might do so strategically, to prevent A from becoming president; if they fear that they cannot get their choice of B, they might settle for C as preferable to A. Think of the Federalists in 1800, unable to re-elect Adams, preferring Burr to Jefferson and causing Burr to end up not in a tie with Jefferson, but actually having more electoral votes. In this situation, the 100 votes for C (75 + 25) would cause C to become president, instead of A, even though the majority of electors—95—wanted A to become president. By contrast, only 25 of C's votes come from electors preferring him to A for the presidency. In this situation, as Clopton saw it, "the will of the majority is defeated" by the "anomalous effect" of the original Electoral College's faulty mechanics, a "serious evil" that would be prevented "if the proposed amendment should be adopted."[23]

In making this argument, Clopton was speaking for his fellow Republicans. Indeed, Clopton summed up his position by explicitly linking it to the fundamental tenets of Republican political philosophy: "Essential means of human happiness are best secured in the agency of those organs of public authority whose creation springs from the public will."[24] Accordingly, "the elective principle in its practical operations" should always "be directed through the channel of that public will." This principle, Clopton exclaimed, "is the life, the soul, of the Republic." Consequently, he concluded:

[I]t must be a consideration of primary importance that the modes of election be so established that in their event they may always secure full expression of the public will, and the appointment of all public agents conformably thereto.

With these impressions on my mind, Mr. Chairman, and from the evident risk attendant on the present mode of choosing the President and Vice President of the United States, that the election of those high and important officers of the Government may terminate contrary to the public will, I am thoroughly convinced of the expediency of the proposed amendment to the Constitution, directing a designation of them in the electoral votes.[25]

Benjamin Huger of South Carolina delivered the Federalist response to Clopton's speech. He endeavored to defend the decision in 1787 to give two undifferentiated votes for president to each elector. Attempting to reframe and revitalize the goal of a consensus-based presidency, Huger argued that the 1787 Electoral College mechanism facilitated the election of a president who would have broader acceptability than just a simple "majority of all the inhabitants of the Union, taken in the aggregate."[26]

But Huger's argument missed Clopton's point. Clopton had not been advocating for electing a president by means of a national popular majority. Instead, Clopton had been promoting an Electoral College revision that, unlike the 1787 version, would actually achieve the federal conception of a compound majority-of-majorities. Huger's effort to cling to the consensus-seeking feature of the 1787 system was a nonstarter now insofar, as Clopton showed with his example, that this feature actually frustrated the achievement of a federal majority-of-majorities.

The Senate Takes Up the Topic

When the debates moved to the Senate, the leading speeches on each side were delivered by Uriah Tracy, a Federalist from Connecticut, and John Taylor, a Republican from Virginia. Tracy, a Yale-trained attorney, was part of the New England cohort so opposed to Jefferson's presidency, including his Louisiana Purchase, that they flirted with secession.[27] Taylor, as mentioned earlier, was a leading constitutional scholar of the era, having studied law at William and Mary.

Tracy's speech was first. John Quincy Adams, who had just arrived to the Senate that year and was aligned with the Federalist Party, noted the quality of the two speeches in his diary. He judged Tracy's "particularly excellent," but "Mr. Taylor's was unquestionably the best."[28]

Tracy, like Huger in the House, endeavored to justify each elector's casting two undifferentiated presidential votes. His argument was that this feature of the 1787 system was more consistent with the federal nature of the United States, properly understood. Federalism, Tracy claimed, required giving small states the power either to choose the president between two candidates favored by the large states, or to select a vice president if the large states control the presidency:

> The Electors are to nominate two persons, of whom they cannot know which will be President; this circumstance not only induces them to select both from the best men; but gives a direct advantage into the hands of the small States even in the electoral choice. For they can always select from the two candidates set up by the Electors of the large States, by throwing their votes upon their favorite, and of course giving him a majority; or, if the Electors of the large States should, to prevent this effect, scatter their votes for one candidate, then the Electors of the small States would have it in their power to elect a Vice President.[29]

Tracy saw this federalism-promoting feature of the 1787 Electoral College design as challenging the Republican argument that "the public will"—by which the Republicans "mean the will of a popular majority"—should prevail. Do Republicans, Tracy asked rhetorically, "suppose that the public will, when Constitutionally expressed by a majority of States, in pursuance of the federative principle of our Government, is of less validity, or less binding upon the community at large, than the public will expressed by a popular majority?" Tracy answered his own rhetorical question: "The framers of your Constitution, the people who adopted it, meant, that the public will, in the choice of a President, should be expressed by Electors, if they could agree, and if not, the public will should be expressed by a majority of the States, acting in their federative capacity, and that in both cases the expression of the public will should be equally binding."[30]

Taylor took up Tracy's challenge. Taylor rejected Tracy's claim "that the federal principle of the Constitution of the United States was founded in the idea of minority invested with operative power."[31] Instead, he saw federalism very differently, as entirely consistent with majority rule—once majority rule was understood in a compound way: "Two principles sustain our Constitution: one a majority of the people, the other a majority of the States; the first was necessary to preserve the liberty or sovereignty of the people; the last, to preserve the liberty or sovereignty of the States." "But both are founded in the principle of majority," Taylor continued, emphasizing that neither supported Tracy's "evidently incorrect" idea that federalism seeks to establish "a government of a minority."[32]

Taylor elaborated this thesis at length. First: "It is the intention of the Constitution that the popular principle shall operate in the election of a President and Vice President." Second: "It is also the intention of the Constitution that the popular principle, in discharging the functions committed to it by the Constitution, should operate by a majority and not by a minority." Third, and most importantly: "If, however, it is admitted that in an election of a President and Vice President by Electors, that the will of the electing majority ought fairly to operate," then "an election by the will of the minority would be an abuse or corruption of the principles of the Constitution."[33]

Taylor continued by explaining that the proposed amendment was intended to enable "the popular principle, applied by the Constitution in the first instance, to operate perfectly, and to prevent the abuse of an election by a minority." The 1787 mechanism, by giving two undifferentiated votes to each elector, caused an unintended frustration of the majority will. Directly contradicting Tracy's contention, Taylor proclaimed: "Sir, it could never have been the intention of the Constitution to produce a state of things by which a majority of the popular principle should be under the necessity of voting against its judgment to secure a President, and by which a minor faction should acquire a power capable of defeating the majority in the election of President, or of electing a Vice President contrary to the will of the electing principle."[34]

Taylor described the stakes as nothing less than a stark choice between *either* that "the people—a fair majority of the popular principle—should elect Executive power" *or* "that a minor faction should be enabled to embarrass and defeat the judgment and will of this majority." As between the two, Taylor had no doubt which was "better." The Constitution never should "intend any minor faction" to control the federal executive.[35]

Taylor concluded by recognizing that the Constitution properly protects "the rights of the minorities." He quoted the aphorism " 'that every individual in society has equal rights, whether he belongs to a majority or minority.' " But this truth did not mean that a "minor faction" had the right to govern "as a faction"; no, that "idea" was "incomprehensible." Thus, the proposed amendment "will have the effect of depriving a minor faction of the possibility of getting possession of Executive power." Instead, the amendment will restore the essential republican principle "that the election of a President and Vice President should be determined, by a fair expression of the public will by a majority," understood in the specific federal form of a compound majority-of-majorities.[36]

During the Senate debates, Taylor was hardly the only Republican to support the proposed amendment on the ground that it was conducive to majority rule. Robert Wright of Maryland, who later would be governor of his state,[37] thought it "absurd" to have a president elected contrary to the fundamental principle of representative government, "the will of the majority."[38] William Cocke, one of Tennessee's first US senators, expounded: "I do not understand the principle of minorities governing majorities. The law of the minority is not the law of the Constitution, and it is not the law for me." He accused opponents of the amendment as "favoring minority government," as much as they might try to "disguise it." Whether or not he was correct in that characterization—the Federalists themselves denied it, saying they only wanted protection of minority rights—Cocke wanted to "speak out" against that position. "I think the majority should govern," he insisted. "I do not wish to have a man put upon us contrary to our wishes."[39]

One specific way in which the senators made clear their support for majority rule was by a change they made to the draft of the amendment. As initially adopted by the House, and as introduced in the Senate, the proposed draft provided only for the designation of separate ballots to be cast by the electors for president and vice president.[40]

This initial draft, like the 1787 Constitution, had the effect of requiring that a presidential candidate receive votes from a majority of electors, or else the election would go to a runoff in the House using the special one-vote-per-state procedure. But the draft permitted a vice president to win simply by receiving the most votes from electors—a plurality, rather than a majority. This feature was left over from the fact that the 1787 Constitution did not require votes from a majority of electors to become vice president.

This lack of a majority requirement to win the vice presidency was objectionable to senators. Stephen Bradley of Vermont first raised the point: "He could not see why the Vice President should not be chosen by a majority, as well as the President."[41] Focusing on "the possibility of the Vice President becoming President by any casualty," he "considered" that "a good reason for both being chosen by the same ratio of numbers."[42] Otherwise, it might so happen that a citizen chosen only for the office of vice president might, upon death of the president, though "chosen only by a plurality, become President." Such a mere-plurality president was so problematic, in Bradley's view, that "he could not give [the amendment] his vote in the present shape."[43]

Other senators quickly concurred with Bradley on this point. Robert Wright of Maryland, for example, declared that "admitting a choice by a plurality" was "contrary" to "principles received" from sound republican philosophy. By contrast, Bradley's proposed revision to the pending draft, "so far as it went to decide the choice of Vice President by a majority instead of a plurality," should be adopted, "as it was the principle most consonant with the spirit of representative democracy."[44] Bradley's proposal was so widely agreeable that it was adopted by the Senate without need of a recorded vote.[45]

Bradley's proposal was not the only change that the Senate made to the pending amendment. The Senate also reduced the number of candidates that the House could consider in the event of a runoff. Like the 1787 Constitution, the version of the amendment already approved by the House (on October 23, 1803)[46] set this number at five. But the Senate switched it to three (and attempted to clarify that, in the event of multiple candidates receiving the same number of votes, the House could choose from among all the candidates receiving the three largest numbers of votes).[47]

The senators made this switch from five to three because they thought it would require the House to choose a candidate with more popular support, whereas if the House had the freedom to elect a president who was a *fifth*-place finisher in the Electoral College voting, then the nation might end up with a president lacking any significant popular support. This point was one that many senators made repeatedly during the debates. For example, Wilson Nicholas of Virginia explained: "By taking the number three instead of five, you place the choice with more certainty in the people at large, and render the choice more consonant to their wishes."[48] This view—like the basic preference for keeping a presidential election out of the House insofar as possible (consistent, of course, with the overriding requirement that a candidate receive a majority of Electoral College votes)—stemmed directly from the deep republican philosophy held by most senators.[49] As Nicholas himself expressed his republican reasoning: "The people hold the sovereign power, and it was intended by the Constitution that they should have the election of the Chief Magistrate."[50]

Back in the House

Because of the changes that the Senate made to the draft, the proposed amendment needed to return to the House for another round of debate. Although some representatives grumbled about the need to accept the Senate's changes, they acquiesced because some essential senators already had left town, and it was necessary for the House to send the Senate's version on to the states in order for the amendment to be in effect for the 1804 election.[51] Consequently, the final discussion of the amendment in the House did not break new ground, but it did give representatives the opportunity to confirm their commitment to majority rule and their conception of the Electoral College, when repaired by the proposed amendment, as fulfilling that commitment in the specific context of the federal chief executive.

For example, James Holland of North Carolina deemed "the will of the majority in their election of the Chief Magistrate" as "the first principle of our Government." He supported the proposed amendment because it is "possible" that in the future "a faction may exist, and on the existence of such a faction, how easy would it be for them, under the existing provisions of the Constitution, to defeat the public will." As others had, he provided the example of "Electors [who] compose part of this faction . . . giving their suffrages to the person intended [by the majority] to fill the second office." In this way, "the minor faction will accomplish their design," electing a president who was not the majority's choice for the office "and by this means contravene and totally defeat the will of the majority."[52]

Among the many voices that echoed this theme, it fell to George W. Campbell of Tennessee to provide the primary summation of the case for the amendment. Campbell, who later would serve as Secretary of the Treasury in James Madison's cabinet, was educated, like Madison, at the College of New Jersey, later known as Princeton.[53] Like Taylor in the Senate, Campbell made clear the amendment's derivation from the foundational commitment to majority rule inherent in republican philosophy:

> It will, I presume, be admitted that in all free Governments the will of the majority must be considered for the purposes of Government as the will of the nation, and that it ought, therefore, to prevail, and control the will of the minority when opposed to it. This, I conceive, sir, is a fundamental principle of our Government.[54]

From this first principle, it necessarily followed that "whatever part of our Constitution is found in its operations to contravene this principle ought to be altered, and so modified that the will of the majority of the people should be pursued." Turning to the specifics at hand, Campbell declared: "This, I conceive, sir, is the case with that part of the Constitution prescribing the mode of electing the President and Vice President now proposed to be amended; it puts it in the power of the minority to control the will of the majority, and elevate a man to the Presidential chair who did not receive a vote from the majority for that office."[55] Campbell, too, explained specifically how "the minority, by voting for the person intended by the majority to be the Vice President"—given the existing defect in the 1787 Electoral College mechanism—"will contravene the intentions of the majority, and place in the Presidential chair a person not designated by the majority."[56] Just imagine, as Campbell did, if Burr had received the vote of one

Federalist elector, and Burr became president instead of Jefferson, without the election even going to the House.[57] That result would be the opposite of how "the representative principle in Government" was supposed to work. Instead, according to that principle, which the proposed amendment would effectuate, "a fair and unequivocal expression of the public will may be obtained, and will have its due weight— the man declared best qualified by the general voice of the nation to direct the Government, will by that voice be placed in the Presidential chair."[58]

As Taylor had in the Senate, Campbell directly tackled the Federalist contention "that the minority ought to have some share in the Government." To this, Campbell forcefully responded:

> I am, sir, of opinion the voice of the minority should be expressed, and fairly heard in Government, and that it should have its due weight consistent with the principles on which that Government is founded; but I am not willing that the minority should rule the nation, or have it in their power to defeat the will of the majority, as I conceive this would sap the very foundation of our Government.[59]

Because "the present mode of electing the President and Vice President, without designation, cannot strengthen the minority, or give them a share of the Administration of Government, in any other way than by enabling them to contravene the will of the majority," Campbell determined that it was imperative to adopt the amendment, so that the Constitution would be restored "to the true spirit of that instrument, that the Chief Magistrate shall be chosen by the people."[60]

As evidenced by the speeches of Campbell, Taylor, Clopton, and the like—and there were many others—a fair reading of the debates in Congress over the redesign of the Electoral College in 1803 yields only one conclusion: the Jeffersonian Republicans were animated by a vision of electing presidents by means of majority rule. Contrary to the mischaracterization by the Federalists, this Jeffersonian vision of majority rule for presidential elections was not a simple national popular majority. Instead, it was a special compound majority whereby achieving a federal majority in the Electoral College vote was itself achieved by virtue of majority rule in the states that provided the electoral votes for the federal majority.

The Federalists resisted this Jeffersonian conception of compound majority rule, clinging futilely to the 1787 idea of a consensus-based presidency. But in 1803 the Federalists could not block adoption of the constitutional amendment that the Jeffersonians had crafted to implement their vision of majority rule appropriate for electing the chief executive of the United States. The Jeffersonians had the necessary votes, two-thirds in each chamber of Congress, to send their amendment to the states, where it was ratified in time for the 1804 election by state legislatures also controlled by Jeffersonian Republicans. In this way, the Jeffersonian redesign of the Electoral College took the form of the Twelfth Amendment to the US Constitution, and in that form it remains the constitutional law that governs the operation of the Electoral College to this day.

Part Two

The Demise of the Jeffersonian Electoral College

4

The Jeffersonian Electoral College in the Nineteenth Century

SINCE ITS ADOPTION, the Electoral College of 1803 has mostly performed in accordance with its original Jeffersonian expectations. That is, the winning candidate in the Electoral College usually has achieved the kind of compound majority-of-majorities that the Jeffersonians in 1803 wanted their redesigned system to produce, and which they considered the key hallmark of legitimacy for the chief executive of a federal republic. Putting the same point somewhat more precisely, in most presidential elections since 1803 the candidate who receives the majority of Electoral College votes has secured that victory by being the majority-preferred candidate in the states providing the electoral votes sufficient to reach that Electoral College majority.

But the 1803 Electoral College has not always performed as expected. There have been three clear instances in which the Electoral College winner failed to achieve the compound majority-of-majorities necessary for Jeffersonian legitimacy. Moreover, in these three cases, the opposing (and losing) major-party candidate was actually the majority-preferred candidate in enough states to have achieved a majority of Electoral College votes. In these three elections, therefore, the Electoral College awarded the presidency to the wrong candidate according to the Jeffersonian objective that the 1803 redesign was supposed to secure. The three were the elections of 1844, 1884, and 2000. As we shall see, the first and third of these Electoral College malfunctions were especially consequential to the unfolding of history.

In addition to these three clear malfunctions of the Jeffersonian Electoral College, there have been other elections in which it is debatable whether the official Electoral College winner was the proper winner from a Jeffersonian perspective. In other words, it is debatable whether the Electoral College winner was the majority-preferred candidate in the states that provided the winner with a majority of Electoral College votes. For these debatable elections, it is indeed possible that the opposing major-party candidate was the one preferred by a majority of voters in enough states to make an Electoral College majority. Therefore, in these years also the Jeffersonian system may have malfunctioned. As we shall analyze, 2016 was one of those debatable years.

Why did the Electoral College of 1803 malfunction at all? The Jeffersonians, as we discussed in the previous chapter, were endeavoring to correct for the breakdown that had occurred in 1800 under the initial Electoral College of 1787. The Jeffersonians knew what they wanted to accomplish (a redesigned system that would produce winners with a compound majority-of-majorities), and they were striving to prevent any sort of malfunction from happening again. So how did they fail? And, perhaps even more important, after their system malfunctioned in the way that it demonstrably did—first in 1844, again in 1884, and also in 2000—why has it not been fixed, just as the Jeffersonians remedied the 1800 breakdown? Furthermore, if the Jeffersonian system may also have malfunctioned in other years as well, including the most recent election of 2016, one must wonder how vulnerable it is to malfunctioning again, and whether this vulnerability is increasing.

To address these and related questions, it is necessary to examine in detail how the Jeffersonian Electoral College has performed in practice since its adoption in 1803. In conducting this examination, we shall see that a key assumption of the Jeffersonians had become invalid after the ascendancy of Andrew Jackson in 1828. Beginning that year, plurality winner-take-all elections became the overwhelmingly dominant method that states used to appoint their presidential electors.

This Jacksonian development meant that it was possible for a candidate to win all of a state's electoral votes without being the majority-preferred candidate in that state and, consequently, that a candidate could assemble an Electoral College majority from states in which the majority of voters preferred another candidate. The Jeffersonians did not think this was possible: as we have seen, based on their experience with the first four presidential elections, they confidently expected that a presidential candidate would receive all of a state's electoral votes only if that candidate was the one whom the majority in that state wanted to win. But once the plurality winner-take-all method of appointing electors took hold in the Jacksonian era, this fundamental Jeffersonian assumption no longer was true. At that point, contrary to the basic majoritarian tenets underlying the Jeffersonian redesign of the Electoral College in 1803, a candidate could win the presidency without the federally legitimating majority-of-majorities. Indeed, as we shall observe, a minority-preferred candidate could win by defeating an opponent who was exactly the kind of majority-preferred candidate that the Jeffersonian system was supposed to install in the presidency.

Despite this pernicious appendage grafted onto the system in the 1820s, the Electoral College of 1803 did not begin to malfunction immediately. Instead, the Jeffersonian Electoral College continued to produce the intended compound-majority winners, notwithstanding the latent new vulnerability. It was not until the election of 1844 that an actual malfunction occurred.

For reasons we shall consider, the malfunction of 1844 could easily be viewed as aberrational, and thus there was no perceived urgency to fixing the defect. The system then continued to function properly according to its Jeffersonian expectations, or so it seemed, until the next malfunction in 1884. That second misfire also appeared aberrational, with again the consequence being no urgent calls to fix the defect.

Both these nineteenth-century malfunctions, moreover, were caused by a single state—New York—making it seem that systemic changes nationwide were unnecessary. New York also was particularly wedded to plurality-based elections, as our historical exploration shall show. Thus, the nineteenth century ended without any rectification of the Jacksonian defect that had crept into the Jeffersonian system and remained mostly hidden.

The story of how the Electoral College has operated in the twentieth century, and so far in the twenty-first, is for the next two chapters. But as a preview of where our historical journey is heading, it is helpful to have this basic point in mind: for most of the twentieth century the Jeffersonian system worked as intended, producing winners that satisfied the compound-majority criterion. Only at the end of the century, in 2000, was there another unambiguous failure. But this malfunction, too, was confined to a single state (Florida) and considered aberrational (on account of those "hanging chads" and "butterfly ballots"). Its significance from a Jeffersonian perspective could thus be easily overlooked.

But when combined with two ambiguous outcomes of the last quarter-century, 1992 and 2016, the malfunction in 2000 takes on another hue. More ominously, in this light it appears that the Jeffersonian system is now significantly more vulnerable as a result of its Jacksonian appendage than it historically has been. The addition of plurality winner-take-all in the Jacksonian era has for the most part not caused the monumental damage of imposing on America minority-preferred presidents while depriving the nation of the candidate who was actually majority-preferred in the appropriately Jeffersonian way. But now it seems as if this latent Jacksonian defect is poised to cause this kind of malfunction much more readily. A careful assessment of this apparently heightened risk, along with an appropriate sense of how urgent the current situation actually is, requires a review of America's experience with the Electoral College of 1803.

As we conduct this historical review, it will assist our assessment of the system's performance to use a mathematical measure. For each election, we will count the number of electoral votes that a candidate received in states where the candidate won a majority of the popular vote, and we will compare that number—which we shall label the ">50" number—with the threshold necessary to achieve an Electoral College majority. If a winning presidential candidate's >50 number reaches an Electoral College majority, then we can call the candidate a *clear Jeffersonian winner*. But if a winning presidential candidate's >50 number fails to reach an Electoral College majority, we can consider the candidate a *dubious Jeffersonian winner*.

Of the 48 presidential elections that have occurred since Andrew Jackson's ascendancy in 1828 (including his victory that year), 32 of them, exactly two-thirds, have produced clear Jeffersonian winners. The remaining 16, exactly one-third, have yielded dubious Jeffersonian winners (see Table 4.1, presenting the 16 dubious Jeffersonian winners, and Table 4.2, presenting the 32 clear Jeffersonian winners). When we

Table 4.1 Dubious Jeffersonian Winners

Year	Winner	Minimum	Received	>50	<50
1844	Polk	138	170	129*	41
1848	Taylor	146	163	103	60
1884	Cleveland	201	219	153	66
1888	Harrison	201	233	105	128
1892	Cleveland	223	277	138	139**
1912	Wilson	266	435	126	309
1916	Wilson	266	277	238	39
1948	Truman	266	303	219	84
1960	Kennedy	269	303	260	43
1968	Nixon	270	301	79	222
1976	Carter	270	297	254	43
1980	Reagan	270	489	254	235
1992	Clinton	270	370	9	361
1996	Clinton	270	379	230	149
2000	Bush	270	271	217	54
2016	Trump	270	304	197***	107

Minimum: minimum number of electoral votes needed for Electoral College majority
Received: actual number of electoral votes the winner received
>50: number of electoral votes from states where winner had more than 50 percent of the popular vote
<50: number of electoral votes from states where winner had less than 50 percent of popular vote
*South Carolina's legislature appointed the state's nine electors; in Polk's >50 tally because that method is a form of Jeffersonian majority rule.
**Several states split their electoral votes in 1892 for various reasons. Of the 139 electoral votes that Cleveland received in states where his share of the popular vote was under 50 percent, 132 came from states in which he won all of the state's electoral votes, and the remaining seven came from states in which he received only some of the state's electoral votes. For an explanation of the split electoral votes in several states in 1892, see George Harmon Knowles, *The Presidential Campaign and Election of 1892* (Stanford, CA: Stanford University Press, 1942), 229.
*** Trump won 1 electoral vote from Maine's Second Congressional District with 51.26 percent of the popular vote.

examine these 16 dubious Jeffersonian winners, we will see that for some of them the doubt is easily dispelled. For example, as indicated in the introduction, Nixon's victory in 1968 was genuinely Jeffersonian even though mathematically it is one of the 16. But for others in this category, including most significantly 2016, the doubt remains. And then there are the three elections—1844, 1884, and 2000—for which

Table 4.2 Clear Jeffersonian Winners

Year	Winner	Minimum	Received	>50	<50
1828	Jackson	131	178	178*	0
1832	Jackson	145	219	208	11
1836	Van Buren	148	170	170	0
1840	Harrison	148	234	234	0
1852	Pierce	149	254	222	32
1856	Buchanan	149	174	152	22
1860	Lincoln	152	180	169	11
1864	Lincoln	118	212	212	0
1868	Grant	148	214	214	0
1872	Grant	184 (177)**	286	286	0
1876	Hayes	185	185	185	0
1880	Garfield	185	214	198	16
1896	McKinley	224	271	251	20
1900	McKinley	224	292	292	0
1904	Roosevelt	239	336	317	19
1908	Taft	242	321	283	38
1920	Harding	266	404	404	0
1924	Coolidge	266	382	296	86
1928	Hoover	266	444	399	45
1932	Roosevelt	266	472	430	42
1936	Roosevelt	266	523	519	4
1940	Roosevelt	266	449	449	0
1944	Roosevelt	266	432	432	0
1952	Eisenhower	266	442	431	11
1956	Eisenhower	266	457	446	11
1964	Johnson	270	486	486	0
1972	Nixon	270	520	520	0
1984	Reagan	270	525	525	0
1988	Bush (41)	270	426	426	0
2004	Bush (43)	270	286	274	12
2008	Obama	270	365	338	27
2012	Obama	270	332	332	0***

See Table 4.1 for explanation of columns.

*South Carolina's legislature appointed its electors. Maine and Maryland used districts. Both methods are consistent with Jeffersonian majority rule.

**Congress rejected the electoral votes from Arkansas and Louisiana, causing a debate (unnecessary to resolve that year) whether their exclusion affected the minimum number necessary for an Electoral College majority.

***The National Archives and FEC both show Obama in Florida winning 4,237,756 votes, out of a statewide total of 8,474,179, just 666 more than a bare majority. (For 2012, David Leip incorrectly puts Obama below 50% in Florida.)

it is certain that the officially winning candidate was not genuinely Jeffersonian insofar as it is demonstrable in those years that the other major-party candidate was the one preferred by a majority of voters in enough states to reach an Electoral College majority.

These three malfunctions, of course, will factor prominently in the historical review of the Jeffersonian Electoral College's performance that we now shall undertake. But a full assessment must consider all the instances in which the 1803 version of the Electoral College has produced a dubious Jeffersonian winner. And to fully understand how the Jeffersonian Electoral College became vulnerable after Andrew Jackson's ascendancy, and to assess the degree to which its vulnerability is currently at a historically unprecedented level, we must start with that Jacksonian development and continue through the election of 2016.

From Jefferson to Jackson

By the time the 1804 presidential election took place, the Jeffersonians were even more dominant throughout the nation than they had been only months before. Accordingly, while they had the power in most state legislatures to appoint presidential electors directly or choose a method of appointment that would be especially advantageous to Jefferson's re-election, their political dominance was such that the particular method of appointment largely would not have made much of a practical difference. Even if Republican-majority states used a district-based system for appointing electors, thereby theoretically giving Federalists a chance to pick up a few electors in an otherwise Republican-controlled state, Jefferson was poised to win most if not all districts, and therefore districting was not a real threat to Jefferson's victory.[1]

As a result, states felt free to adopt whatever method of appointing electors they thought most suited to the values of their local political culture. Six states chose to retain direct legislative appointment of their electors: Connecticut, Vermont, New York, Delaware, South Carolina, and Georgia. Tennessee moved from its unique form of legislative appointment to a district-based system in which the voters of each district chose an elector by popular ballot. By making this move, Tennessee joined Maryland, North Carolina, and Kentucky, all of which had used this method of appointing electors in 1800.[2]

New Jersey and Pennsylvania switched from direct legislative appointment to a statewide popular vote for all their electors, joining Rhode Island and Virginia, both of which had used this system in 1800. Ohio, participating in a presidential election for the first time in 1804, also adopted this system.[3] The prevailing practice in these states, as it would be throughout the nineteenth century whenever voters cast ballots for presidential electors, was for the voter's ballots to name the electors they wanted (not the presidential candidate whom they wanted the electors to choose). Since the practice of balloting in the nineteenth century, prior to the adoption of the so-called Australian ballot printed by the government, was for each party to print "tickets" with the names of its candidates, each party would undertake the task of printing tickets with the names of the individuals it wanted to serve as presidential electors.[4]

Massachusetts and New Hampshire both reverted to methods of guaranteeing majority rule, as they had before 1800. Massachusetts used its own distinctive system in which a person would be appointed elector from a district if that individual received a majority of the votes cast statewide for anyone seeking to be that district's elector.[5] But if in a particular district no one received a majority of the votes, then the Massachusetts legislature would appoint the elector for that district.[6] New Hampshire used a statewide popular vote, and the individuals receiving the most votes would be appointed electors as long as their popular votes were from a majority of the voters. But if any elector position remained unfilled because there were not enough individuals with popular-vote majorities, then the New Hampshire legislature would fill these vacant positions. Jefferson, however, was so popular that Republican electors won majorities even in Massachusetts and New Hampshire, formerly Federalist strongholds, so that no legislative runoffs were needed there that year.[7]

The 1804 election thus ended in a rout. Jefferson won 162 of the 176 electoral votes cast (this time there being only one electoral vote cast for president by each elector). Jefferson's Federalist opponent, Charles Pinckney, who had been the vice presidential running mate for Adams in 1800, received the remaining 14 electoral votes. Jefferson won all the electoral votes from 14 of the 17 states then in the union, including states that used district-based systems to appoint their electors.[8] Jefferson's triumphant victory in 1804 genuinely reflected exactly the kind of compound majority-of-majorities that the Republican architects of the redesigned Electoral College believed was required to make legitimate the chief executive of a federal republic. Jefferson easily achieved his majority of Electoral College votes from states where he was the majority-preferred candidate.

The Electoral College continued to perform exactly as the Jeffersonians intended for the remainder of the Virginia dynasty: Madison's two terms that followed Jefferson's, and then Monroe's two victories that followed Madison's. In each of these four elections, the winner's Electoral College majority was derived from the electoral votes of states where the winner was the majority-preferred candidate. In 1808, Madison won 122 electoral votes. His Federalist opponent was Charles Pinckney again, who did better than he had against Jefferson in 1804, this time winning 47 electoral votes. Even discounting Madison's electoral votes from states that split their votes between candidates—New York, Maryland, and North Carolina—Madison still won an Electoral College majority, 89 votes out of a total of 176, from states in which he won all of the state's electoral votes, and in all those states Madison was the majority-preferred candidate. The split electoral vote in New York was caused by some legislatively appointed electors giving their presidential vote to George Clinton, Madison's running mate for vice president, who had been a long-time New York governor and remained popular in his home state. Clinton, however, was a factor only in New York, not an independent candidate for president nationally, and so did not undercut Madison's 1808 victory being a genuinely Jeffersonian compound majority-of-majorities.

In 1812, Madison's margin of victory was narrower than it had been four years earlier. He received 128 electoral votes to 89 for the Federalist candidate, who this time was Dewitt Clinton (George's nephew). But Madison still received a majority of Electoral College votes, 122, in states where he won all the state's electoral votes, and in all those states he again was the majority-preferred candidate.[9]

In 1816, Monroe trounced Federalist candidate Rufus King, 183 to 34. No state split its electoral votes, and Monroe was clearly the majority-preferred candidate in all the states that gave him their electoral votes. In 1820, during the so-called Era of Good Feelings, Monroe essentially had no opponent to his bid for re-election, the Federalist Party having withered into oblivion. A sole electoral vote, from New Hampshire, was cast for John Quincy Adams, son of the former Federalist president—but even Adams's ex-president father, a Massachusetts elector, voted for Monroe's re-election. In any event, there is no doubt that both of Monroe's victories easily satisfied the Jeffersonian majority-of-majorities standard.[10]

In this Virginia-dynasty era, states continued to use various methods to appoint their electors. Direct legislative appointment remained the most common method during this period, employed by seven states in 1808 and nine in each of the three following elections. By 1820, statewide popular voting caught up with legislative appointment in frequency of use, employed by six states in 1808 (Rhode Island, New Hampshire, New Jersey, Pennsylvania, Virginia, and Ohio); five in 1812 (New Jersey reverting to legislative appointment that year); seven in 1816 (New Jersey returning to the method, and North Carolina joining in); and nine in 1820 (Connecticut and Mississippi coming on board). Districting remained less frequently used than the two predominant methods, but still had substantial—and indeed increasing—support among the states, growing from four states in both 1808 and 1812 to six in 1820 (after a dip to just three in 1816). Table 4.3 summarizes which of the three methods were used by how many, and which, states in these four elections.[11]

Massachusetts switched back and forth between direct legislative appointment (in 1808 and 1816) and a district-based system (in 1812 and 1820).[12] New Hampshire, by contrast, consistently used statewide popular votes for all its electors, and also consistently insisted that a candidate receive a popular-vote majority in order to avoid a legislative runoff. In these four elections, however, New Hampshire never needed to use a legislative runoff because of a mere plurality, rather than majority, in the popular vote.[13] Although the Federalists were dwindling even in New England, there was no third-party alternative to the two-party competition between Republicans and Federalists, such as it

Table 4.3 Method of Choosing Electors by State

Year	Direct Legislative Appointment	Statewide Popular Vote	District-Based Popular Vote
1804	6: CT, VT, NY, DE, SC, GA	6: RI, NH, NJ, PA, VA, OH	5: MA, MD, NC, KY, TN
1808	7: MA, CT, VT, NY, DE, SC, GA	6: RI, NH, NJ, PA, VA, OH	4: MD, NC, KY, TN
1812	9: CT, VT, NY, NJ, DE, NC, SC, GA, LA	5: RI, NH, PA, VA, OH	4: MA, MD, KY, TN
1816	9: MA, CT, VT, NY, DE, SC, GA, LA, IN	7: RI, NH, NJ, PA, VA, NC, OH	3: MD, KY, TN
1820	9: VT, NY, DE, SC, GA, AL, LA, IN, MO	9: RI, NH, CT, NJ, PA, VA, NC, OH, MS	6: MA, ME, MD, KY, TN, IL

existed during this period of Republican dominance. Even when the Federalists entirely collapsed in 1820, they were not yet replaced either by a single new party to compete against the Republicans (as would later be the case with the rise of the Whigs in opposition to what would become the Democrats), or by multiple new parties jousting to become the major opposition force.

The situation changed in 1824. That year there were four main candidates, all ostensibly from the same party known by then as the Democratic-Republicans. William Crawford, the incumbent secretary of the treasury, was the most establishment, or old guard, candidate. John Quincy Adams, the incumbent secretary of state, had Federalist roots and regional strength in New England. Henry Clay was Speaker of the House and, being from Kentucky, had particular appeal in more western (frontier) states. Andrew Jackson, the military hero from the War of 1812, was the insurgent populist of his era.[14]

The Electoral College vote split among the four candidates, with none getting an Electoral College majority. Consequently, the election went to the House of Representatives for its runoff procedure in which each state's delegation cast a single vote. The use of this legislative runoff is exactly what the Jeffersonian architects of the Electoral College redesign in 1803 intended to happen in this situation. None of the four candidates in 1824 were capable of achieving through the Electoral College the kind of compound majority-of-majorities that the Jeffersonians considered essential for a chief executive of a federal republic. Therefore, having failed to achieve a federally legitimating majority-of-majorities through the primary Electoral College mechanism, a candidate would need to reach a different form of federal majority through the backup mechanism of the House runoff procedure. Winning a majority of state delegations in the House would have to suffice to demonstrate that a candidate had adequate majority support from enough states to warrant being the president of the federal union. Indeed, this majority of state delegations in the House could be considered a different kind of compound majority-of-majorities, insofar as no House delegation would cast its single vote for a candidate unless that candidate achieved, in the particular context of the legislative runoff, majority support from that state.[15]

Andrew Jackson thought he was entitled to win the House runoff because he was the candidate with the most Electoral College votes: 99. Adams was next with 84, and then Crawford with 41. These were the three whom the House could choose among in the runoff, as revised by the Jeffersonians in 1803. If the Jeffersonians had kept the number at five, rather than limiting it to three, then Clay could have been considered as well. With only 37 electoral votes, Clay just fell short of third place; as Speaker of the House, he likely would have won the runoff if he had been eligible.[16]

Jackson's sense of entitlement had no basis in the Jeffersonian Electoral College of 1803 or its underlying commitment to majority-rule principles of republican political philosophy. Jackson merely had a plurality of Electoral College votes, meaning that the majority of electors who had not voted for him preferred someone else. Nor could Jackson claim to have majority support within the electorate of America as a whole—not that a unified national electorate was relevant to the federal system that the Jeffersonians wholeheartedly embraced in their 1803 redesign. At most, Jackson had a plurality, barely above 40 percent, of the national popular vote, such as it was in 1824. Six states, including populous New York, used direct legislative appointment of electors that year. New York gave most of its electoral votes to Adams, reflecting his popularity in the state, and indeed had New York appointed its electors in 1824 by means of a popular vote, Jackson might not have had a national plurality in popular votes.[17]

Thus, Jackson entered the House runoff procedure with no presumptive claim to the presidency under the Jeffersonian system created in 1803. In this thoroughly majoritarian system, no kind of plurality was enough: not popular votes nationwide, not electoral votes, and not the votes of states in the House runoff. Instead, Jackson would have to earn the presidency by convincing a majority of all the state delegations that of the three eligible candidates, he was the best man for the job. This he was unable to do.

Instead, Adams was the one for whom a majority of state delegations voted. Jackson and his supporters bitterly and vociferously complained that Adams had made a "corrupt bargain" with Clay in order to secure enough support in the House. But it was not corruption in the conventional form of bribery or other financial inducement. There was essentially a policy agreement between Adams and Clay, used as a basis for coalition-building. Clay became secretary of state. Historians debate whether Adams explicitly offered Clay the job as part of the deal. There is no clear evidence that he did. But even if Adams had promised Clay a position in his administration, that kind of agreement between politicians is internal to a political system in which groups lacking a majority coalesce to reach a governing majority. (It is like putting together a cabinet in a multiparty parliamentary system.)[18]

In any event, Jackson and his supporters insisted that the House vote to make Adams president was incorrigibly corrupt, and they spent the next four years endeavoring to undo that result. In this, they smashingly succeeded. In 1828, in a two-person race against the incumbent Adams, Jackson easily trounced him by an Electoral College vote of 178 to 83.[19]

The Jacksonian Move to Plurality Winner-Take-All

As part of this conquest, Jackson and his supporters transformed the Electoral College of 1803, unmooring it from its majoritarian premises. This process was not entirely deliberate or even intellectually coherent. Indeed, it did not take place all at once, as a product of any single decision. Instead, it was the somewhat unintended byproduct of multiple moves undertaken in many states. Nonetheless, the result was a set of state laws that let a presidential candidate receive all of a state's electoral votes based on winning just a plurality of the state's popular vote. For the 1828 election, 15 states had laws of this kind (five more than in 1824), making it by far the most widely used method of appointing electors that year (there being a total of 24 states for that election).[20]

With the benefit of hindsight, we can see that 1824 was the pivot point in this transformation from a Jeffersonian insistence on majority winners to a Jacksonian willingness to accept plurality results. We see this if we compare maneuverings over the Electoral College procedures that occurred leading up to the fractured 1824 election with the procedural changes that were adopted in its aftermath. Shortly before this election, both nationally and locally, efforts to change to a plurality-based system were rejected—most crucially, in the decisive state of New York. Afterward, however, although these efforts failed at the federal level, they began to take hold in New York and other states.

In Congress, by 1823 it had become evident that the multicandidate race that was looming in 1824 might end without a majority winner in the Electoral College. Accordingly, members seriously considered various ideas for replacing the backup mechanism that gave one vote to each state's delegation in the House. Twenty years after the Twelfth Amendment, this equality of electoral power for the states regardless of population seemed out of step with developing democratic norms. Among the ideas contemplated was to let a candidate win with only an Electoral College plurality. But this idea never gained traction. Rather, much creative energy was expended to develop an alternative backup procedure that would conform to the Jeffersonian commitment to majority rule, but in an updated form. One possibility was an Electoral College runoff, which would have had the electors reconvene for a second round of balloting limited to the top two vote-getters if no candidate won an Electoral College majority in the first round. Another proposal was for a joint session of Congress, with each member (not state) having one vote, to select between the top two finalists. Even venerable James Madison weighed in from the sidelines, reaffirming his longstanding preference for a majority-based rather than plurality-based system for electing a president. As a means to this end, Madison offered a prototype of ranked-choice balloting (with electors listing second choices as well as first choices on their ballots).[21] Despite all this brainstorming, none of the alternatives achieved enough congressional support to dislodge the existing backup procedure, which therefore remained in place for 1824.[22]

In New York, as the presidential election approached that year, local politics became engulfed in the question of how the state's presidential electors should be appointed. The dominant faction in the state legislature, known pejoratively as the Albany Regency, favored the old-guard candidate Crawford. From the beginning, New York law had given its legislature the power to appoint electors, and the Regency wanted to exercise this power on Crawford's behalf. With New York having 36 electoral votes in 1824, more than any other state (Pennsylvania being the next with 28), the Regency would hold considerable clout in Electoral College dynamics if it could deliver all 36 of New York's votes to Crawford.[23]

Opposed to the Regency was a loose coalition of factions that backed Adams primarily, but also Clay to a lesser extent. (Jackson did not have much strength in the state.) They advocated energetically for appointment of the state's presidential electors by means of a statewide popular vote, which they called "the general ticket" method to distinguish it from a district-based system. They even endeavored to organize themselves into a "People's Party" to galvanize support on the issue.

Early in 1824, these self-proclaimed "People's men" introduced in the state legislature a bill to adopt a version of the general-ticket method that would appoint electors based on a plurality, rather than a majority, of the popular vote. In committee deliberations on the bill, Regency members objected that plurality-based appointment of electors—in contrast to the "present system" of majority-based legislative appointment—would be "at war with the spirit of our republican government." Expressing this view in a report of the committee to the assembly (the lower house of the legislature), Regency leader Azariah Flagg explained: "By the existing law of this state, a majority of all the representatives of the people is required to choose electors of president." The committee saw this requirement as reflecting the "broad republican principle of securing electors of president and vice-president who will speak the sentiments of a majority of citizens of the state." The committee wanted no "departure" from this essential principle, declaring instead that "the same republican principle ought to control" any new "mode" of appointing electors that might be adopted.[24]

In defending majority rule at the state level in the appointment of electors, Flagg linked this particular feature of the Electoral College system to its overall majoritarian structure: "The same principle governs in the choice of president by the electoral colleges of the several states: a majority of all electors being necessary to a choice." He even observed that the backup House procedure contained its own version of majority rule: "And in the last resort, when the question is decided by the states, in their capacity as independent sovereigns, a majority of all states is necessary to decide the question." In this way, Flagg faithfully summarized the essence of the compound majority-rule system that the Jeffersonians adopted in their 1803 version of the Electoral College.

In his report, Flagg made clear that the Regency-dominated committee did not insist on legislative appointment of electors. Nor did the committee object to all forms of popular voting by general ticket. Rather, it was only the plurality-based element of the People Party's proposal for a general-ticket system that was objectionable. Thus, the committee moved to amend the People Party's proposal by adding a majority-winner requirement. "In recommending the system of a general ticket," Flagg reported, "the committee are of the opinion that a majority of all votes of the state ought to be required to make a choice."

The committee's reason for this modification was simple: "Without such a provision, a minority might control the electoral vote of this state." To illustrate the basic point, Flagg gave an example not unlike the one that opens this book: "In choosing by plurality, if there were only three candidates before the public, the thirty-six electoral votes of this state might be controlled by little more than one-third of the voters." This result would be inherently unacceptable from the perspective of fundamental democratic principles underlying the Jeffersonian mechanism for presidential elections.

A district-based system would be preferable to a plurality-based general ticket, Flagg explained. A district-based system does not run the risk of "having the whole influence of the state brought to act contrary to the wishes of a large majority of its citizens." A plurality-based general ticket, by contrast, necessarily makes "it possible for a minority to wield the whole power of the state." While not wishing to dilute the bloc power of New York's 36 electoral votes as a district-based system would, the committee considered it essential that "the strength of the state" not be given over to a mere minority but instead "ought to be secured to a majority of the freemen of the state."

When the assembly took up the committee's report, the People's Party balked at the committee's modification of its bill. They specifically objected to the committee's requirement of a majority vote for the popular appointment of presidential electors on the ground that there was insufficient time to hold a runoff vote in the event that no ticket of electors achieved a majority in the first round of popular voting. In response to this objection, Flagg offered that the legislature could appoint the electors as a fallback in the event that the popular vote failed to produce a majority. (This fallback would be the equivalent of what Massachusetts and New Hampshire had adopted.) The People's Party viewed Flagg's fallback as little better than the status quo—legislative appointment with no initial popular vote—given the high unlikelihood of a majority winner in the first round of voting (at least in 1824, with its multicandidate field). The People's Party thus moved to undo the committee's modification and return the bill to its original plurality-based form. But Flagg and his Regency allies were dominant in the assembly, and this motion failed, 64–52.[25]

The committee's version, with its insistence on a majority winner, had the votes to pass the assembly. But it died in the state senate. There, too, the People's Party pressed for a plurality-based general ticket. Again they were defeated, this time by a 17–14 vote. With more deliberation, the senate might have passed a majority-based version of the general ticket, comparable to that proposed in the committee report in the assembly. But a motion to postpone consideration of the issue prevailed, by the same 17–14 margin, and no further action was taken until after the 1824 election later that year.[26] Thus, New York retained its legislative appointment of electors and exercised that power in a way that ultimately favored Adams over Jackson. (Ironically, intervening events caused a diminution of Crawford's status, and although the Regency had wanted to retain this legislative power to promote his candidacy, the struggle in the state over the method of appointment had ended up benefiting Adams anyway.)

Immediately after the election of Adams by the House of Representatives, New York's legislature changed its procedure for appointing the state's presidential electors. Although there were advocates continuing to push for the People Party's plurality-based general ticket, including the state's newly inaugurated governor (DeWitt Clinton, who had been the Federalist presidential candidate back in 1812), the legislature was not yet ready for that major a transformation. Instead, as an interim step the legislature adopted a district-based system for the next election in 1828.[27] The year after that election the legislature would complete the process, installing the plurality form of the general ticket for 1832 in New York.[28]

Meanwhile, five other states did not wait. Illinois, Kentucky, Louisiana, Missouri, and Vermont all switched to plurality-based versions of winner-take-all for 1828. These enactments, however, do not reveal a philosophical commitment to plurality rather than majority winners. Rather, they simply provide for winners based on the "highest" or "greatest" number of votes cast, thereby putting in place a plurality-winner system with no explicit requirement of obtaining a majority. Adoption of these new rules may have reflected confusion, or at least a lack of conscious choice, on the part of the legislatures concerning the distinction between plurality and majority winners. For example, in supporting Vermont's move to a popular vote for the appointment of its electors, the state's governor said that it would cause these appointments to accord with the "sentiments" held by "a majority of the people."[29]

Georgia also switched from legislative appointment of its electors in 1824 to a statewide popular vote as the method of appointment in 1828. But in making this switch Georgia explicitly required that the electors win a majority, and not merely a plurality, of the popular vote. Otherwise, the state's legislature (by a joint ballot of the two chambers) would appoint the state's electors. In this respect, Georgia followed the majority-rule model used in Massachusetts and New Hampshire.[30]

This statutory distinction between Georgia and the five other states that switched to a general-ticket vote did not make a practical difference in the 1828 election, as Jackson had no need for plurality victories. He was the majority-preferred candidate, not merely the plurality-preferred candidate, in all of the states in which he won electoral votes (see Table 4.2).[31] Thus, despite unleashing a political movement that undermined the majoritarian basis of the Jeffersonian system adopted in 1803, Jackson himself was a genuinely Jeffersonian winner in 1828. That year, unlike in 1824, he achieved the kind of compound majority-of-majorities that the Jeffersonians considered as legitimating for a federal president.

Moreover, Jackson himself never specifically advocated for a plurality-based system of electing presidents. On the contrary, after becoming president with the clear support of the majority of America's voters in 1828, Jackson called for Electoral College reform that he thought would better conform to majoritarian principles. In his first presidential message (what we today would call a "state of the union" address, although then it was delivered in writing), Jackson declared: "Let us, then, endeavor so to amend our system that the office of Chief Magistrate may not be conferred upon any citizen but in pursuance of a fair expression of the will of the majority."[32]

Jackson, not surprisingly, targeted for amendment the one-state-one-vote House backup procedure, which had delivered the 1824 election to Adams. In addition to fostering the selling of "offices" for "votes" (the kind of "corruption" that Jackson saw inherent in the Adams-Clay alliance), the House backup procedure may cause "a minority" of citizens to "elect a President" given the equal voting rights of states regardless of population. This result was pernicious, Jackson explained, because "a President elected by a minority can not enjoy the confidence necessary to the successful discharge of his duties."

Accordingly, Jackson recommended replacing the existing backup procedure with a runoff: "A failure in the first attempt may be provided for by confining the second to a choice between the two highest candidates." Jackson also urged eliminating the Electoral College insofar as it involved the "intermediate agency" of actual human electors casting their own ballots. But Jackson was willing to keep the existing federalist structure insofar as it would "preserve to each state its present relative weight in the election." Jackson's vision of Electoral College reform was entirely consistent with the basic Jeffersonian idea that the system should be designed to achieve a compound majority-of-majorities, as the form of majority rule appropriate for a federally elected chief executive. Indeed, Jackson described his proposal as premised on "the first principle of our system—that the majority is to govern."

Nor did Jackson's supporters in Congress challenge this first principle or offer a philosophical claim for plurality-based voting as preferential to majority rule. To be sure, in the immediate aftermath of the 1824 election, among the flurry of proposals offered in Congress was the idea of electing presidents based on a mere plurality of votes. But this idea went nowhere. Much greater attention was devoted to adopting some form of Electoral College runoff, which would have been fully consonant with the Jeffersonian commitment to majority rule. The runoff proposal floundered, however, as it had before the 1824 election, because members of Congress could not agree on the particular form the runoff should take. There was certainly no full-throated or concerted effort in Congress, along the lines of what had transpired in New York, to replace the goal of achieving a compound majority-of-majorities with a new majority-of-*pluralities* system.[33]

Even so, within the states, Jacksonians after 1828 continued to consolidate plurality winner-take-all as the prevailing method of appointing presidential electors. For Jackson's own re-election victory in 1832, every state but four used this system—including New York, as we have seen.[34] Only South Carolina clung to direct legislative appointment, which it would use until the Civil War.[35] Maryland stuck with its districting system for 1832, but switched to plurality winner-take-all for 1836 and thereafter.[36] Massachusetts and New Hampshire remained holdouts as they continued to insist upon majority winners and still required legislative runoffs, if necessary, to avoid appointing any electors by merely a plurality of popular votes.[37]

But, as in 1828, Jackson did not need any plurality wins to achieve an Electoral College majority in 1832. He needed 145 electoral votes and won 219, of which 208—or almost three-quarters of the total cast that year—came from states in which he won a majority, not just a plurality, of the popular vote (see Table 4.2). Once again, Jackson achieved a genuinely Jeffersonian victory, a thoroughly validating majority-of-majorities, even as his supporters continued to alter the Jeffersonian system in a way that would cause it to contradict its majoritarian premises.

The Jacksonian transformation of the Electoral College system was thus unorchestrated, even unintentional. It contravened Jackson's self-professed "first principle." It was rather like a virus that, having stealthily invaded the body, remained latent—not yet visibly erupting into disease.

This pathogen of plurality winner-take-all did not immediately produce an anti-majoritarian, un-Jeffersonian outcome. In 1836, Jackson's protégé Martin Van Buren received all 170 of his electoral votes, a sizable majority (58 percent) of the 294 cast, from states in which he won a majority, not just a plurality, of the popular vote (see Table 4.2). The fact that the new Whig Party fielded several candidates in opposition to Van Buren caused the Whigs to fracture their minority of electoral votes into even smaller shares, but this multiplicity of Whig opponents did not cause Van Buren to fall below a majority of the popular vote in any state that gave him its electoral votes.[38] He, too, was a genuinely Jeffersonian winner.

So was William Harrison, the Whig winner in 1840, who crushed Van Buren's bid for re-election. Although the prevailing party was different, the Jeffersonian nature of the victory was the same. Harrison, like Van Buren four years earlier, received all of his electoral votes— 234, or 80 percent of 294 total—from states where he won a majority of the popular vote (see Table 4.2).

There was another candidate in the race that year: James Birney of the abolitionist Liberty Party. In 1840, however, Birney did not win enough votes to be a factor in the competition between Whigs and Democrats. In the state where Birney won his largest number of votes—2,809, in New York—Harrison still received 51.2 percent, which amounted to 226,001 ballots. Harrison's Electoral College win was a solid federal majority-of-majorities.

Four years later, circumstances were entirely different.

The First Failure of the Jeffersonian Electoral College

In 1844, the Democratic candidate was James Polk. As the champion of Manifest Destiny, he called for westward expansion and the annexation of Texas by force if necessary. The Whig candidate was Henry Clay, who favored annexation and expansion only by peaceable means.

James Birney ran again as the candidate of the abolitionist Liberty Party.[39]

This time Birney was crucial to the outcome. Although other factors undoubtedly were at play as well, including some errors in judgment on the part of Clay in how he handled the Texas issue during his campaign, it is not too much to say that Birney's presence in the race made the difference in who won. The leading account of the era summarizes: "Birney took enough anti-annexation votes away from Clay to cost him New York," and New York was the pivotal state. "If New York had gone the other way, Clay would have won the election."[40]

The numbers tell the basic story. Polk won a majority of Electoral College votes, 170 of 275, but he did so only because he, not Clay, received all of New York's 36 electoral votes. Without these New York votes, Polk's total would have dropped to 134, below the majority threshold of 138 (see Table 4.1).[41]

Moreover, if Clay had received New York's 36 electoral votes, then he—not Polk—would have won an Electoral College majority. Without New York's electoral votes, Clay's total was 105. Adding New York's to these would have given Clay 141, putting him above the majority threshold in the Electoral College and thus making him president.

Polk did not win a majority of the popular vote in New York. His official total there was 237,588, which was 48.90 percent of all presidential ballots cast in the state. Clay's total was 232,482, which was 47.85 percent and 5,106 fewer than Polk's. In New York that year Birney got 15,812 votes, 3.25 percent of presidential ballots in the state and an amount three times as large as Polk's margin over Clay. As the preeminent historian of the Whigs has observed, "If Clay had captured only a third of Birney's 15,800 votes in New York, he would have won the election."[42] In the same vein, antebellum historian Amy Greenberg writes: "Had just 5,000 Liberty Party supporters voted for Henry Clay, whose views they most certainly preferred to Polk's, Clay would have won the state and with it the electoral vote and the national election."[43]

There is no doubt that Birney "siphoned significant antislavery votes from Clay," not Polk.[44] Clay was not the abolitionist that Birney was, but Clay was far less pro-slavery than Polk. If Birney had not been in the race, or if there had been a popular-vote runoff between Clay and Polk in New York after Birney had been eliminated from contention, enough Birney supporters would have found their way to Clay's column to make Clay victorious in New York.

Both Clay and his leading supporters saw Birney as a key factor causing Clay's defeat. Writing to a Delaware supporter a month after his defeat, Clay lamented that "if the Abolitionists had been true to their avowed principles"—meaning if they had voted for him rather than Birney as the only practical means of curtailing slavery—"we should have triumphed."[45] Thurlow Weed, the prominent Albany editor, was much more blunt about the "disastrous" consequences of "Birneyism" and the "fatal tendencies of ultra Abolitionists": "The fifteen thousand votes which were worse than squandered in New York, to say nothing of the thousands thrown away elsewhere, have not only made a shipwreck of every other public interest, but threaten to extend and strengthen the links of slavery." Abraham Lincoln, then a Whig disciple of Clay, made the same point: " 'If the Whig abolitionists in New York had voted with us last fall, Mr. Clay would now be President."[46] Elaborating on the folly of voting for Birney if one opposes slavery, Lincoln added: "If the fruit of electing Mr. Clay would have been to prevent the extension of slavery, could the act of electing have been *evil*?"[47]

To be sure, not every Birney voter would have cast a ballot for Clay if confined to a choice between him and Polk. Rather, some of these Birney supporters would have abstained from selecting what they indeed perceived as an evil, even though Clay was obviously the lesser one from their abolitionist perspective. Such "indomitable firmness" in support of an unwinnable third-party candidacy might not make sense; indeed, it could be called sheer "obstinancy," as the early historian Jabez Hammond observed.[48] Nonetheless, it was a real phenomenon and would have put a limit on the percentage of Birney votes that would have been available to Clay if the election had been confined to a two-candidate race (or runoff).[49]

Even so, the opposite extreme must also be rejected: not every Birney voter in New York was irreconcilably opposed to casting a ballot for Clay under any circumstances. On the contrary, Horace Greeley, who as editor of the *New York Daily Tribune* observed the 1844 election in the state as closely as anyone, later estimated that "at least half" of Birney's votes would have been available to Clay.[50] That number would have been far more than enough to tip New York, and thus the entire election, to Clay. The analysis of a new Clay biography reaches the same conclusion. Even recognizing it "uncertain" how many "Liberty Party voters" would have "voted at all," what "certainly" remains true is this: "Had that third party not been in the field, most of those ballots would have been cast for Clay" and, consequently, "he would have won."[51] Or as the distinguished historian Sean Wilentz frames it, anticipating the structural similarity between the 1844 and 2000 elections: "The Liberty Party candidate James G. Birney looks like the Green Party candidate Ralph Nader."[52]

Thus, in understanding the significance of 1844 for today—and the future—it is fair to conclude that as between Clay and Polk, Clay unquestionably was the majority-preferred candidate in New York. Polk's election was an "accident," as one Clay supporter put it in a letter reprinted in multiple newspapers. "The victor has nothing to boast of," this writer explained, because Polk was a "minority" candidate who "owes his success to the fatuity of a political sect who have been cajoled into a position that deprived the Whigs of the majority [which genuinely was theirs] and given to their opponents a base plurality." This widely circulated missive was hardly alone in questioning Polk's legitimacy as a "minority Chief Magistrate," placed in the presidency "against a majority of the people's suffrages." Indeed, even a pro-Polk paper in New York acknowledged that he "gained the Presidency by a plurality, not a majority" and that his status as "chief magistrate" was compromised by having "been elected by a minority of the popular vote."[53]

Clay was the genuinely Jeffersonian choice in the race because, with New York's electoral votes, he would have achieved an authentically compound majority-of-majorities. His Electoral College majority, unlike Polk's, would have been assembled entirely with electoral votes from states where he, Clay, was the candidate preferred by a majority of the state's voters. Given that the goal of the Jeffersonian Electoral College of 1803 was to make president the candidate capable of attaining this kind of compound majority-of-majorities, the system badly misfired in 1844 by producing Polk and not Clay as the winner. In short, given its own Jeffersonian objectives, the system reached the wrong result that year.

To be clear, there was one state, Ohio, that Clay won in which he received only a plurality, not a majority, of the popular vote: 49.68 percent for Clay, to 47.74 percent for Polk, with 2.58 percent for Birney. Without Birney in the race, Clay easily would have crossed 50 percent in Ohio. All the rest of Clay's electoral votes came from states where even with Birney as candidate, Clay had more than 50 percent. The conclusion is inescapable that in a two-person race between Clay and Polk, Clay would have won a majority of Electoral College votes from states where he would have won the majority of the popular vote.

But it was not a two-person race, and today one might speculate how an Electoral College system designed with Jeffersonian principles and objectives could have resulted in Clay, rather than Polk, prevailing with Birney in the race. A legislative runoff, as both Massachusetts and New Hampshire law required at the time in the event of a statewide plurality winner, is one possibility.[54] But in 1844 the New York legislature was controlled by Democrats, and so if it used a legislative runoff that year, New York might have given its electoral votes to Polk, the Democrat, even though Clay was the major-party candidate preferred by a majority of the state's voters.[55] Only a popular-vote runoff, of the kind New Hampshire used in 1792, would have guaranteed that Clay received New York's electoral votes because a majority of the state's voters preferred him to Polk.

The key point is that in 1803, when the Jeffersonians redesigned the Electoral College with the idea of a compound majority-of-majorities in mind, they did not anticipate the need to require states, like New York, to use a runoff in this kind of situation. They did not envision a three-way race that would end up with a candidate winning an Electoral College majority without being the majority-preferred candidate in the states that generated that federal majority. Instead they foresaw two-party disputes in which states would support one party or the other, and if there were a three-way dispute, it would deprive any candidate of an Electoral College majority—as occurred in 1824. But if they could have foreseen what happened in 1844, we know that their principles would have caused them to believe that Clay, rather than Polk, was the true federal-majority candidate in the race and thus deserving to serve as chief executive of the federal republic.

The fact that Polk won a plurality of the national popular vote in 1844 does not alter this conclusion. Winning a national plurality was entirely irrelevant according to the federal-majority premises of the Jeffersonian redesign of the Electoral College in 1803. Clay, indeed, might actually have won a national popular majority if there had been a national popular runoff in 1844. (If Birney's 2.30 percent nationally is added to Clay's 48.09 percent nationally, it reaches 50.39 percent, more than Polk's 49.54 percent nationally.) But the Jeffersonians of 1803 did not want to elect a president based on a national popular vote, whether plurality or majority. Instead, they wanted to elect a president with an Electoral College majority based on being the candidate preferred by the majority of the electorate in the states forming that Electoral College majority.

Given the failure of the Jeffersonian Electoral College in 1844, why was the system not changed afterward?

There are two main reasons. First is the extraordinary difficulty of amending the Constitution. Although the Jeffersonians were able to clear that high hurdle in 1803, there has been no comparable constitutional retooling of the Electoral College since. That absence is not for lack of effort. As the historian Alex Keyssar portrays, there have been repeated attempts since the Twelfth Amendment to make further constitutional changes to the Electoral College or even abandon it altogether in favor of a national popular vote. All those efforts have come up short, even those in the wake of 1824, when the Jacksonians were complaining so vociferously about the alleged "Corrupt Bargain."[56]

The second reason, more particular to 1844, is that what happened in New York to deprive Clay of victory that year seemed an anomaly. There were serious allegations that Polk received his New York plurality only by fraud in the state.[57] New York's "dogs and cats must have been affected with an unusual dose of civic pride," one historian has quipped.[58] In other words, even with Birney on the ballot, Clay might well have won New York—and thus the presidency—if the voting process there had been conducted properly, untainted by fraud. Rather than the result appearing to require a legislative change, it seemed only to demand that the existing system operate honestly. Why add the mechanism of a runoff, with the extra costs associated with that change, if the correct result would have occurred simply by employing existing procedures accurately and fairly?

New York, moreover, was not predisposed to require that electors receive a majority of popular votes, or else face some form of runoff (either legislative or popular), since the state had failed to adopt that requirement during its debates over the People Party's general-ticket proposal back in 1824. More than any other state, New York had become devoted to the idea of plurality-based, rather than majority-based, voting for presidential electors as its response to the rise of Jacksonian populism.[59] After the debacle of 1844, leading Whigs in New York also expected that abolitionists in the state had learned their lesson from causing Polk's presidency, thereby accelerating the expansion of slavery contrary to their own professed goals.[60] If they would not make the same mistake twice, there was no pressing need for structural reform to handle the problem of a misguided third-party candidacy. Instead, the existing system—built for two-party competition—could continue unamended.[61]

In any event, after Clay's loss to Polk, the Whigs accepted the defeat and turned their attention to opposing his aggressive expansionism.[62] But the consequences of Polk's victory were enormous. As promised, he took the nation to war against Mexico to conquer new territory for the United States. "A wicked war," because it was a war of aggression undertaken by the United States, one officer called it. That officer was Ulysses Grant, who certainly did not shirk from battle when he saw the cause as just.[63]

Also, in keeping with Polk's pro-slavery views, the territory acquired from this war were largely domains seeking entry to the Union as slave states, not free. Some have speculated that the disequilibrium of Polk's expansion put the nation on the path to the Civil War. Daniel Walker Howe has endorsed this view, and Sean Wilentz has lent it credence.[64] We can never know for sure, but it is reasonable to assume that history would have unfolded very differently if Clay, rather than Polk, had become president.[65]

Insofar as Clay, not Polk, should have been the winner given the Jeffersonian premises of the 1803 Electoral College, the malfunctioning of the system that gave Polk the presidency was all the more monumental in light of the military aggression that Polk pursued. "The country owes much of its misrule and misery," Thurlow Weed presciently agonized, to the "actions of minorities." By this, Weed meant the capacity of the Liberty Party voters in New York—"well-meaning, patriotic, but misguided"—to derail Clay's presidency, thereby frustrating what actually was "the popular will" and what should have prevailed if America had "practically a representative government."[66] It is astonishing how little Americans today know about the election of 1844, its pivotal role in making the United States an imperial power as a result of its territorial conquests, and most crucially its antidemocratic character insofar as its outcome was contrary to majority rule.

Comparing 1844 and 1848

Four years later, the system came close to another malfunction. It certainly did not produce a clear Jeffersonian winner in the strict mathematical sense defined at the outset of this chapter. The Whig candidate, General Zachary Taylor, won an Electoral College majority: 163 of 290. But he did so by winning four states with popular-vote pluralities: New York (36), Massachusetts (12), Connecticut (6), and Vermont (6). Without these states Taylor would have only 103 electoral votes, well below the majority threshold of 147. Thus mathematically, Taylor is in the category of a dubious Jeffersonian winner (see Table 4.1).

In 1848, Taylor faced two opponents. Senator Lewis Cass was the Democrat. Martin Van Buren, the former president and former Democrat—indeed a leader of shaping the Democratic Party into its Jacksonian form during the prior two decades—was now the presidential candidate of the new Free Soil Party.[67]

Although Van Buren's presence in the race surely cost Cass votes, it is far from obvious that Cass would have picked up all of Van Buren's votes if Van Buren had not run. The Free Soil ticket, with Charles Francis Adams as Van Buren's running mate, attracted some support from so-called conscience Whigs, who could not support Taylor—a slaveholding southerner—as their party's presidential candidate. Also, most of those who had supported Birney and the Liberty Party in 1844 gravitated to the Free Soil ticket, and these abolitionists would not have voted for Cass if limited to just him and Taylor as the only two options;

they either would have sat the race out or reluctantly voted Whig as the more antislavery alternative.

Moreover, Van Buren, not Cass, was the second-place finisher in three of the four states where Taylor had pluralities: New York, Massachusetts, and Vermont. Thus, the relevant question is whether Taylor would have achieved majorities in these states if Cass had been eliminated from the race in runoffs there.[68]

There are reasons to think that Taylor would have beaten Van Buren in these runoffs. For one thing, Massachusetts held a legislative runoff pursuant to its statutory requirement to resolve three-way splits that caused the kind of plurality that Taylor had. Using this runoff procedure, Massachusetts gave its electoral votes to Taylor, not Van Buren.[69] Taylor might have won a popular runoff there as well, and also in New York, with these two states being enough to reach an Electoral College majority. (Winning a runoff in Vermont as well would have been superfluous.) Taylor was already close to 50 percent of the popular vote in both Massachusetts (45.32 percent) and New York (47.94 percent), whereas Van Buren was far from it—with only about a quarter of the vote in each state (28.45 percent in Massachusetts and 26.43 percent in New York). If only a fairly small percentage of Cass voters would have refused to vote Free Soil in a popular runoff (perhaps because they shared the pro-slavery sympathies of the Democratic Party), even if they had just stayed home rather than voting Whig in the runoff, Taylor easily could have ended up the runoff winner in both states.[70]

Despite the ambiguities caused by the three-way race in 1848, it is probable that Taylor actually was a Jeffersonian winner, reaching an Electoral College majority by being the majority-preferred candidate in enough states, including Massachusetts and New York, once one analyzes what results popular-vote runoffs probably would have produced in those states. Although 1848 again demonstrated the vulnerability to malfunctioning that plurality winner-take-all had introduced into the Jeffersonian system, 1848—unlike 1844—most likely was not an actual malfunction. Instead, the best analysis is that Taylor would have won the presidency even if the Jeffersonian system had worked exactly as designed, in a way that unambiguously guarantees that the Electoral College winner had achieved the requisite compound majority-of-majorities. This analysis accords with the assessment of historians who have concluded that in contrast to four years earlier, "the third party does not appear to have determined the outcome of the election, which Taylor would have won even without its intervention."[71]

Whatever our assessment of 1848, the system returned to producing clear Jeffersonian winners in both 1852 and 1856. Franklin Pierce, in 1852, won 222 electoral votes, well above the majority threshold of 149, from states in which he won a majority of the popular vote. James Buchanan's victory in 1856 was narrower, but he still secured 152 electoral votes—three more than the majority threshold of 149—from states where he had popular-vote majorities (see Table 4.2). The 1850s brought the increasing threat of Civil War, but that impending crisis was not exacerbated by the particular way in which the Electoral College operated in the two elections during that decade. In both of those elections the Jeffersonian Electoral College performed exactly as planned, yielding presidents with demonstrably appropriate majority-of-majorities. If the Electoral College system had contributed to the onset of the Civil War, it was because of the monumental malfunctioning that had occurred back in 1844 and the flow of history that ensued from that mistake.

Lincoln, Grant, and the Reconstruction of the Electoral College

It is often remarked that the election of Abraham Lincoln in 1860 was the immediately precipitating spark that led to the conflagration of the Civil War. As David Donald put it in his prize-winning biography of Lincoln: "At the news of his election, disunion erupted in the South." Even moderate Southerners proclaimed that "the Election of Lincoln is Sufficient Cause for Secession." Indeed, every representative in Congress from South Carolina had announced that they would support secession if Lincoln were elected.[72]

Some also consider Lincoln's 1860 victory to be a massive failure of the Electoral College system. Lincoln's Electoral College majority was produced with only 40 percent of the popular vote nationwide, and even that requires rounding up from 39.65 percent. And Lincoln was entirely a regional candidate. His support came solely from the North.

He won no electoral votes from southern—or even border—states. Even more startlingly, he won zero popular votes in nine southern states: Alabama, Arkansas, Florida, Georgia, Louisiana, Mississippi, North Carolina, Tennessee, and Texas.

If there had been a nationwide runoff between Lincoln and Stephen Douglas, the Democratic nominee, without John Breckinridge and John Bell in the race, Douglas undoubtedly would have won a majority of that nationwide popular runoff. Breckinridge was the candidate of the splinter Southern Democrats. Bell was the nominee of the new Constitutional Unionist Party, which drew its support from border states and was much more moderate toward the South and slavery than Lincoln and his fellow Republicans. If faced with a choice between only Lincoln and Douglas, Breckinridge's supporters clearly would have preferred Douglas. The same is true for many of Bell's supporters, at least enough to make Douglas majority-preferred nationally over Lincoln.[73]

That truth is used to argue that the Electoral College picked the wrong winner in 1860. Douglas should have been the one elected, so the argument goes, based on being the majority-preferred candidate nationally. The fact that Lincoln won the Electoral College with so little national support demonstrates the Electoral College's mistake, according to this argument, and justifies—at least to some extent—the Southern outrage at Lincoln's victory.[74]

This argument, however, misses the Jeffersonian premises of the Electoral College as redesigned in 1803. As we have seen, mere national popularity—without regard to its distribution among states—was irrelevant to the Jeffersonian quest for a federally appropriate winner. Douglas was not a genuinely Jeffersonian candidate in 1860. He was incapable of assembling the kind of compound majority-of-majorities necessary for federal legitimacy.

In fact, Lincoln was the genuinely Jeffersonian candidate in 1860. He received 180 electoral votes, 169 of which came from states in which Lincoln won a majority—not merely a plurality—of the popular vote. The total number of electoral votes in 1860 was 303, and so the threshold for an Electoral College majority was 152. Thus, Lincoln's 169 electoral votes from states where he was a majority winner of the popular vote mean that Lincoln achieved the kind of compound majority-of-majorities that the Jeffersonian authors of the 1803 Electoral College wanted to elect a president (see Table 4.2).

True, Lincoln achieved his compound majority-of-majorities without any support from the South. But the Jeffersonians specifically anticipated in 1803 that a presidential candidate, perhaps even Jefferson himself in 1804, might win an Electoral College majority without any support from one specific region of the federal union. In 1804, a candidate could lose all of New England's 45 electoral votes and still have far more than the majority needed for an Electoral College victory. In redesigning the Electoral College the Jeffersonians certainly did not believe that losing all of New England, because a Republican would lack popular support in that Federalist-dominated region, would deprive a Republican winner of federal legitimacy.

In that situation, the New England Federalists would need to recognize that they were the minority within the federal union, and to accept that this minority status did not empower them to block a Republican from becoming president. It certainly would not justify New England seceding from the union, as some New England Federalists were contemplating in 1803. No, the Jeffersonians considered this very situation as they were thinking through their Electoral College redesign. After all, the Federalists in Congress themselves raised the point in the 1803 debates on what would become the Twelfth Amendment. The Federalists kept contending that their minority status, confined essentially as it was to the region of New England, required that they retain the mechanism of the 1787 Electoral College that gave them blocking power over the Republican Party's first-choice candidate for president. That blocking power, argued the New England Federalists (like Senator Tracy of Connecticut, a leader of those contemplating secession), was the price necessary for keeping the regionally confined minority within the federal union. But the Jeffersonians repeatedly and emphatically rejected that Federalist argument. Instead, they energetically maintained that as long as a presidential candidate had majority support in the states that gave the candidate an Electoral College majority, then this compound majority-of-majorities sufficed to make the candidate a legitimate chief executive for the federal union. Therefore, the regionally confined minority had no right either to veto that federally legitimate choice or to leave the union because of it.

The Jeffersonians of 1803 had contemplated exactly the kind of winning candidate that Lincoln was in 1860, and the Jeffersonians had specifically determined this kind of candidate to be federally legitimate. To be sure, in 1860 the regionally confined minority was the South, not New England as had been the case in 1803. But the principle was exactly the same.

The Electoral College did not malfunction in 1860. Lincoln's election was not at all a breach of federalist principles as hammered out in the context of presidential elections in 1803. The Federalist version of federalism had failed in 1803. It was the Republican version of federalism that was constitutionalized in the Electoral College redesign that year. Insofar as the South in 1860 was now repudiating Lincoln's election, it was Southerners—not Lincoln and his supporters in the North—who were attempting to undo the conception of a federally appropriate president made part of the Constitution by adoption of the Twelfth Amendment.

Accordingly, if the Electoral College was a cause of the Civil War, it was only because the South was unwilling to abide by the terms of the federal arrangement embodied in the Electoral College of 1803. Lincoln's election was fully faithful to both the letter and spirit of that arrangement. He was entitled to govern the South as part of the federal union on the basis of his compound majority-of-majorities, just as Jefferson had been entitled to govern New England on the very same basis. In rejecting Lincoln's legitimacy, the South was in the wrong from a Jeffersonian perspective.

The Civil War, moreover, did not abolish or even alter the Electoral College of 1803. Instead, while the war was still raging, Lincoln's re-election in 1864 again complied with the system's Jeffersonian principles and expectations. All 212 of Lincoln's electoral votes that year came from states in which Lincoln won the majority of the popular vote. Those 212 electoral votes gave Lincoln a landslide in terms of the electoral votes actually cast that year: only 234, because the South did not participate. But even if all the Confederate states were counted against Lincoln, his 212 votes still would have been a strong Electoral College majority. Lincoln thus remained a genuine Jeffersonian winner for the entire United States throughout the Civil War.

Given the federal legitimacy of both Lincoln's victories, Reconstruction then proceeded on the premise that no constitutional change to the Electoral College of 1803 was needed. All that was necessary was for the Southern states to return to the union and for the Electoral College to operate according to its Jeffersonian premises, as it had before. Grant's two victories, in 1868 and 1872, occurred entirely on this basis. Each time, all of Grant's electoral votes—well in excess of the threshold necessary for an Electoral College majority—came from states where Grant won a majority of the popular vote (see Table 4.2). There was thus no doubt that Grant was twice a genuine Jeffersonian winner, suitable for the presidency of the reconstructed federal union.

The election of 1876 was hugely controversial, as Republicans and Democrats fought over the outcome of the popular vote in three southern states: Florida, Louisiana, and South Carolina.[75] But easily overlooked when focusing on that controversy is the fact that the ultimate resolution of that election represents a reaffirmation of the Jeffersonian Electoral College, with a commitment to continue its use as the method for electing a federally legitimate president. Officially, the Republican candidate Rutherford Hayes won all three of the disputed states by popular majorities, albeit slim ones. Hayes, moreover, won his other states with popular majorities, not pluralities. (Colorado, newly admitted to the Union, and acting quickly to participate in the election, had its legislature appoint its electors directly, but there is no doubt that this legislative appointment reflected the majority view within the state's electorate, and in any event direct legislative appointment of electors was a method of achieving the majority will of a state consistent with the Jeffersonian redesign of the Electoral College in 1803.[76]) Accepting the official results from the three disputed states, as Congress did using the special procedure that it devised when faced with the dispute, Hayes managed to eke out a compound majority-of-majorities. With the electoral votes of Florida, Louisiana, and South Carolina in his column, Hayes won the bare minimum necessary for an Electoral College majority: 185. And because that Electoral College majority was predicated on his official wins in those three states, it entirely comprised states where Hayes officially won a majority of the popular vote.

Beyond this official result, there was even better reason to believe that Hayes was a genuine Jeffersonian winner in 1876. The only reason why the tallies in Florida, Louisiana, and South Carolina were at all close was that black voters had been unlawfully and systematically denied the right to vote. Given their overwhelming support for Hayes, the Republican, the circumstance was that if they had been permitted to cast ballots as they were entitled—and tried—to do, Hayes would have won those three states by comfortable majorities, and his compound majority-of-majorities would have been abundantly clear.

Thus in 1876, Hayes actually won the presidency by being the majority-preferred candidate in enough states. The fact that Hayes did not win the national popular vote remained irrelevant for the federal union that the United States, as reconstructed, continued to be. Indeed, insofar as acceptance of Hayes's victory marked the end of Reconstruction, it was confirmation that the Jeffersonian method of electing presidents continued to be accepted as the constitutionally appropriate way to choose the chief executive of the federal United States.

The Second Failure of the Jeffersonian Electoral College

The system still had its latent Jacksonian vulnerabilities, and these began to resurface almost immediately after the end of Reconstruction. To be sure, the 1880 election went smoothly according to the Jeffersonian plan. Four years later, however, the system failed again, as it first had four decades earlier in 1844. This second failure is not as historically significant or memorable as the first—no major war occurred as a result—but for the purpose of assessing the Jeffersonian system's susceptibility to failure it is worth considering nonetheless.

The 1884 election involved four candidates. Grover Cleveland was the Democrat, and James Blaine the Republican. Two minor-party candidates became key factors in the race. Benjamin Butler ran as the Greenback Party candidate, and John St. John for the Prohibition Party.[77]

New York again was the pivotal state. There, Cleveland had a plurality of 563,048 votes, only 1,047 more than Blaine's 562,001. In percentage terms, the New York numbers for both major-party candidates rounded to 48.2 percent, and thus both were almost equally short of a majority.[78]

Had they been the only two candidates in the race, Blaine in all probability would have pulled ahead of Cleveland and been the majority-preferred candidate. Butler, the Greenback, who won 16,955 votes in New York (1.5 percent), most likely hurt Cleveland much more than Blaine.[79] But crucially, the converse was true of St. John, the Prohibitionist. Historians have concluded that he got votes that otherwise would have gone to Blaine; he also won 24,999 (2.1 percent) in New York, much more than Butler, and much more still than Cleveland's sliver of a plurality over Blaine.[80]

Without Butler and St. John in the race, Blaine also would have won majorities in the two states where he was the plurality winner over Cleveland: Massachusetts and Michigan. With Blaine as the actual majority-preferred candidate in these states as well as New York, Blaine would have won an Electoral College majority from states where he was the majority-preferred candidate. As it was, Blaine won 182 electoral votes, all of these except the 14 from Massachusetts and 13 from Michigan from states where he did achieve popular-vote majorities even with Butler and St. John in play. Adding New York's 36 electoral votes to Blaine's column would have given him 218, more than the 201 needed for an Electoral College majority.

Thus, Blaine rather than Cleveland was the genuinely Jeffersonian choice in 1884. In letting Cleveland prevail based on his New York plurality, the Jeffersonian Electoral College malfunctioned, just as it had 40 years earlier in letting Polk prevail over Clay based on a New York plurality.

The consequences of the 1884 mistake were not nearly as severe as the one in 1844. Cleveland, unlike Polk, did not take the nation to war. Control of Congress, moreover, was divided between Republicans and Democrats.[81] Therefore, the long-term historical significance of Cleveland, rather than Blaine, in the White House from 1885 to 1889 was not momentous.

Nor did the nation, or even just New York, remedy the mistake. As in 1844, it was easy to see the mistake as isolated and aberrational, and for the same reason. Just as in 1844, there were significant allegations of fraud with respect to the administration of New York's voting process in 1884. Although historical analysis shows that fraud most likely did not determine the outcome in New York in 1884, at the time many Blaine supporters believed that it did.[82] What matters is that attributing the 1884 outcome to New York political corruption deflected attention from the need to change New York's plurality winner-take-all system of appointing its electors. The state by then had been using this plurality-based method for a half-century, having adopted it deliberately in the aftermath of the People's Party movement of 1824, and thus the state was not predisposed to alter it. If only New York could have run a clean election, one could rationalize, the majority-preferred candidate would have won the presidency anyway. The more urgent imperative appeared to be to clean up New York's elections for the future, so as to reduce the risk that fraud again might taint the result.

But the Jacksonian vulnerabilities remained, and they continued to produce dubious results from a Jeffersonian perspective. In 1888, Cleveland ran for re-election. He lost the Electoral College to his Republican challenger, Benjamin Harrison. But Harrison was not a clear Jeffersonian winner (see Table 4.1). He achieved his Electoral College majority only because of popular-vote pluralities in seven states: New York, Ohio, Illinois, Michigan, Indiana, Wisconsin, and California. In all, these seven states amounted to 128 of Harrison's 233 electoral votes, and without them he would have fallen far below the majority threshold of 201.[83]

There was a Prohibition Party candidate in the race, Clinton Fisk. He almost certainly was the reason Harrison fell below 50 percent in these seven states.[84] Harrison most likely would have achieved majorities in these states if the race had been between only him and Cleveland. In this sense, then, Harrison most probably was an actual Jeffersonian winner, being the majority-preferred candidate in enough states for an Electoral College majority, even though based on the simple math of the election returns he was not clearly so.

The Jeffersonian system thus narrowly escaped another malfunction in 1888, which would have made two in a row. Many consider 1888 an Electoral College mistake because Cleveland won a plurality of the national popular vote yet lost the election. But Cleveland's national plurality was entirely irrelevant from a Jeffersonian perspective. For one thing, Harrison—not Cleveland—might have won a national majority if there had been a nationwide popular runoff between just those two candidates. More importantly, the Jeffersonian question is which candidate, Harrison or Cleveland, was capable of achieving a compound majority-of-majorities. The answer appears to be Harrison, although the use of Jacksonian plurality winner-take-all inevitably muddies that answer.

The situation was even muddier four years later. The 1892 election involved a rematch between Harrison and Cleveland. This time Cleveland prevailed in the Electoral College. But again there were minor-party candidates in the race, and Cleveland achieved his Electoral College victory only because of popular-vote pluralities in nine states: New York (not surprising), Illinois, Indiana, Wisconsin, Missouri, North Carolina, West Virginia, California, and Washington. These states counted for half of Cleveland's 277 electoral votes. Without them he would have had only 138, well below the 223 necessary for an Electoral College majority (see Table 4.1).

Moreover, it is unclear what would have happened if the 1892 rematch had involved a head-to-head runoff between just Cleveland and Harrison, without the minor-party candidates in the race. The Prohibitionist candidate, John Bidwell, probably hurt Harrison. But more significant was James Weaver, the Populist, who actually won 22 electoral votes of his own and was a major factor in other states. Weaver might have suppressed Cleveland's totals more than Harrison's, at least in some of the states where Cleveland won pluralities. It is possible that in a two-person race Cleveland would have won popular-vote majorities in enough states for an Electoral College majority. But Weaver himself had been a Republican before becoming a Populist, and so it is at least conceivable that he prevented Harrison from achieving majorities in some states that Cleveland carried only by pluralities. One cannot be confident either way. And it is even theoretically imaginable that given Weaver's 22 electoral votes, if runoffs were conducted state-by-state rather than nationally, there could have been a three-way split in the Electoral College, with no candidate achieving a majority and the election needing to be decided by the House (as in 1824).[85]

The most that can be said about 1892 is that the Jeffersonian Electoral College did not obviously produce the wrong result, in the way that it did eight years earlier. This time, unlike in 1884, Cleveland might have been the Jeffersonian winner. But because of the system's Jacksonian vulnerabilities, one cannot know for sure. Taking all three of these Gilded Age elections together—1884, 1888, and 1892—the system does not inspire confidence in its ability to achieve its intended compound-majority results.

In sum, the key point is that the system adopted in 1803 had only two outright failures in all of the nineteenth century, and only one of these two (1844) was hugely consequential. That is not a bad track record. When one combines it with the fact that the entire twentieth century went without another outright failure until 2000, one can understand why the system was never fixed despite its longstanding risk of misfiring.

Still, the second failure 10 elections after the first shows that neither was a fluke. Indeed, when 1884 is considered in context with the two elections that immediately followed it—both of which are dubious enough to be sobering, although not outright failures—the appropriate assessment is that during the Gilded Age the United States had entered a period of increased risk of un-Jeffersonian outcomes as a result of plurality winner-take-all. The Gilded Age, as historians remind us, was a period of heightened partisan polarization, not unlike our own era.[86] The political cleavages of the time caused incipient third-party movements to take advantage of ideological space left open by the warring major parties—a dynamic that, again, is not dissimilar to our era. The combination of this increased third-party activity and plurality winner-take-all made the Electoral College system more susceptible during the Gilded Age to outcomes inconsistent with the original intent of the Jeffersonians in 1803. The Gilded Age thus offers a lesson to us now: insofar as current political conditions replicate or even accentuate those existing then, America today may have entered another period of susceptibility to Electoral College failures. Yet Americans may be unprepared to learn from this Gilded Age history, because between then and now the risk diminished.

The system righted itself in 1896. That year McKinley was an unambiguous Jeffersonian winner. He won 251 electoral votes, more than the 224 minimum for a majority, from states where he was the majority winner of the popular vote. Then, in his 1900 re-election, all of his 292 electoral votes came from states where he won a majority of the popular vote (see Table 4.2).

As the Jeffersonian Electoral College entered the twentieth century, it seemed to have recovered its ability to produce presidential winners based on their having achieved the federally legitimating majority-of-majorities.

The Jeffersonian Electoral College in the Twentieth Century

THE ELECTORAL COLLEGE had a remarkable run in the twentieth century. Of the 25 elections from 1904 to 2000, only in the final one did the Electoral College clearly fail to award the presidency to the candidate capable of achieving the requisite majority-of-majorities. The year 1912 was an exceptional case: that year's three-way split between Wilson, Taft, and Roosevelt produced an outcome without any obvious Jeffersonian winner. Eighty years later, in 1992, there was another ambiguous outcome due to another three-way split (between Clinton, Bush, and Perot). But neither of those uncertain results was a clear failure like 2000: denying the White House to the obviously Jeffersonian candidate (Gore).

Moreover, because the 80-year interval between those two questionable cases went altogether smoothly, without any instance in which the Electoral College might have produced a problematic result, it had become easy to believe that the Electoral College system was operating without need of repair. The fact, too, that the failure in 2000 was confined to what happened in a single state—Florida—which had run an election plagued with multiple administrative fiascos (butterfly ballots, hanging chads, and erroneous purging of voter rolls, among others) made it easy to miss the systemic significance of 2000. When combined with the dubious result eight years earlier, however, 2000 becomes a harbinger of the acute vulnerabilities that surfaced 16 years later. As we shall see in the next chapter, collectively 1992, 2000, and

2016 force a reappraisal of the risks that the current Electoral College system poses in the early decades of the twenty-first century despite its generally remarkable track record of success in the twentieth.

The Bull Moose Election

The Electoral College of 1803 began its second century auspiciously. Teddy Roosevelt's landslide victory in 1904 was quintessentially Jeffersonian. He won 317 electoral votes, two-thirds of the total available (476), in states where he won a popular majority (see Table 4.2). To be sure, all of his electoral votes came outside the South, but that was no different than previous Republican victories—Lincoln's, or Garfield's, or McKinley's. Nor was it any different, in principle, than the idea of Jefferson or one of his successors (Madison or Monroe) winning without any electoral votes from New England. The same was true in 1908, when Roosevelt's handpicked successor, William Taft, achieved a compound majority without any electoral votes from the South.

Then came 1912.

Teddy soured on Taft and decided to challenge his protégé. Roosevelt first sought to wrest the Republican nomination from the incumbent president. When that failed, the Bull Moose bolted from the GOP and ran as the nominee of the newly formed Progressive Party.[1]

The former president thus created a three-way race: the Republican incumbent, Taft; the Democratic nominee, Governor Woodrow Wilson of New Jersey; and himself. The result was a triangular fracturing of the electorate in most states, which the Jeffersonian Electoral College system could not handle consistently with its own values and expectations.

The problem, again, was plurality winner-take-all, adopted in the Jacksonian aftermath of 1824. If states in 1912 had required candidates to win a majority of a state's popular vote in order to receive all of the state's electoral votes, it is quite likely that the three-way split between Wilson, Taft, and Roosevelt would have caused the election to go the House of Representatives, as in 1824. As undesirable as that situation might have been according to democratic values that had developed since the early nineteenth century, given the archaic one-vote-per-state House procedure, the use of that procedure is what the

Jeffersonians of 1803 would have wanted and expected if indeed no candidate was capable of achieving a compound majority-of-majorities in the Electoral College. As it was, the use of plurality winner-take-all masked the inability of any of the three contenders to secure an appropriately Jeffersonian victory.

Wilson won the Electoral College without need of the House procedure, but only because Roosevelt and Taft, two Republican presidents, divided what otherwise would have been clear majorities in enough states to reach an Electoral College majority. Without Taft in the race, Roosevelt unquestionably would have achieved a genuinely Jeffersonian majority-of-majorities, as he had in 1904. Roosevelt may not have been as economically conservative as some Taft supporters would have liked, but they almost certainly would have favored the former president (running as the Republican nominee) over Wilson, the populist-sounding Democrat.[2] Roosevelt had reason to believe that he was the stronger choice for the Republican nomination, even though Taft was the incumbent president, because in the general election more voters would prefer him to Taft. Roosevelt proved this prediction true, winning more votes than Taft nationally in November, 27.39 percent to 23.18 percent. A two-person race between Wilson and the more popular Republican would have resulted, almost certainly, in another term for Roosevelt.

Wilson was able to attain an Electoral College majority only by winning popular-vote pluralities, not majorities, in 29 states—an astonishingly large portion of the 48 states then in the union. Only in the South, where Democrats had attained essentially one-party dominance after the demise of Reconstruction, did Wilson receive more than half of a state's ballots. Wilson won 13 northern and western states with less than 40 percent of the popular vote, including Illinois and Massachusetts (and their combined 47 electoral votes), with barely 35 percent of the ballots cast (see Table 5.1). With three-quarters of his electoral votes from states where he was short of a popular majority, Wilson was the opposite of a Jeffersonian winner.

Although Roosevelt would have won a national popular runoff against Wilson, it is unclear exactly what would have happened if runoffs had occurred on a state-by-state basis. The situation was complicated by the fact that there were more than three candidates in

Table 5.1 States Wilson Won with Less Than 40 percent

State	Wilson's Popular Vote %	Electoral Votes
Idaho	32.08	4
North Dakota	34.14	5
Oregon	34.34	5
Montana	35.00	4
Illinois	35.34	29
Massachusetts	35.53	18
Iowa	37.64	13
Wyoming	36.20	3
Rhode Island	39.04	5
Connecticut	39.16	7
Kansas	39.30	10
Maine	39.43	6
New Hampshire	39.48	4
Nevada	39.70	3

contention. Eugene Debs, the Socialist, was also a factor in some states. So too was the Prohibitionist candidate, Eugene Chafin.

Nevertheless, it seems likely that Roosevelt would have won two-candidate runoffs in 10 states where both (a) he finished second to a Wilson plurality and (b) adding Taft's third-place total to his would have given him a majority.[3] Collectively, they would have given Roosevelt 102 electoral votes (see Table 5.2). One can add to these the states in which Roosevelt was the plurality winner ahead of Wilson. Roosevelt's vote combined with Taft's would have made a majority. Also, in Michigan, Taft came in second to Roosevelt, and Wilson would have been the one knocked out in a runoff; there Roosevelt would have picked up most of Wilson's votes (being, like Wilson, much more progressive in philosophy than Taft), thereby giving Roosevelt a majority over Taft (see Table 5.3). Together, these Roosevelt-plurality states amount to 72 electoral votes, making 174 when combined with the 102. Roosevelt also won South Dakota with a majority of the popular vote. Its five electoral votes would bring his total to 179, still far short of the 266 necessary for an Electoral College majority.

Table 5.2 States Wilson Won but Roosevelt + Taft Is a Majority

State	Electoral Votes	Wilson	Roosevelt	Taft	Roosevelt + Taft
Illinois	29	35.34	33.72	22.13	55.85
New Jersey	14	41.20	33.60	20.53	54.13
Iowa	13	37.64	32.87	24.33	57.20
Kansas	10	39.30	32.88	20.47	53.35
Nebraska	8	43.69	29.13	21.74	50.87
West Virginia	8	42.11	29.43	21.11	50.54
Maine	6	39.43	37.41	20.48	57.89
North Dakota	5	34.14	29.71	26.67	56.38
Oregon	5	34.34	27.44	25.3	52.74
Montana	4	35.00	28.13	23.19	51.32

Table 5.3 Roosevelt Plurality Plus Taft Makes Majority

States	Electoral Votes	Roosevelt	Taft	Roosevelt + Taft	Wilson
Michigan	15	38.95	27.63	66.58	27.36
Minnesota	12	37.66	19.25	56.91	31.84
Pennsylvania	38	36.53	22.45	58.98	32.49
Washington	7	35.22	21.82	57.04	26.90

One can even put in Roosevelt's column Vermont, where he came in second to Taft's plurality, not Wilson's. With Wilson excluded from a runoff, his voters would have preferred Roosevelt to Taft (as in Michigan, where Roosevelt and Taft were the top two in reverse order), and so Wilson's 24.43 percent there can be added to Roosevelt's 35.22 percent, making a majority of 59.65 percent. But adding Vermont's 4 electoral votes would increase Roosevelt's total to only 183.

There were 13 states (with a total of 160 electoral votes) in which Taft came in second to Wilson's plurality, and so a runoff would have been between those two, with Roosevelt knocked out (see Table 5.4). Who would have won these runoffs? It depends on whether Roosevelt's voters would have considered Taft or Wilson the better second choice. If we assume that these voters would have preferred a Republican, since

Table 5.4 Wilson Plurality and Taft in Second

States	Electoral Votes	Wilson	Taft	Roosevelt
Kentucky	13	48.40	25.46	22.65
Missouri	18	47.35	29.75	17.80
Oklahoma	10	46.95	35.77	0.00
Delaware	3	46.48	32.85	18.25
New Mexico	3	41.39	35.91	16.90
New York	45	41.27	28.68	24.56
Wisconsin	13	41.06	32.65	15.61
Ohio	24	40.96	26.82	22.16
New Hampshire	4	39.48	37.43	20.23
Connecticut	7	39.16	35.88	17.92
Rhode Island	5	39.04	35.56	21.67
Wyoming	3	36.20	34.42	21.83
Massachusetts	18	35.53	31.95	29.14
Idaho	4	32.08	31.02	24.14

Roosevelt only months before had been one, then Taft could have won the electoral votes from these states. That assumption seems more likely in traditionally Republican states, where Wilson's plurality was very low. For example, in Massachusetts, where Taft got 31.95 percent and Roosevelt 29.14 percent, giving the two Republicans together a combined 61.09 percent, it seems unlikely that Wilson would have attracted enough Roosevelt voters to bring his own meager 35.53 percent above a majority. (If Roosevelt voters split two-to-one for Taft, that would have been enough to put Taft above 50 percent.) Conversely, in New York, a perennial swing state in which Democrats often did well, Wilson's plurality was 41.27 percent, with Taft at 28.68 percent and Roosevelt at 24.56 percent. There, Taft would have needed to pick up almost 90 percent of Roosevelt's supporters in order to reach 50 percent and overtake Wilson in a runoff.

Wilson would not have faced a runoff in the eleven southern states where he won majorities. These gave him 126 electoral votes no matter what. He would have needed 140 more to reach an Electoral College majority of 266, but only 95 more if one assumes he would have beaten Taft in a New York runoff. In 10 states where Wilson won only with pluralities, the combined vote for Roosevelt and Taft was also below 50 percent (because of the presence of Debs and, to a lesser extent, Chafin; see Table 5.5). In six of these—Arizona, Kentucky, Maryland, Missouri, Nevada, Oklahoma—the vote for Debs, if added to Wilson's, would have given Wilson majorities. If one assumes that Debs supporters would have preferred Wilson, the Democrat, as more pro-labor than even the Progressive version of Roosevelt, then Wilson could have won runoffs in these states by picking up the votes of Debs supporters. They would have added 55 electoral votes to Wilson's total, bringing him to within 40 of an Electoral College majority.

In the other four states, adding Debs's votes to Wilson's would not have been enough. Chafin, the Prohibitionist, might have made the difference there. And some believe his votes more likely would have gone to Roosevelt or Taft than Wilson.[4]

In short, it is possible that with both Taft and Roosevelt in the race against Wilson, the use of runoffs state-by-state would have caused no candidate to achieve an Electoral College majority. Taft could have won enough states, with Wilson and Roosevelt splitting the rest, to require an Electoral College runoff in the House under the archaic one-vote-per-state procedure. Who would have prevailed in that process is unclear. Democrats controlled 23 House congressional delegations, Republicans controlled 22, and three were evenly split between the

Table 5.5 Wilson Plurality; Effect of Debs and Taft

State	Electoral Votes	Wilson	Debs	Wilson + Debs	Roosevelt	Taft	Roosevelt + Taft
Oklahoma	10	46.95	16.42	56.85	0.00	35.77	35.77
Arizona	3	43.52	13.33	56.85	29.29	12.74	42.03
Nevada	3	39.7	16.47	56.17	27.94	15.89	43.83
Missouri	18	47.35	4.07	51.42	17.8	29.75	47.55
Kentucky	13	48.4	2.57	50.97	22.65	25.46	48.11
Maryland	8	48.5	1.7	50.29	24.91	23.69	48.6
Ohio	24	40.96	8.69	49.65	22.16	26.82	48.98
Wisconsin	13	41.0	8.37	49.43	15.61	32.65	48.2
Colorado	6	42.8	6.15	48.95	27.09	21.88	48.97
Indiana	15	43.07	5.64	48.71	24.75	23.11	47.86

two parties.[5] With the Constitution requiring an absolute majority of 25 states to elect a president, it is anybody's guess which of the three candidates would have been able to attain the necessary number of states.

But that process is what the Jeffersonians of 1803 would have wanted for this situation. If in a genuine three-way race no candidate is capable of securing a compound majority by having majority support in enough states to win the Electoral College, then the Jeffersonian commitment to federalism required a candidate to win a majority of states in the House. If employing that procedure to resolve the 1912 election would have seemed archaic and undemocratic, then it might have served as a catalyst to replace the Electoral College of 1803 with a better system.[6] But that opportunity never arose because the problematic three-way split in 1912 was papered over by the use of plurality winner-take-all.

Perhaps the best that can be said about how the Electoral College performed in 1912 was that it did not award the presidency to a candidate who obviously should have lost. With Taft in the race, that assertion could not be made about Wilson. Yet there is a lingering sense that Roosevelt had the most majoritarian claim to victory. Not only would Roosevelt have won a national runoff against Wilson (with Taft eliminated as the third-place finisher in a nationwide tally), but crucially for Jeffersonian purposes, Roosevelt would have achieved the requisite compound majority-of-majorities if Taft had stepped aside to let his mentor have the Republican nomination. Based on this analysis, 1912 was another year in which the Jeffersonian system failed to achieve its Jeffersonian objectives.

Insofar as Wilson's election was an accidental outcome, contrary to how the Electoral College system was supposed to work, it was an accident with major repercussions. Wilson kept the nation out of war, or so his slogan said in 1916 when he ran again. But delaying America's entry into World War I caused the peace to be that much harsher when it came. Roosevelt, some historians believe, would have gotten the United States much more quickly into the war, and then more quickly out of it, with a peace treaty rooted in realism rather than idealism and therefore much less punitive toward Germany. If so, then Hitler may never have come to power, and the horrors of World War II potentially would have been averted. All this is speculation, to be sure, but it suggests that the

Electoral College's mishandling of the 1912 election may have altered the course of world history.[7]

The Return to Two-Party Normalcy

The breach in the Republican Party between Roosevelt and Taft was repaired by 1916 under the banner of Charles Evans Hughes, the progressive-leaning Supreme Court Justice and former New York governor. The year 1916 also ushered in an 80-year period in which the Electoral College did what its Jeffersonian architects had wanted, producing winners who were the majority-preferred candidates in the states that generated their Electoral College majorities. These two facts illuminate why, from a Jeffersonian perspective, there was no urgent need for Electoral College reform for most of the twentieth century. The fractured election of 1912 could be dismissed as the aberrational byproduct of the internecine feud within the GOP, driven in part by the personal rift between Roosevelt and Taft. Once this temporary anomaly had passed and the regular two-party competitive system was back on track, the Electoral College was capable of identifying appropriately Jeffersonian winners.

This fundamental truth does not deny that various third-party and independent candidates arose from time to time during this 80-year period. But they did not affect the outcome of any races. In none of the 19 elections between 1912 and 1992 is there a reason to think that the winner was not the majority-preferred candidate in enough states to achieve an Electoral College majority.

In 13 of these, the elected candidate was indisputably a clear Jeffersonian winner, as mathematically defined at the outset of Chapter 4. For the six elections lacking that precise mathematical clarity, further analysis confidently concludes that the Electoral College winner was indeed the majority-preferred candidate in enough states for a genuinely Jeffersonian victory. As a practical matter, for most of the twentieth century—from World War I through the collapse of the Soviet Union—the Electoral College of 1803 operated as originally designed and expected, identifying which candidate in a competitive two-party race was the one appropriate to become the chief executive of the federal government.

A brief review of the six elections without mathematical clarity will confirm what simple math alone cannot.

1916

Wilson, running for re-election against Hughes, won popular-vote majorities in 25 states amounting to 238 electoral votes, 28 shy of the 266 needed for an Electoral College majority. Wilson also was the plurality winner in five more states, for an additional 39 electoral votes (see Table 5.6). There is little doubt that Wilson would have won runoffs in those states, converting his pluralities into majorities. Also on the ballot that year was a Socialist candidate, Allan Benson. Socialists in 1916, as in 1912, presumably would have preferred Wilson, the more labor-friendly Democrat, over Hughes (who, despite progressive leanings, was more business-friendly as a Republican, compared to Wilson). Also, Socialists were strongly against entry into World War I, and Wilson had kept his promise (so far) to keep America out of the war. If Benson's votes are added to Wilson's in the five states where Wilson was a plurality winner, Wilson's total in each becomes a majority. This would have made Wilson's Electoral College majority genuinely Jeffersonian, entirely comprising majority wins.[8]

After 1916, there came a period in which presidential elections were not close. First, in the 1920s, the Republicans won by landslides. Then, it was Franklin Roosevelt's turn for four elections. In all of these elections, the winner easily won Electoral College majorities on the basis of state-based popular majorities. Indeed, in 1920 Warren Harding won all of his electoral votes this way, and the same was true for all of FDR's electoral votes in both 1940 and 1944 (see Table 4.2).

Table 5.6 States with Wilson Pluralities in 1916

State	Electoral Votes	Wilson	Benson (Socialist)	Wilson + Benson	Hughes
California	13	46.65	4.29	50.94	46.27
Kansas	10	49.95	3.92	53.87	44.09
N. Hampshire	4	49.12	1.48	50.60	49.06
N. Dakota	5	47.84	4.95	52.79	46.34
Washington	7	48.13	5.98	54.11	43.89

1948

Harry Truman's victory in 1948 was much closer. He needed popular-vote pluralities in six states in order to achieve his Electoral College majority of 303 (see Table 5.7). But Truman was outflanked on the left by Henry Wallace, FDR's previous vice president, who was running as a Progressive. Wallace's supporters almost certainly would have tended to prefer Truman, the pro-labor Democrat, to Dewey, the pro-business Republican. Adding Wallace's totals to Truman's would put Truman above 50 percent in four of his six plurality-victory states (California, Florida, Idaho, and Ohio), with a combined 62 electoral votes. These, plus the states where Truman won a popular-vote majority, which collectively gave him 219 electoral votes, would have totaled 282—more than enough to reach the majority threshold of 266.[9]

1960

Eisenhower's two wins in the 1950s were much the same as the Republican landslides of the 1920s. But 1960 was very close, even closer than 1948, and technically Kennedy's Electoral College victory depended upon his popular-vote plurality in Illinois or New Jersey. Without those two states Kennedy's electoral vote total would have fallen to 260, below the 269 threshold for a majority that year (see Table 4.1). If Kennedy had been above 50 percent in either of these two states, then he would have achieved a mathematically clear majority-of-majorities. But Kennedy

Table 5.7 States with Truman Pluralities in 1948

State	Electoral Votes	Truman	Wallace	Truman + Wallace	Dewey
California	25	47.57	4.73	52.30	47.13
Florida	8	48.82	2.01	50.83	33.63
Idaho	4	49.98	2.31	52.29	47.26
Ohio	25	49.48	1.28	50.76	49.24
Tennessee	11*	49.14	0.34	49.48	36.87
Virginia	11	47.89	0.49	48.38	41.04

*The 12th elector in Tennessee, who had pledged to support Truman, was "faithless" in casting a vote for Strom Thurmond, the Dixiecrat candidate. "Presidential Electoral Vote, 1948," CQ Press, http://library.cqpress.co.

was just below 50 percent in both states: 49.98 percent in Illinois, and 49.96 percent in New Jersey.

The Socialist Labor candidate, Eric Haas, as weak as his support was, was enough to pull Kennedy below 50 percent in those two states. In Illinois Haas got 0.22 percent, and in New Jersey he got 0.15 percent. Since these voters would almost certainly have preferred Kennedy to Nixon, Kennedy was in fact the majority-preferred candidate in those two states. This analysis accepts as valid the officially certified vote totals in Illinois, about which there was controversy, although Nixon ultimately chose not to pursue a recount there. In any event, even without Illinois, Kennedy had a genuinely Jeffersonian majority-of-majorities as long as New Jersey is counted among the states where a majority of voters preferred him to Nixon, and New Jersey's vote totals in 1960 were never controversial in the way that the ones from Illinois were.[10]

1968

After another landslide in 1964 (this time for the Democrats), 1968 could have been a seriously problematic three-way split, similar to what had occurred in 1912. George Wallace, the segregationist, was a significant third-party candidate, winning 46 electoral votes and 13.5 percent of the popular vote nationally. Even more importantly, he caused Nixon to be a plurality winner in 17 states amounting to 222 electoral votes (see Table 5.8). Without those, Nixon's Electoral College total would have fallen to just 79, far below the 270 threshold for a majority.

If there were doubt whether Nixon would have won runoffs in these states against his Democratic opponent, Hubert Humphrey, then there would be reason to treat 1968 (like 1912) as a year where the Jeffersonian system proved incapable of handling a three-way race. But political science has shown that Wallace supporters preferred Nixon to Humphrey because, unlike in 1948, Republicans pursued their new southern strategy and signaled sympathy with opponents of busing and other measures to achieve racial integration. Adding Wallace's votes to Nixon's would put Nixon above 50 percent in all of the states where he won only pluralities. We can confidently say that the majority of voters preferred Nixon to Humphrey in all of the states where Nixon won

Table 5.8 States with Nixon Pluralities in 1968

State	Electoral Votes	Nixon	Wallace	Nixon + Wallace	Humphrey
Alaska	3	45.28	12.07	57.35	42.65
California	40	47.82	6.72	54.54	44.74
Delaware	3	45.12	13.28	58.4	41.61
Florida	14	40.53	28.53	69.06	30.93
Illinois	26	47.08	8.46	55.54	44.15
Kentucky	9	43.79	18.29	62.08	37.65
Missouri	12	44.87	11.39	56.26	43.74
Nevada	3	47.46	13.25	60.71	39.29
New Jersey	17	46.10	9.12	55.22	43.97
N. Carolina	13*	39.51	31.26	70.77	29.24
Ohio	26	45.23	11.81	57.04	42.95
Oklahoma	8	47.68	20.33	68.01	31.99
Oregon	6	49.83	6.06	55.89	43.78
S. Carolina	8	38.09	32.30	70.39	29.61
Tennessee	11	37.85	34.02	71.87	28.13
Virginia	12	43.36	23.64	67.00	32.49
Wisconsin	12	47.89	7.56	55.45	44.27

*One Nixon elector in NC cast his electoral vote for Wallace, giving Nixon 12.

electoral votes, totaling 301, and in this way he qualifies as a genuinely Jeffersonian winner.[11]

1976

Nixon's re-election in 1972 was another monumental landslide. Conversely, 1976 was a close race that from a Jeffersonian perspective resembled 1960. Jimmy Carter won 254 electoral votes based on popular majorities, but that was 16 short of the 270 required for an Electoral College majority (see Table 4.1). He won three more states, for an additional 43 electoral votes, with only pluralities. Eugene McCarthy, the former Democrat running as an independent, cut into Carter's totals. Without McCarthy in the race, Carter would have won majorities in the three states where he had only pluralities—even in Mississippi, where McCarthy was less of a factor than in Ohio and Wisconsin (see Table 5.9).

Table 5.9 States with Carter Pluralities in 1976

State	Electoral Votes	Carter	McCarthy	Carter + McCarthy	Ford
Mississippi	7	49.56	0.53	50.09	47.68
Ohio	25	48.92	1.42	50.34	48.65
Wisconsin	11	49.50	1.66	51.16	47.83

The majority of voters undoubtedly preferred Carter to Ford in all the states that Carter won, making him a genuinely Jeffersonian winner, just like Kennedy in 1960.

1980

Ronald Reagan defeated Carter's re-election bid in 1980, a year with some similarity to 1968. There was a third candidate in the race whose presence potentially could have affected which of the two major-party candidates prevailed, but who ultimately did not. John Anderson was a Republican offering himself as a more moderate alternative to Reagan. But even with Anderson on the ballot, Reagan won 254 electoral votes by popular majorities—a very impressive number. (Recall that Nixon in 1968 had won only 79 electoral votes this way, because of Wallace on the ballot). Even so, it was not quite enough for an Electoral College majority.

But Reagan won 19 more states with pluralities, amounting to 235 additional electoral votes, for a total of 489 (see Table 5.10). Had there been runoffs between him and Carter in those states, Reagan surely would have won enough of them to be the majority winner in states amounting to an Electoral College majority. In Illinois alone, Anderson's home state, Reagan almost reached a majority as it was, winning 49.65 percent. Carter there had only 41.72 percent. Anderson had 7.30 percent. Even if in a runoff Carter rather than Reagan would have been the second choice of many Anderson voters in Illinois, Carter surely would not have picked up all of Anderson's votes. Reagan would have needed less than 5 percent of Anderson's voters to choose him instead of Carter in an Illinois runoff in order for Reagan to reach a majority in the state. Reagan surely would have obtained at least this small percentage and, with it, the state's 26 electoral votes, giving him

Table 5.10 States with Reagan Pluralities in 1980

State	Electoral Votes	Reagan	Anderson	Reagan + Anderson	Carter
Washington	9	49.66	10.62	60.28	37.32
Illinois	26	49.65	7.30	56.95	41.72
Pennsylvania	27	49.59	6.42	56.01	42.48
South Carolina	8	49.57	1.59	51.16	48.04
Mississippi	7	49.42	1.35	50.77	48.09
North Carolina	13	49.30	2.85	52.15	47.18
Kentucky	9	49.07	2.40	51.47	47.61
Michigan	21	48.99	7.04	56.03	42.50
Alabama	9	48.75	1.23	49.98	47.45
Tennessee	10	48.70	2.22	50.92	48.41
Oregon	6	48.33	9.51	57.84	38.67
Connecticut	8	48.16	12.22	60.38	38.52
Arkansas	6	48.13	2.68	50.81	47.52
Wisconsin	11	47.90	7.07	54.97	43.18
Delaware	3	47.21	6.91	54.12	44.87
New York	41	46.66	7.54	54.20	43.99
Maine	4	45.61	10.20	55.81	42.25

283—more than the 270 threshold for an Electoral College majority. There is no doubt whatsoever that in 1980 Reagan was the majority-preferred candidate in enough states to achieve an Electoral College majority.[12]

He was again in 1984, when all 525 of his electoral votes came from states in which he won a majority of the popular votes (see Table 4.2). Indeed not since Monroe, who ran unopposed in 1820, had a winning candidate won a higher percentage of electoral votes based on majority support from the states providing those electoral votes. In this sense, Reagan's re-election victory over Walter Mondale in 1984 has the status of being the most Jeffersonian victory ever in a competitive presidential election: the largest compound majority-of-majorities, and thus the most impressive electoral mandate for the chief executive of a federal union.

Reagan's vice president, George H. W. Bush, could not reach quite that same extraordinary level of support. Still, his victory in 1988 was impressive by historical standards: all 426 of his electoral votes, far above the 270 minimum to win, came from states where he was the majority winner of the popular vote (see Table 4.2). Like the many previous Republican landslides of the twentieth century, this one made Bush 41 an unambiguously Jeffersonian winner in 1988. Moreover, it capped the remarkable eight-decade period in which the actual outcome of all presidential elections was uncontrovertibly the same as it would have been if the two major-party candidates had been the only ones in each race.

But then came Bush's bid for re-election in 1992.

Ross Perot, Ralph Nader, and the Renewed Third-Party Problem

George H. W. Bush faced two opponents when he ran for re-election in 1992. One was the Democratic nominee, Bill Clinton. The other was Ross Perot, a populist-sounding billionaire from Texas running as an independent.

The race ended up a three-way split not unlike what happened 80 years before, in 1912. Bill Clinton's Electoral College victory depended entirely on popular-vote pluralities, even more so than Wilson's in 1912. In fact, the only state where Clinton won a majority of the popular vote was his home state of Arkansas, which gave him six electoral votes. (Clinton also won the District of Columbia's three electoral votes with a popular majority.) His other electoral votes, 361 of them, came from states in which Clinton's share of the popular vote was under 50 percent. He even won four states with less than 40 percent of the vote: Maine (38.77 percent), Montana (37.63 percent), Nevada (37.36 percent), and New Hampshire (38.86 percent).[13] Clinton's middle name may be Jefferson, but in no way was Clinton's 1992 victory clearly Jeffersonian. On the contrary, it was far from evident that he had the kind of compound majoritarian support that Jeffersonians in 1803 considered the basis for a chief executive's legitimacy in the federal United States.

Bush himself, along with many other Republicans, believed that Perot's presence in the race caused Bush's defeat.[14] Much like the split between Taft and Roosevelt leading to Wilson's victory in 1912, Bush believed that Perot got votes that otherwise would have gone to him.

Certainly, if one adds Perot's share of the popular vote to Bush's in those states that Clinton won by pluralities, Bush then would have popular-vote majorities in far more than enough states for an Electoral College majority. Essentially, 361 electoral votes would swing from Clinton to Bush. Moreover, with majorities and not merely pluralities in all these states, Bush would be the Jeffersonian candidate in the race.

But despite Bush's belief that "Perot cost me the election," it is far from clear that Bush would have won all—or even any—of the states Clinton won with pluralities had there been runoffs (or had Perot withdrawn from the race).[15] Political science analysis indicates that Perot actually pulled more votes away from Clinton than from Bush, and thus Clinton, not Bush, would have won runoffs. If so, that would make Clinton and not Bush the genuinely Jeffersonian candidate in 1992, similar to Nixon in 1968.[16]

Given the degree of debate and uncertainty on this point, however, it is better to classify 1992, like 1892 a century earlier, as an election for which we simply cannot be sure whether or not from a Jeffersonian perspective the correct candidate won. We cannot say about Bush, as we can about Henry Clay in 1844, for example, that he certainly would have won if the Jeffersonian system had operated as intended.

But we can say for certain that after 80 years of unproblematic outcomes, 1992 again exposed the system's Jacksonian vulnerabilities. Even if the system in 1992 did not actually malfunction as it had in 1844 and 1884 (by awarding the presidency to the candidate who clearly should have lost), for the first time since 1912 the system demonstrated its difficulties in handling a significant three-way split.

It took only two more elections, eight years later, for a true breakdown to occur.[17] But the real significance of 2000, in terms of the implication of plurality winner-take-all for the Jeffersonian Electoral College, was buried beneath an avalanche of other problems in the administration of the voting process that year.

The myriad problems are well known. They occurred most critically in Florida, involving the state's use of punch-card voting technology, which produced so-called hanging chads that the machines could not identify as votes and ended up in litigation that twice went to the US Supreme Court. Many observers believe that if Florida had used sound voting equipment, permitting voters to cast their ballots as they intended, and if the state then had counted those ballots correctly, Al Gore would have won Florida (and with it the presidency). Indeed, if Palm Beach County had not used a defective butterfly ballot that caused Gore voters to mistakenly cast their votes for Pat Buchanan—a conservative candidate who acknowledged he was not the intended recipient of these miscast votes—Gore definitively would have prevailed over Bush.[18]

From a Jeffersonian perspective, however, the problem with the 2000 election is more fundamental than Florida's substandard voting machinery and related administrative deficiencies concerning the casting and counting of ballots. Instead, even with those problems unfixed, Gore still should have been recognized as the majority-preferred candidate in Florida, along with enough other states for an Electoral College majority. Thus, 2000 is a year in which there was an indisputable Jeffersonian winner, and yet the system did not produce that candidate as the winner.

Al Gore won a majority of the popular vote in 15 states, amounting to 222 electoral votes. He won pluralities in six more states, adding 44 electoral votes, for a total of 266—just four short of the 270 majority threshold. And then there was Florida with 25 electoral votes, where officially he was just 537 ballots behind George W. Bush.

But Gore would have won majorities in his six plurality-victory states plus Florida if he and Bush had been the only two candidates on the ballot—or, which amounts to the same thing, if there had been a head-to-head runoff between him and Bush in those states. Ralph Nader was also on the ballot, as the nominee of the environmentally inclined Green Party. Gore, known for his environmental advocacy, undoubtedly was preferred over Bush by most of Nader's supporters. Adding Nader's votes to Gore's would give Gore a majority in all six states, including Florida (see Table 5.11). Indeed, Gore could have lost more than a quarter of Nader's supporters in Florida and still had a majority in the state.[19]

Gore was the genuinely Jeffersonian candidate in 2000, with majority support in enough states for an Electoral College majority, and the Jeffersonian system should have recognized him as such and elevated him to the presidency on that basis. Because it did not, the system failed according to its own majority-rule values, objectives, and

Table 5.11 States with Gore Pluralities in 2000

State	Gore	Nader	Gore + Nader
Florida	48.84	1.63	50.47
Iowa	48.54	2.23	50.77
Maine	49.09	5.70	54.79
Minnesota	47.91	5.20	53.11
New Mexico	47.91	3.55	51.46
Oregon	46.96	5.04	52.00
Wisconsin	47.83	3.62	51.45

expectations. Instead, it gave the presidency to a candidate incapable of achieving majority support in enough states for an Electoral College majority.

In this respect, the Electoral College of 1803 had a major malfunction in 2000. The problem was not that Bush did not win a plurality of the national popular vote. That fact was irrelevant given the majoritarian philosophy and design of the 1803 Electoral College. Rather, the grievous error was that violating its own principles and premises, the 1803 Electoral College declared the winner a candidate who lacked the federally legitimating compound majority-of-majorities. Even worse from the system's own perspective, it elected the wrong candidate when it was so obvious that a different candidate in the race had precisely the right kind of federally majoritarian support.[20]

The system's error in declaring Bush president instead of Gore was essentially the same mistake that it had made in declaring Polk president instead of Clay. The accident in 2000 was also similarly consequential to the accident in 1844. Bush took the nation to war in Iraq, just as Polk had taken the nation to war against Mexico. To be sure, the exact circumstances of the two wars were very different. But both were viewed by many as wars of choice, not necessity, and both dramatically altered the course of history. Many believed that Clay would not have undertaken the war that Polk instigated, and many similarly believe that Gore would not have gone to war in Iraq as Bush did. Insofar as these beliefs are sound, then the two mistakes of 1844 and 2000 gave the nation not only the wrong presidents according to how the

Electoral College was supposed to work, but also unnecessary wars that properly identified winning candidates would not have undertaken. Grave mistakes indeed.[21]

To be clear, the point is not that presidents elected in accordance with the Electoral College's Jeffersonian precepts (including mathematically demonstrable clear Jeffersonian winners) have unblemished records in office. Lyndon Johnson is an obvious example to the contrary. In his 1964 landslide, all 486 of his electoral votes came from states in which he won a majority of the popular vote. Yet his escalation of the Vietnam War was an egregious blunder, requiring him to abandon his re-election bid in 1968. Conversely, just because a particular election is an accident from a Jeffersonian vantage, it does not follow automatically that the accidentally elected president will perform poorly in office. Grover Cleveland's first term may have been altogether competent despite his un-Jeffersonian victory in 1884. Rather, the point is that if a president is to commit a calamitous error, at least it should be a president who was elected properly according to the system created for identifying the American people's collective choice of which candidate should hold the office. It is a particularly vexing sin against democracy if a major calamity is committed by a president who reached office without majority support and, therefore, inconsistently with how the system of electing presidents is supposed to work. It is easier, in other words, for a democracy to accept the failures of a leader who was democratically elected, rather than those of an officeholder imposed upon the populace through an undemocratic process.

In sum, although the Electoral College functioned without incorrect results for most of the twentieth century, by the century's end it had shown itself twice in the same decade (1992 and 2000) vulnerable to serious error and had indeed committed one such blunder. The urgency of the problem, however, was obscured in part by the ambiguity of the result in 1992 from a Jeffersonian perspective and, even more so, by the glaring administrative defects that surfaced in the counting of Florida's ballots in 2000. Just as Clay's defeat in 1844 could be attributed to New York's failure to count votes fairly, thereby causing observers to overlook the deeper structural problem associated with the embrace of plurality winner-take-all, so too was it commonplace to attribute Gore's defeat to Florida's inability to fairly count its hanging chads.

But as the twenty-first century began, the anti-majoritarian component of the Electoral College system, added in the Jacksonian era but largely inconsequential apart from a couple of major exceptions, was poised to cause problems more frequently and on a larger scale.

6

The Jeffersonian Electoral College in the Twenty-First Century

THE FIRST THREE elections of the current century reverted to normal two-party competition, in which the winner was mathematically a clear Jeffersonian winner. The fourth, however, did not. Indeed, the 2016 election indicated that the Jeffersonian Electoral College of 1803 is much more susceptible to its Jacksonian vulnerabilities than previously realized. Moreover, when combined with the uncertain outcome of the three-way split in 1992 and the undeniable major malfunction in 2000, the 2016 election reveals that the last quarter-century has challenged the 1803 Electoral College more than any other period in US history. Rather than surmounting this challenge successfully, the Jeffersonian system has shown its urgent need for repair—to purge the Jacksonian accretions that undermine its own commitment to a federally appropriate form of majority rule.

The Electoral College's functioning in the new century began innocently enough with the 2004 election. Although it was another nail-biter, coming down to just Ohio in the early hours of the morning after Election Day, it turned out the Electoral College worked properly according to the Jeffersonian vision of 1803. In winning re-election, George W. Bush received 274 electoral votes—enough for an Electoral College majority—from states where he was the majority winner of the popular vote. He also received an additional 12 electoral votes from states where he won a plurality, icing on the cake from a Jeffersonian perspective (see Table 4.2).

Both of Barack Obama's elections, in 2008 and 2012, also fully complied with the Jeffersonian standard. Indeed, in 2012 all 332 of Obama's electoral votes came from states where he had popular-vote majorities (see, again, Table 4.2). The Jeffersonians of 1803 might not have envisioned an African American becoming president, but they would have recognized his victories as entirely legitimate according to their conception of a presidential election for the federal United States.

Not so for Donald Trump's victory in 2016. From a Jeffersonian perspective, Trump's Electoral College win is problematic at best and possibly another major malfunction. Unlike Bush in 2004 or Obama twice, Trump in 2016 was unable to achieve a mathematical majority-of-majorities. On the contrary, Trump received only 197 electoral votes from states in which he won a majority of the popular vote—far short of the 270 necessary for an Electoral College majority (see Table 4.1). Trump was entitled to two more electoral votes from Texas, which he did not receive because two "faithless electors" there broke their pledge to cast their electoral votes for him. But this fact does not affect the analysis of Trump's failure to reach an Electoral College majority based on state majorities.

Trump won the Electoral College only by obtaining pluralities in seven states amounting to 107 electoral votes, one-third of the electoral votes he ultimately received (see Table 6.1). More significantly, it is not clear that Trump would have won six of these seven states if only he and Hillary Clinton had been on the ballot or, equivalently, if there had been runoffs between the two of them in those states. Two

Table 6.1 States with Trump Pluralities in 2016

State	Electoral Votes	Trump % (Popular Vote)
N. Carolina	15	49.83
Florida	29	48.60
Pennsylvania	20	48.17
Arizona	11	48.08
Michigan	16	47.25
Wisconsin	10	47.22
Utah	6	45.05

additional candidates in the race, Jill Stein and Gary Johnson, may have caused Trump to be the plurality winner in these states, whereas Clinton might have prevailed in a two-candidate matchup against Trump. The seventh state, Utah, presents a separate situation because of the presence of yet another candidate, Evan McMullin.[1]

Jill Stein was the Green Party candidate in 2016, running considerably to Clinton's left. In three of the states with Trump pluralities—Michigan, Pennsylvania, and Wisconsin, the so-called Rust Belt states that received so much attention after Trump's victory—Stein's share of the vote was larger than the difference between Trump and Clinton. Together, these three states had 46 electoral votes. If Clinton had beaten Trump in all three, then she would have won the Electoral College (see Table 6.2).

Stein in 2016, in other words, might have played a similar role to that of her Green Party predecessor Ralph Nader in 2000. To be sure, the populist Trump was hardly the typical Republican nominee, and one cannot necessarily assume that Clinton would have received all of Stein's votes in a runoff. Indeed, depending upon the type of runoff (regular or instant), one cannot assume that all of Stein's voters would have bothered to cast runoff votes. If there had been a regular runoff, held sometime later in 2016, Stein voters might have decided to stay home and abstain from choosing between Clinton and Trump. Even with the convenience of an instant runoff ballot, voted on Election Day, they might have declined to express a preference for either major-party candidate as a second choice after Stein. In other words, some

Table 6.2 Trump's Margin Compared to Third-Party Share

State	Electoral Votes	Trump	Clinton	Trump-Clinton (Margin)	Stein	Johnson
Michigan	16	47.25	47.03	0.22	1.07	3.57
Pennsylvania	20	48.17	47.46	0.71	0.81	2.38
Wisconsin	10	47.22	46.45	0.77	1.04	3.58
Florida	29	48.60	47.41	1.19	0.68	2.18
Arizona	11	48.08	44.58	3.50	1.32	4.08
N. Carolina	15	49.83	46.17	3.66	0.26	2.74

Stein voters might have viewed themselves as equally indifferent, or hostile, toward both Trump and Clinton. Even so, there were enough Stein voters in the three key Rust Belt states that it is at least theoretically possible that with the bulk of them preferring Clinton to Trump, Stein's presence in the race pulled Clinton's level of support below Trump's in these states.

Ultimately, however, the analysis must depend on another minor-party candidate in the race: Gary Johnson, the Libertarian. In the states with Trump pluralities, Johnson received a far larger share of the vote than Stein. Thus, it matters whether Johnson's voters preferred Clinton or Trump and in what ratios in these states. If Johnson voters liked Trump more than Clinton, then even if Clinton would have received the bulk of Stein's votes in a runoff, Trump would have remained ahead of Clinton by netting enough Johnson votes. Conversely, if Johnson voters actually preferred Clinton to Trump, then perhaps Clinton could have won runoff majorities in the three Rust Belt battlegrounds.

But Johnson's voters also might have declined to participate. Or the race might have been close enough that not just Stein and Johnson voters would have been the deciding factors. Even Evan McMullin's miniscule 0.07 percent in Pennsylvania might have made a difference there, depending on how many of Johnson's voters would have cast runoff votes for Clinton in the state. Yet another minor-party candidate was also in the race: Darrell Castle of the ultra-conservative Constitution Party. At 0.35 percent in Pennsylvania, five times McMullin's amount, Castle might have mattered even more than McMullin in potentially offsetting any pro-Clinton runoff preference among Johnson and Stein voters.

Moreover, the existence of a runoff procedure in 2016—either instant or otherwise—almost surely would have affected the dynamics of campaigning in the states. The minor-party candidates might have received even larger shares of the first-preferences votes, with their supporters knowing that they had an opportunity to make a choice between the two major-party contenders at the runoff stage of the process. As has happened in other elections with runoff procedures, the two major-party candidates might have tailored their messages in an effort to pick up support among voters whose first choice was a minor-party candidate. If either Trump or Clinton had been able to do a better job of appealing to these voters in that kind of electoral environment, that major-party candidate would have been the one to prevail with the runoff procedure in place.

We can never know for sure what would have happened if the three Rust Belt states had employed some sort of runoff in 2016. But it is at least conceivable that if they had, Clinton would have won the runoffs in those three states and, with them, the presidency. It is thus possible that with majority-preference victories in those states, Clinton was the genuinely Jeffersonian candidate—capable of accumulating a majority of Electoral College votes from majority-preference wins in enough states.

To be fair, Trump also might have been an actual Jeffersonian winner. Apart from the three Rust Belt states, it seems more likely that he rather than Clinton would have won runoffs in the four other states where he was only a plurality winner: almost certainly Utah, where Clinton received barely a quarter of the vote; probably Arizona, Florida, and especially North Carolina, where Trump was barely below 50 percent and Clinton barely above 46 percent. These southern and western states were harder for Clinton than the northeastern Rust Belt. Not only was she far behind Trump in these states, but Johnson voters there more likely would lean toward Trump in their runoff preferences. Assuming that Clinton could not have beaten Trump in a runoff in Florida (the Trump-plurality state outside the Rust Belt where the numbers show her as having the best chance), then Trump would have reached an Electoral College majority by winning a runoff against Clinton in Pennsylvania (of the three key Rust Belt states, the one in which she was the weakest). Being the majority-preferred candidate in Pennsylvania, on this analysis, would have made Trump a genuinely Jeffersonian winner even if Clinton had been the majority-preferred candidate in Michigan and Wisconsin.

Clinton would have needed to win runoffs in *all three* of the crucial Rust Belt states to be the true Jeffersonian candidate in 2016 (assuming, again, that she would not have won a Florida runoff). Even so, she would have needed to do more. She also would have needed to win runoffs in the seven states where she, rather than Trump, was only a plurality winner.

Table 6.3 States with Clinton Pluralities in 2016

State	Electoral Votes	Clinton	Trump	Clinton-Trump (Margin)	Johnson	Stein
New Mexico	5	48.26	40.04	8.22	9.34	1.24
Virginia	13	49.75	44.43	5.32	2.97	0.69
Colorado	9	48.16	43.25	4.91	5.18	1.38
Maine (a-l)	2	47.83	44.87	2.96	5.09	1.91
Nevada	6	47.92	45.50	2.42	3.32	*
Minnesota	10	46.44	44.93	1.51	3.84	1.26
N. Hampshire	4	46.83	46.46	0.37	4.14	0.87

*Stein did not qualify for the ballot in Nevada. Sean Whaley, "Green Party Presidential Candidate Jill Stein Won't Appear on Nevada Ballot," *Las Vegas Review-Journal*, September 2, 2016.

These seven states amounted to 49 electoral votes (see Table 6.3). Clinton was the plurality winner of Maine's two at-large electoral votes. (She won a single district-based electoral vote in Maine by a popular-vote majority.) Indeed, she received only 177 electoral votes from states in which she won a majority of the popular vote. (Were it not for faithless electors, Clinton would have received five additional electoral votes in Washington and Hawaii, where she won popular-vote majorities.[2]) But if it is reasonable to believe that Clinton might have won enough Johnson and Stein votes in combination to win runoffs in all three Rust Belt states with Trump pluralities, then it is also reasonable to think that she could have won runoffs in the seven Clinton-plurality states. Of these, Trump came the closest in New Hampshire, where he was only 0.37 percent behind. But if Clinton would have overtaken Trump in a Pennsylvania runoff because enough Johnson and Stein voters favored her there, then it is hard to imagine Trump overtaking Clinton in New Hampshire because of the Johnson and Stein voters in that northeastern state.

Nor would New Hampshire be enough. Trump would also have needed to win a runoff in another Clinton-plurality state—Minnesota most likely—in order to prevent Clinton from achieving a majority-of-majorities (based, hypothetically, on Rust Belt runoffs).[3] But, again, if Clinton could have come from behind to win runoffs in Michigan and Wisconsin, as well as Pennsylvania, there is no reason to think that she would not have confirmed her first-place finish in a Minnesota runoff. Simply put, as between Trump and Clinton, it may have been that Clinton is the one who should have prevailed according to the fundamental majoritarian precepts underlying the redesign of the Electoral College in 1803.

Perhaps not. We of course cannot turn back the clock to rerun the race with a runoff system in place in those three Rust Belt states. But for anyone who values the basic democratic principle of majority rule, especially once one understands that the goal of the Jeffersonian Electoral College was to produce a president with a majority-rule pedigree, it must remain frustrating that we will never know which candidate, Clinton or Trump, would have reached an Electoral College majority if there had been runoffs to determine which of the two was preferred by a majority of voters in the pivotal states.

Thus, 2016 may have been another malfunction of the Jeffersonian Electoral College, like 2000 was. The point is not that Clinton won more popular votes nationwide than Trump. That fact is irrelevant from a Jeffersonian perspective. For one thing, Clinton had only a national plurality (48.18 percent), not majority, of the popular vote.[4] Trump might have been able to win a national runoff against Clinton. It depends upon what the Johnson and Stein voters would have done in a national runoff, along with the McMullin and Castle voters (and still others). It is also possible that if America's electoral system included a national runoff, then at the outset other candidates, like Michael Bloomberg, would have entered the race. But who would have won a national runoff is not the key point, given the Jeffersonian commitment to federalism.[5]

Instead, the key point is that Hillary Clinton might have been the majority-preferred candidate in enough states for an Electoral College majority. If so, then the Electoral College of 1803 delivered the presidency to the wrong candidate in 2016 according to its own Jeffersonian objectives and expectations. Moreover, it would have been the second malfunction of this kind in less than 20 years.

Considering 2016 together with 1992 and 2000, one reaches the alarming conclusion that the last quarter-century has been the most problematic period in the history of the Jeffersonian Electoral College. It is not clear that the Jeffersonian system identified the correct winner, from its own perspective, in 1992. It is absolutely clear that the system misidentified the correct Jeffersonian winner in 2000. In 2016, it is again unclear whether the system was correct or incorrect, according to its own principles. This record of three fumbles in the space of seven elections is cause for great consternation.

One can identify other 25-year periods in which the Jeffersonian system had significant lapses. The era that covers 1824 through 1848 includes the major malfunction that occurred in 1844. It also includes 1848, which requires close scrutiny to be reassured that the system reached the right result. Moreover, many might consider 1824 to be a problematic election because it needed to be resolved by the House using the Twelfth Amendment's runoff procedure. But by the Jeffersonian standards of 1803, going to the House runoff is exactly what should have happened given the absence of a genuinely Jeffersonian winner that year. All in all, the period from 1824 to 1848 does not look nearly as bad as the period from 1992 to 2016.

The Jeffersonian Electoral College hit another rough patch from 1884 through 1892. There was another malfunction in 1884, although not as consequential as either 1844 or 2000. The outcome could also have been a mistake in 1888 but probably was not, and 1892 was one of those about which one cannot be confident one way or the other. Not a great run, and even more problematic if one extends the period another 20 years to 1912. But by itself the trilogy of 1884, 1888, and 1892 is not nearly so troublesome as the trilogy of 1992, 2000, and 2016.

There is another aspect of the most recent quarter-century that makes it especially worrisome. Both 1992 and 2016 were elections in which the inability of the system to identify which candidate was the Jeffersonian winner was not caused by a problem confined to a single state—like New York in 1844 and 1884, or Florida in 2000. Instead the difficulty extended across many states, reflecting a systemic inability to cope with significant independent or third-party candidates.

Yes, presidential elections had seen prominent third-party candidacies before, like George Wallace's in 1968 or John Anderson's in 1980—or most especially Teddy Roosevelt's in 1912. But not since Roosevelt's Bull Moose candidacy confounded the Jeffersonian system had a comparable third-party effort caused a problem until Ross Perot's appearance in 1992. For 80 years, the Jeffersonian system had been able to accurately identify the genuinely Jeffersonian winner in each race, and that was true even with the presence of prominent third-party candidates like Wallace or Anderson. As a practical matter, the system seemed to be working just fine.

That complacency has now been shattered. The combination of 1992, 2000, and 2016 demonstrates beyond all doubt that the Jeffersonian system, as it currently operates with its Jacksonian appendage of plurality winner-take-all, cannot adequately handle multicandidate races. When a third or fourth candidate is a factor—as Perot was in 1992, as Nader was in 2000, and as Stein and Johnson together were in 2016— the Jeffersonian system in its current configuration cannot operate as it was originally intended (to identify which candidate, if any, is the one with majority support in enough states for an Electoral College majority).

The fact that the system has proved so problematic in the most recent quarter-century suggests that the problem is worsening. The conditions of contemporary American politics—including extreme polarization, the emphasis on negative messaging, and the ability of celebrity candidates to self-finance or raise campaign funds outside the traditional party apparatus—all contribute to the likelihood that independent and third-party candidates will seek to capture support from voters disaffected by the dysfunctional status quo. The consideration of an independent candidacy in 2020 by John Kasich among others, as mentioned in the introduction, is an indication of this developing trend. Consequently, the chances of another three-way split that the system cannot handle are far from trivial. Understanding how and why the presently accelerating risk is more severe than ever before is a predicate to recognizing the urgency of the need for reform.

Given the Jeffersonian goal of electing presidents who have the federally appropriate majority-of-majorities, and because the Jacksonian move to plurality winner-take-all elections undermines that basic Jeffersonian objective, the task then must be to undo that Jacksonian move and restore the Jeffersonian system to its original commitment to a federal form of majority rule.

Part Three

The Potential Restoration of the Jeffersonian Electoral College

7

A Recommitment to Majority Rule

NO STATE SHOULD award all of its Electoral College votes to a presidential candidate unless that candidate wins a majority of popular votes cast by the citizens of the state.

This principle, which we can simply call the *majority-rule requirement*, should be embraced by states in the exercise of their constitutional power to appoint presidential electors. Adopting this principle would enable states to restore the original Jeffersonian expectation that an Electoral College winner would be the presidential candidate preferred by a majority of the electorate in the states providing the electoral votes for that victory. The Jeffersonians did not think they needed to spell out this expectation as part of their 1803 redesign, because they never imagined states deviating from it. But states did so after the rise of Andrew Jackson, with the consequences catalogued in Part Two of this book. However, states can repledge themselves to the original Jeffersonian expectation by embracing the majority-rule requirement as part of their participation in the Electoral College process.[1]

In theory, this majority-rule requirement could be codified in the form of a federal constitutional amendment. As we have discussed, Article II of the original Constitution authorizes each state to appoint its presidential electors "in such manner as the Legislature thereof may direct," and the Jeffersonian redesign of the Electoral College in 1803 retained this particular provision. A new constitutional amendment could merely append to this original authorization the following qualification: "except that no state shall appoint electors in a manner that causes all of the state's electors to vote for the same individual unless the individual wins a majority of popular votes cast by the citizens of the state."

This constitutional amendment, while perhaps desirable as a means of confirming a commitment to the majority-rule requirement, is impractical and unnecessary. It is impractical for the basic reason that the hurdle for obtaining any constitutional amendment is too high under contemporary conditions of polarized American politics: a two-thirds vote in each house of Congress, and then ratification by three-fourths of the states.[2] It is unnecessary because without the amendment, each state individually already has the constitutional power to commit itself to the majority-rule requirement. Indeed, the very virtue of the existing language of the Constitution on this point—explicitly giving each state the power to choose whatever method of appointing electors that it prefers—means that each state undoubtedly has the authority to embrace the majority-rule requirement as part of its own law for the appointment of electors.

Multiple Ways to Comply with Majority Rule

There are a variety of ways in which a state could appoint its presidential electors that would be consistent with this majority-rule requirement. From purely a policy perspective, the most preferable method may well be the kind of instant runoff voting system that Maine has adopted for its congressional elections (and which will be discussed later in this chapter). From a historical perspective, the most obvious method would be for a state to use the kind of popular-vote runoff that New Hampshire adopted in 1792. Because it was adopted essentially at the beginning of the Electoral College's existence, and because the Electoral College was retooled in 1803 on the assumption that states could continue with this kind of runoff if they wished, it is impossible to argue that this kind of runoff is incompatible with the Twelfth Amendment and the Electoral College system as the Jeffersonians recreated it. On the contrary, this kind of runoff is an entirely appropriate way to implement the specific majoritarian premise of the 1803 reform.

This runoff system guarantees that if no candidate wins a majority of the initial popular vote, then a second popular vote limited to the two candidates with the most first-round votes will produce a single winner with a majority of second-round ballots. If all states used this runoff system to appoint their electors, it would guarantee that the Electoral College winner would have the federally appropriate compound majority-of-majorities. (If no candidate achieved an Electoral College majority, in the unusual circumstances that more than two candidates won enough runoffs in the states, then the election would go to the House—just as the Jeffersonians intended for a fragmented result caused by several candidates having strong support in multiple states.) The kind of runoff system that New Hampshire used in 1792, and continued to employ until 1848 with a different form of a runoff, fully accords with Jeffersonian values underlying the redesign of the Electoral College in 1803 and would be perfectly constitutional for any state to use today.[3]

Moreover, for a state to conduct a runoff would also be lawful under the modern calendar that Congress has created for presidential elections. The Constitution gives Congress the authority to specify the "time for choosing the electors," and Congress has used this authority to set "the Tuesday next after the first Monday in November" as the familiar Election Day on which states appoint their presidential electors. But Congress has also explicitly permitted states to appoint their electors "on a subsequent day" if an initial popular vote for the appointment of electors "has failed to make a choice." Congress, in fact, specifically adopted this safety valve in 1845 at the behest of New Hampshire, which wanted to preserve its right to use a runoff in the event that the initial popular vote for presidential electors did not produce a majority winner.[4]

To be sure, given contemporary voting procedures, the timetable for holding a runoff would be extremely tight. As the world learned in 2000 with the disputed election between George Bush and Al Gore, there are only five weeks between Election Day and the date by which states are expected to resolve any disputes over the appointment of their presidential electors.[5] Then, six days later, in mid-December, the electors themselves meet to cast their official votes for president. If a state were to hold a runoff sometime during this five-week period between Election Day and early December, it would need to do so toward the end of November—around Thanksgiving—and it would need to determine exactly how many days to allocate for absentee (or so-called early) voting in the runoff as well as for any recount of runoff ballots that might be necessary.[6] It would be no easy task. Nonetheless, if in the future a state wanted to use an actual runoff as the way to comply with the majority-rule requirement for the appointment of its presidential electors, it would be legally permissible for it to do so, just as it always has been, for New Hampshire or any other state.

An Alternative Two-Round System

An electoral system that has a general election followed by a runoff, if necessary to yield a majority winner, is what political scientists call—quite straightforwardly—a "two-round" system. But there are other versions of a two-round system that do not use the term "runoff" to describe their second round. For example, the "top-two" system used in California and Washington has a first round of voting in advance of the November general election, and the two candidates with the most votes in that initial round move on to the second round in November.[7]

As currently operated in both states, the first round of this top-two system is open to multiple candidates from the same political party, and the top two finalists on the November general election ballot are the two candidates with the most votes in the initial round regardless of party affiliation. Thus, it is possible for the two finalists to come from the same political party. But there is no inherent need for a top-two system to operate this way. The initial round could be limited to a single candidate from each party (with the party's candidate chosen by an even earlier primary election open only to voters who are members of that political party), in which case the November general election in this top-two system would function as the equivalent of a runoff.

Along the same lines, in the context of presidential elections we can imagine a state wanting to conduct a two-round system but wanting more time between the two rounds than is available between November and early December, when a runoff would need to be complete in order for the presidential electors to assemble on the date Congress has specified. If so, then using the top-two system as something of a model, a state could adopt an initial round of voting before Election Day and make Election Day the second round. For example, a state could set

Labor Day (the first Monday in September) as the date for an initial round of popular voting relating to the appointment of the state's presidential electors. The Labor Day ballot would contain the two major-party candidates, who by then would have received their nominations at the national conventions held by the two major parties during the summer (as is traditional).[8]

Also on the Labor Day ballot would be any minor-party or independent candidates wishing to participate in the presidential election and capable of satisfying the state's ballot-access requirements, such as the collection of a sufficient number of signatures.[9] (This Labor Day ballot would be much like the November ballot under current practice.) The voters would select their preference among the various options on the ballot, and the top two vote-getters would advance to the second round on Election Day in November. The Labor Day ballot would differ from the existing system of presidential primaries and caucuses that states hold before the nominating conventions to choose a major party's candidate.[10] The purpose of the Labor Day ballot would not be to help select a party's nominee, but instead to let each party compete against all others as well as any independent candidates in the first stage of a two-stage general election. Also, unlike with the top-two system currently in use in California and Washington, multiple candidates from the same party would not be permitted on this first-stage ballot.[11]

This version of a two-round system would be consistent with existing federal law as long as the Labor Day voting did not conclusively determine the winner of the state's Electoral College votes. Even if one candidate or party won a decisive majority of the popular vote on Labor Day, the state would need to hold the second round of voting between the top two vote-getters on Election Day in order to comply with the congressional mandate that the state appoint its presidential electors on Election Day. In other words, Election Day would not be a runoff used only in the absence of a majority winner in the first round. Nonetheless, it otherwise would function as a two-round system similar to a runoff mechanism, the main difference simply being that Election Day voting would be the second rather than first round. Either way, the two-round process guarantees that the winner receives a majority, and not merely a plurality, of popular votes.

One option that would not be available under current constitutional law would be for a state to limit the Election Day ballot to only the Democratic and Republican candidates, with no opportunity for minor parties or independent candidates to participate in the popular vote that determines the appointment of presidential electors. In a series of cases, including one that involved the independent candidacy of John Anderson in 1980, the US Supreme Court has held that the Fourteenth Amendment to the federal Constitution requires states to give minor parties and independent candidates a fair chance to convince voters that they, rather than either of the major parties, should win the presidency in a particular election.[12] Crucially, the Court has acknowledged that states have a valid concern that "the election winner be the choice of a majority of its voters" rather than a "plurality winner."[13] But the Court ruled that states must pursue this valid interest by laws that do not arbitrarily prevent the two major parties from facing fair competition from minor parties or independent candidates.[14]

A two-round system of the kind described here would not run afoul of this constitutional requirement. On the contrary, it would give minor parties and independent candidates a full and equal opportunity to compete for votes in the initial round. Indeed, they would have an equal chance of making it to the second round, displacing a major-party candidate, if that were the choice of voters in the first round. Moreover, the Supreme Court itself has expressly recognized that runoffs and other forms of two-round systems are a constitutionally appropriate way for states to winnow a field of multiple candidates to a single winner supported by a majority of the state's voters.[15]

Instant Runoff Voting

There are strong reasons why a state might prefer not to adopt a two-round system as its way to comply with the majority-rule requirement. First, there is the considerable public expense of holding two rounds of voting, rather than just one. Second, there are also the additional costs of campaigning that the candidates would have during the time between the two rounds (costs the candidates would need to defray with additional fundraising). Third, and arguably even more significant from the perspective of operating a fair democracy, there is the greater burden on voters of having to cast two ballots rather than just one.

This burden is often reflected in lower turnout rates in runoffs or sometimes in the initial round of voting in a two-round system.[16] Invariably, the electorate is never exactly the same in both rounds of a two-round system, and thus the majority of voters who elect the winning candidate in the second round is not necessarily a majority of the voters who cast first-round ballots. While this fact does not deprive the winner of the second round of being the choice of a majority who cast second-round ballots, it is a reason for combining both rounds into a single ballot.

Instant runoff voting is an electoral mechanism that permits just what its name suggests. It conducts whatever runoff is necessary "instantaneously" by enabling states to hold the first and second rounds of a two-round system at the same time. Often called ranked-choice voting, this system gives voters ballots that enable them to rank the candidates in order of preference. For reasons we shall shortly explore, it would be more accurate to call instant runoff voting a species, or subcategory, of ranked-choice voting.

In any event, as with any voting system that uses ranked-choice ballots, instant runoff voting can be structured so that voters are not obligated to rank candidates if they would prefer to vote only for one. Rather, the system can simply permit—not require—voters to rank candidates if they wish. Moreover, to simplify the ranking process in an election with many candidates, the system can limit the option of ranking to just a subset of candidates, for example just a voter's top three choices from the entire field.[17]

Some have expressed a concern that giving voters the option of ranking candidates would be too confusing for some voters.[18] But many have observed that this option would be no more difficult than inviting voters to identify their top three flavors of ice cream among the varieties offered at their local ice cream parlor.[19] The acclaimed children's author and cartoonist Sandra Boyton even produced an illustration showing how easily kids could rank their favorite animals among the choices of duck, hippo, tiger, rabbit, and pig (see Figure 7.1).[20] In any event, ranked-choice voting is currently experiencing an insurgence of interest, with its recent adoption statewide in Maine, as well as its use in

Figure 7.1 Illustration reprinted with permission of Sandra Boynton and FairVote.org.

many municipalities nationwide, including San Francisco and Santa Fe. Voters who recently cast ranked-choice ballots expressed favorable views of the system in general.[21]

Instant runoff voting would be an entirely constitutional way for a state to comply with the majority-rule requirement in the appointment of its presidential electors. Pursuant to its existing powers to determine the method of appointing its electors, a state could give its voters ranked-choice ballots on Election Day, listing all the participating candidates—including minor-party and independent candidates along with the two major-party nominees—and permit voters to rank a specified number of candidates in order of preference. The state then could mathematically calculate a majority-vote winner from the rankings that the voters provided on their Election Day ballots.[22]

There are several different mathematical methods for calculating an election's winner using ranked-choice ballots. The most common, associated with instant runoff voting, is to eliminate the candidate with the least number of first-choice votes and then, for all the voters who had ranked that candidate first, to re-tally those ballots as ones cast for the candidate each voter ranked second. The process stops, according to this method, as soon as a candidate accumulates a majority of the ballots cast. But if, after eliminating one candidate and taking account of second-choice votes, still no candidate has a majority of ballots, then the remaining candidate with the least number of first-choice votes is eliminated; and again for all the voters who had ranked that candidate highest, those ballots are re-tallied for the candidate ranked next-highest. If necessary, the process continues until there are only two candidates left, and the one with more votes—a majority of ballots at this point—is the winner.[23]

Instead of eliminating the lowest-ranked candidate one at a time, it is also possible to more directly replicate a two-round system by immediately eliminating all but the two candidates with the most first-choice votes. If neither of these candidates already has a majority of first-choice votes, then all of the ballots with first-choice preferences other than these two candidates are redistributed between the two finalists according to which is higher ranked on each ballot. Whichever of the two finalists has the majority of votes after this single redistribution is the election's winner.[24]

Although both methods usually will yield the same result, theoretically it is not always the case. Eliminating candidates one at a time can cause the two remaining finalists to be different from the two candidates with the highest number of first-choice votes, depending on how lower-ranked preferences are redistributed. But the key point is that both methods are consistent with the majority-rule requirement, insofar as both yield a winner who is preferred by more voters than the other candidate who is a finalist according to the procedure.[25] Moreover, both methods are equally permissible for a state to choose as an exercise of its existing constitutional power to select a method for appointing its presidential electors.

It would also be permissible for a state to employ a mathematical method to identify the majority-preferred candidate that is quite distinct from these two alternatives, both of which are best understood as versions of instant runoff voting. Using the same ranked-choice ballots, the third method would compare candidates two at a time. If one candidate beats all others in this series of head-to-head matchups, then that candidate would win the election. For example, imagine an election with candidates A, B, and C. If in their rankings of these candidates a majority of voters prefer A to B, and if a majority also prefer A to C, then A would win. Called "Condorcet voting" after the eighteenth-century philosopher who invented the system (Marquis de Condorcet), this mathematical method currently has among its advocates the Nobel laureate economists Amartya Sen and Eric Maskin. They defend it as the purest form of majority rule, since by definition according to the mathematical properties of this procedure the winner is the candidate whom a majority of voters prefers when compared against all other candidates.[26]

Condorcet voting, however, has its detractors. For one thing, at least theoretically, not every election has a Condorcet winner. Like the game "rock, paper, scissors" (in which paper beats rock, scissors beats paper, and rock beats scissors), an electorate's preferences among three or more candidates can be cyclical: a majority prefers A to B, a majority prefers B to C, and a majority prefers C to A—leaving no single candidate as the Condorcet winner, who beats all others in the series of head-to-head matchups.[27]

But even more fundamentally as a matter of democratic principle, there are reasons to think that a Condorcet winner—even where one exists—is not necessarily the result that best reflects the preferences of the majority of the electorate. In this regard, it is useful to think about the 2016 election. It is quite possible that with ranked-choice ballots, Gary Johnson would have been the Condorcet winner. A majority of voters would have preferred him to Hillary Clinton (all the anti-Clinton voters who cast ballots for Trump plus Johnson's own supporters). A majority of voters also would have preferred Johnson to Trump (all the anti-Trump voters who cast ballots for Clinton plus Johnson's own supporters). Yet even as the Condorcet winner, Gary Johnson was a very weak candidate: only a small percentage of the electorate picked him as its first choice (a little over 3 percent nationally). Johnson would have beaten Clinton and Trump in head-to-head matchups only because both Clinton and Trump were so unpopular among the voters who opposed them. It is not as if a majority of the electorate enthusiastically supported Johnson compared to either Clinton or Trump.

Consequently, the case can be made that in the 2016 election it would have been preferable to use instant runoff voting (in either of its two alternative versions, as described earlier) rather than Condorcet voting. In other words, it would have been better to eliminate Johnson because of his small percentage of first-choice votes, and then redistribute the ballots that ranked him first on the basis of whom those voters ranked second. In this scenario, either Clinton or Trump would win, depending upon which of the two was preferred by the voters who ranked Johnson first. The argument here is that as unpopular as both Clinton and Trump were, they both were the first-choice candidates of many more voters than Johnson was; in other words, they each had their strong supporters, even as they were strongly opposed by others. In this situation, it is better to figure out—or so the argument goes—which of *these two* is preferred by a majority in the head-to-head matchup *between just them*, with Johnson eliminated as the much weaker candidate in comparison, rather than letting Johnson become president simply because he could cobble together weak majority coalitions based on the opponents of each major-party candidate.[28]

The key point here, however, is not to decide which of these arguments is correct: whether instant runoff voting is preferable to Condorcet voting, or vice versa. Instead, the key point is that each method of using ranked-choice ballots is consistent with the majority-rule requirement. And each is completely constitutional under the existing Article II power of states to choose their method for appointing presidential electors. Thus, each would be appropriate for a state to adopt as its means of returning to the Jeffersonian expectation that the winner of the Electoral College be a candidate who has demonstrated the support of the majority of the electorate in the states that produce that candidate's Electoral College victory.

Proportional Allocation and Conditional Winner-Take-All

In addition to various forms of two-round systems or ranked-choice voting, there are still more ways in which a state might comply with the majority-rule requirement in the appointment of presidential electors. A state could adopt a districting system, as several states did both before and after the Jeffersonian redesign of the Electoral College in 1803—and as Maine and Nebraska currently use.[29] A districting system is problematic insofar as it is vulnerable to gerrymanders (in other words, the partisan manipulation of district lines) in the same way that congressional districting is. Still, insofar as the majority-rule requirement prohibits a state from awarding all of its Electoral College votes to a mere plurality winner of the state's popular vote, a districting system conforms to that requirement by splitting the state's Electoral College votes among the candidates depending on which particular district each candidate won. Only if a candidate won all the districts of a state with less than a majority of the state's popular vote, which would amount to an instance of extreme gerrymandering, would a district system run afoul of the majority-rule requirement (as specified herein to be consistent with the original Jeffersonian expectation of how the Electoral College would function).[30]

Better than a districting system, but similar insofar as it is designed to produce a split in the awarding of a state's electoral votes rather than having a single candidate win them all, would be a statewide proportionality system. Under this kind of system, candidates would win a share of the state's electoral votes in proportion to the candidate's share of the statewide popular vote. For example, imagine a state with ten electoral votes, and four candidates with the following shares of the popular vote: A 40 percent, B 30 percent, C 20 percent, and D 10 percent. According to the proportionality system, A would win four of the state's electoral votes, B would win three, C two, and D one. This system would comply with the majority-rule requirement, because no candidate with less than a majority of the state's popular vote would receive all of the state's electoral votes.[31]

This proportionality system would require some kind of rounding formula to handle the many situations in which a candidate's share of the popular vote did not divide evenly into the state's number of electoral votes. Under the existing Constitution, states appoint electors who each cast one whole electoral vote for president. There cannot be fractional electoral votes. In other words, in a state with ten electoral votes, and a candidate who receives 35 percent of the popular vote, the proportionality system must decide whether the candidate receives the appointment of three or four electors; there is no possibility of the candidate receiving the appointment of 3.5 electors. But this rounding problem could be handled mathematically, if a state decided it would prefer to use a proportionality system as a means of complying with the majority-rule requirement.[32]

A more limited use of proportionality would also be permissible. This alternative, which we can call *conditional winner-take-all*, would employ proportionality only when no candidate receives a majority of votes using a conventional (nonranked) ballot. But if one candidate does win a majority, then that candidate would win all of a state's electoral votes. This conditional winner-take-all system complies with the majority-rule requirement because, by definition under this system, no candidate wins all of a state's electoral votes unless that candidate receives a majority of the popular vote. If there is no majority winner of the popular vote, then the contingent proportionality formula kicks in, dividing the state's electoral vote between the plurality winner and any other candidate who qualifies for a share of the state's electoral votes according to the proportionality formula.[33]

Jeffersonian Federalism and the Virtue of Variety

It may seem unsettling that there are so many different ways for a state to comply with the majority-rule requirement. A runoff after Election Day: yes. An initial rounding of voting to produce an Election Day ballot with only two candidates: yes. Instant runoff voting: yes. Condorcet voting: yes. Districting: yes. Statewide proportionality: yes. Conditional winner-take-all: yes. All these options: yes, yes, and more yes!

But this myriad of permissible options is entirely consistent with the original Jeffersonian vision for the Electoral College redesign of 1803. The Jeffersonians wanted to maintain the prerogative of states to choose their preferred method for appointing their presidential electors. They were adherents of federalism in this respect. Their vision of federalism was, of course, different from that of their Federalist opponents. But the Jeffersonians were still believers in federalism insofar as their conception of the Electoral College retained a vital role for the states.

To be sure, the Jeffersonians never imagined that the states would exercise their power to appoint electors in a way that would undermine the very Jeffersonian premises of the Electoral College as they redesigned it. They never expected that states would appoint electors who in the aggregate would create an Electoral College majority for a candidate who lacked majority support in the states forming that Electoral College majority—and in so doing would defeat a candidate who *was* preferred by a majority of voters in enough states for an

Electoral College majority. To prevent the continued undermining of Jeffersonian expectations, the risk of which appears to be increasing with each election, states must supply what the Jeffersonians themselves omitted: a guarantee that they will not deviate from majority rule in appointing their electors.

Within the broad set of options compliant with the majority-rule requirement, states may have strong policy reasons for preferring one option over the others. States, for example, may prefer to avoid proportional allocation, or even conditional winner-take-all, insofar as dividing a state's Electoral College votes among candidates dilutes the strength of a state acting as a single unit within the overall Electoral College system. It was for this reason that states for the most part abandoned the districting system of dividing a state's Electoral College votes.

In the end, instant runoff voting may prove to be the method of complying with the majority-rule requirement preferred by most, if not all, states. There would be nothing wrong with that. As long as states retain the choice of alternative methods, in keeping with the Jeffersonian version of federalism, they are entitled to converge on the same policy preference. An Electoral College system in which all states used instant runoff voting as their method of appointing presidential electors would be fully consonant with the Jeffersonian vision of presidents elected by virtue of achieving the federally appropriate compound majority-of-majorities.

8

An Exploration of Alternatives

IF THE GOAL is to repair America's method of electing presidents—in particular, fixing it to conform to the fundamental democratic principle of majority rule—why bother tinkering with the Electoral College system? Why not, instead, replace the Electoral College with direct election of the president by a majority of American voters nationwide?

The Practical Impossibility of a Constitutional Amendment

For three-quarters of a century Americans have wanted to get rid of the Electoral College, replacing it with a direct vote of the entire American electorate. In 1944, Gallup asked whether the Electoral College system should be "discontinued" and instead presidents "elected by total popular vote alone." Nearly two-thirds of Gallup's respondents, 65 percent, said they favored this change. Less than a quarter, only 23 percent, opposed (with the remaining expressing no opinion).[1]

Gallup received similar responses to the same question, or a substantially equivalent version of it, throughout the twentieth century and into the twenty-first. For example, in 1980 Gallup asked: "Would you approve or disapprove of an amendment to the Constitution which would do away with the electoral college and base the election of a President on the total vote cast throughout the nation?" Again two-thirds, 67 percent, responded favorably. Only 19 percent, opposed (with the rest having no opinion).[2] In 2011, 62 percent of respondents—not quite, but almost, as many as before—told Gallup that they would

135

"prefer" to "amend the Constitution so that the candidate who receives the most votes nationwide wins the election," while this time 35 percent expressed a preference "to keep the current system, in which the candidate who wins the most votes in the Electoral College wins the election" (with a much smaller fraction expressing no preference).[3]

At times, the percentage of Americans wanting to replace the Electoral College with a direct nationwide popular vote has been much higher than even this two-thirds supermajority. In 1968, Gallup received its highest response in favor of this change: 81 percent, or slightly more than four-fifths. Only 12 percent in 1968 wanted to keep the Electoral College (and 7 percent had no opinion). A decade later, in 1977, the percentage supporting this change had dropped to a still extraordinarily high 73 percent, or almost three-quarters, with only 15 percent opposing the change (and 12 percent expressing no view).[4]

Despite this overwhelming level of sustained support over five decades, Americans have never obtained the constitutional amendment that they desired. As the historian Alex Keyssar has analyzed, Americans have been trying to amend the Constitution to jettison the existing Electoral College system for almost two centuries, since at least the 1820s. But after the Jeffersonian redesign of 1803 as adopted in the Twelfth Amendment, none of these subsequent efforts have been successful. The closest a proposal came was in 1969, when popular support for eliminating the Electoral College was at its highest, and in Congress the House of Representatives passed by the necessary two-thirds majority an amendment that would have replaced the Electoral College with a national popular vote. But the amendment died in the Senate, where it was filibustered. As Keyssar explains, the procedural hurdles for a constitutional amendment are too high for even the continued overwhelming sentiment of the American people to prevail on this issue.[5]

Moreover, even if it were possible to amend the Constitution to eliminate the Electoral College, there is the question of exactly what the replacement should be. When Gallup has asked the question over the years, it usually has been vague about the details of a direct nationwide vote: Would a plurality be enough to prevail, or would a majority be necessary and, if so, how would it be assured? More recently, as in 2011,

Gallup phrased its question in a way that suggested that a plurality would suffice (do you "prefer" to "amend the Constitution so that the candidate who receives the most votes nationwide wins the election?"), although even this updated phrasing is not entirely explicit on this crucial point. Perhaps this phrasing is part of the explanation why support for a constitutional amendment has dropped somewhat. Amending the Constitution to permit a mere plurality winner of a nationwide vote to become president would be a terrible idea. It would enable someone to become president no matter how small the plurality: less than 40 percent, or perhaps even less than one-third, if the race were extremely fragmented among multiple candidates.[6]

In theory, it would be possible to amend the Constitution so that America could have the kind of direct nationwide two-round system for presidential elections that France, among many other nations, uses. Under this straightforward system, there are multiple candidates on the first-round ballot, with the top two vote-getters moving on to the second round if no candidate wins a majority in the first round. Because the second-round ballot is limited to only two candidates, it is guaranteed (absent the extremely unlikely event of a tie in a national election with millions of ballots) that the winner receives a majority of the second-round votes.[7]

France's experience shows the significance of the second round. Three times since the beginning of its two-round system in 1965 the first round's runner-up, and not the first round's plurality winner, has been the majority winner of the second round. In 1974, Francois Mitterand was the plurality winner in the first round with 43.25 percent. Valéry Giscard d'Estaing was the runner-up with 32.60 percent. In the second round, Giscard d'Estaing pulled ahead of Mitterand 50.81 percent to 49.19 percent, thereby demonstrating the effect that other candidates on the first-round ballot had in suppressing demonstration of the majority support for Giscard d'Estaing.[8]

Then in 1981, the roles of these two candidates were reversed. This time Giscard d'Estaing was the plurality winner in the first round, with 28.32 percent. Mitterand was the first round's runner-up, with 25.85 percent. In the second round, Mitterand beat Giscard d'Estaing 51.76 percent to 48.24 percent, revealing the majority preference for Mitterand that was disguised in the first round of voting.[9]

Likewise, in 1995 Jacques Chirac was the runner-up in the first round, with 20.84 percent. The plurality winner was Lionel Jospin, with 23.30 percent. In the second round, Chirac beat Jospin 52.64 percent to 47.36 percent.[10]

France's two-round system would be a suitable method of presidential elections for the United States to adopt. It would permit multiple third-party and independent candidates to be on the first-round ballot, without distorting the second-round choice between the two major-party candidates (assuming, as expected, that most often the two major-party candidates would make it to the second round). Looking ahead to 2020, John Kasich or anyone else contemplating a candidacy without a major-party nomination could compete on fair and equal terms in the first round. If they failed to dislodge the Democratic and Republican nominees from the top two spots, then these minor-party and independent candidates would drop aside, and the second round would determine definitively which of the two major-party candidates the American electorate preferred. And in the unusual instance in which a third-party or independent candidate managed to achieve one of the top two spots in the first round, as Teddy Roosevelt did in 1912, then this candidate would have earned the right to compete in the second round.

A two-round system is not perfect. As social scientists have proved, there is no perfect electoral system, since none can satisfy a set of basic criteria that would be reasonable to expect of any system.[11] A two-round system can allow an extremist candidate to reach the second round, as Le Pen father and daughter did in 2002 and 2017, when the nonextremists split their first-round votes among several alternatives.[12] It is also possible that neither of the two finalists in the second round is the election's Condorcet candidate—defined, as discussed in the previous chapter, as the candidate who would beat all others in head-to-head matchups. The Condorcet candidate could have finished third, close behind the top two, and being more moderate and broadly popular than either of them would have won the second round against either, and yet was boxed out of the second round by finishing third. Think of a 32 percent–31 percent–30 percent split among the top three finishers in the first round. Knowing that the 30 percent candidate would have clobbered either the 32 percent or 31 percent candidate in the second round, one easily can understand that the two-round system is far from perfect.[13]

Because of the theoretical imperfections of any electoral system, creative political scientists have conjured up a wide variety of alternatives to consider. In addition to the various forms of ranked-choice voting, which we considered in the previous chapter, there is "approval voting," which would permit voters to designate as "satisfactory" (or "acceptable") any number of candidates on the ballot.[14] More complicated is a system that would let voters grade candidates—Excellent, Very Good, Good, Satisfactory, or Unsatisfactory—much as teachers grade students in school.[15] But as a practical matter, it is not worth dwelling upon the pros and cons of these various alternatives, as none has a chance of being adopted by means of constitutional amendment as the new method of presidential election in America.

Rather than debating what would ideally be the best method of electing US presidents (if we could start from scratch), it is much more useful to accept the inevitability of the Electoral College system insofar as it is embodied in the text of the Constitution—and then ask what reform within this constitutional constraint would be achievable and desirable. It is from this framework that this book advocates restoring the election of presidents based on a federally appropriate majority-of-majorities. Not only is this goal worth striving for as a significant improvement on the status quo, this goal is also achievable by states adopting for themselves the majority-rule requirement (as defined at the outset of the previous chapter).

The National Popular Vote Multistate Compact Plan

There has been a concerted effort in recent years to nullify the effect of the Electoral College without a constitutional amendment, by employing the Electoral College machinery to contravene its essential nature. Because a majority of Electoral College votes wins the presidency, the basic idea is to convince enough states to award their votes not on the basis of the popular vote in their own states, but instead on the basis of the national popular vote. If states that together have a majority of Electoral College votes join the plan, then the winner of the national popular vote would win the presidency. The effect would be the same as a constitutional amendment to eliminate the Electoral College and to replace it with a direct national popular vote, without actually undertaking the steps necessary to adopt a constitutional amendment for this purpose.[16]

The idea was initially developed in the aftermath of the 2000 election, when the Electoral College winner (Bush) deviated from the plurality winner of the national popular vote: Gore won 48.38 percent of the popular vote nationwide, to Bush's 47.87 percent. Becoming operative only when enough states have signed on to reach the 270 electoral votes needed for a majority, the plan was adopted in advance of the 2008 election by only four states (Maryland, New Jersey, Illinois, and Hawaii) amounting to 48 electoral votes. Before the 2012 election, four more states (Washington, Massachusetts, Vermont, and California) and the District of Columbia had signed on, for a total of 132 electoral votes. Two more states (Rhode Island and New York) joined before the 2016 election, reaching 165 electoral votes—still 105 shy of the 270 needed for the plan to take effect.[17]

The outcome of the 2016 election has energized the effort to add enough other states to reach the 270 threshold. Like 2000, 2016 produced an Electoral College winner (Trump) who was not the plurality winner of the national popular vote: Clinton won 48.02 percent of the popular vote nationwide, whereas Trump won only 45.93 percent. A new organization, Make Every Vote Count, led by former Federal Communications Commission chairman Reed Hundt and backed by significant resources including pro bono contributions from the leading DC law firm Covington & Burling, has joined in to jump-start this effort. So far, Connecticut, Colorado, Delaware, New Mexico, and Oregon have joined the multistate compact, for a current total of 196 electoral votes.[18]

Given all this renewed energy and resources directed toward reaching the 270 electoral votes necessary to activate this multistate compact, why detract from this focus by introducing the alternative idea of a recommitment by states to the Jeffersonian principle of appointing presidential electors in accordance with the majority-rule requirement (as defined in the previous chapter)?

The answer is a simple comparison: there are four significant defects with this multistate compact plan, including one huge problem, whereas a Jeffersonian recommitment to majority rule has none of these defects and, instead, is appropriately consonant with the Constitution as it currently exists.

First, the multistate compact idea is arguably unconstitutional.[19] Because its whole purpose is to eviscerate the Electoral College and would be the functional equivalent of a constitutional amendment to eliminate the Electoral College without going through the procedures required for a constitutional amendment, it is easy to imagine that the Supreme Court might be persuaded to invalidate the idea. To be sure, the plan is technically compliant with the text of the Constitution, since the states have the power to choose the method of appointing their electors and it would be the states themselves agreeing to appoint their own electors in conformity to the results of the national popular vote. Still, no one can confidently predict that the Court would sustain the validity of a plan that is so obviously subversive of the way the constitutional mechanism is supposed to work. In particular, the Constitution's federalist character gives each state a distinct number of Electoral College votes to be cast in separate meetings of electors in each state, rather than making the presidential election an undifferentiated amalgamation of nationwide popular votes. In addition to being a procedural end-run around the Constitution's method for amendments, the proposed compact would undermine this federalist structure inherent in the Electoral College.

Second, even if enough states eventually sign on to reach the threshold number of 270 electoral votes, it is unclear that the agreement would be binding upon those states and judicially enforceable in the event that one or more states decided to breach the agreement in a situation where it would make a difference. We can imagine a scenario in which one or more states in the compact, whose votes are necessary to award the presidency to the national popular vote winner, decide to repudiate the deal once it becomes clear that the voters in those states preferred a different candidate and, moreover, their preferred candidate would win the Electoral College if those states reverted to the previous system of awarding their electoral votes based on which candidate won the popular vote in the state rather than in the nation as a whole. The repudiation of the deal would be politically popular in the key states precisely because it would favor the candidate supported by the voters in those states; if the members of the state legislature shared the same partisan allegiance as this preferred candidate, there would be intense political pressure for the state legislature to engage in this repudiation of the deal. Were such a repudiation to occur it undoubtedly would spark litigation, but it is difficult to foresee how the litigation would be resolved given various constitutional principles at play: (1) the right of state legislatures to choose the method of appointing electors, (2) the due process concern about changing electoral rules after an election is already underway, and (3) the potential reluctance of the federal judiciary to involve itself in an Electoral College controversy that Congress is constitutionally empowered to resolve. A fight of this nature might replicate the crisis that occurred over the 1876 presidential election, when Congress was forced to choose which of multiple competing sets of electoral votes from several states were the lawfully authoritative votes entitled to be counted. Significantly increasing the chances of replicating that kind of controversy, as adoption of the multistate compact idea would do, is far from desirable.[20]

Third, despite the reinvigorated push post-2016, it is highly unlikely that the effort to reach 270 will be successful anytime soon. So far, all the states that have adopted the plan are solid blue, strongly Democratic states—based on the perception that the Electoral College favors Republicans, a perception reinforced by the result in 2016. (Colorado, one recent addition, is the least solidly blue based on its status in previous elections, but it has been trending blue in recent years.) Consequently, it is unlikely that red states will join the plan, or even purple states in which Republicans have sufficient power in the state legislature to block its adoption.[21]

With 74 electoral votes still to go, and assuming it is easier to add states in proportion to how blue they lean, the effort would need to pick up Virginia (13), Maine (4), Nevada (6), Minnesota (10), New Hampshire (4), Michigan (16), and Pennsylvania (20), for a total of 73 additional electoral votes, and still it would be one vote short. The next bluest state, Wisconsin (10), would put the effort over the top, with a cushion that would mean that one or two small states (like Nevada, or Maine and New Hampshire) could defect from the coalition. In any event, roughly half as many more states would need to sign on (seven or eight) as already have (fifteen plus the District of Columbia).

Of course, fewer states would be necessary if the proposed compact could pick up Florida (29), Ohio (18), or Texas (38), but these states are redder and thus presumably more difficult to get. And intrinsic to the proposal's being a compact, the effort does not succeed unless and until it achieves legislative victories in enough states to reach the crucial threshold of 270. Coming up short, even by just one electoral vote, is essentially the same as having zero states on board with the plan. For this reason, the celebrated Electoral College prognosticator Nate Silver proclaimed the effort "probably doomed" for the foreseeable future.[22]

Fourth, and most fundamentally, even if the effort managed to make it to 270, the multistate agreement would award the presidency to whichever candidate received the greatest share of the national popular vote, which could be significantly less than 50 percent. In this respect it would fail to solve the most basic problem of the way that the 1803 Electoral College has become defective in practice. Invoking the example that began the introduction to this book, the multistate compact would give the presidency to Tinker, who has a nationwide plurality of 43 percent, even though Evers with 42 percent would beat Tinker in a runoff 52 percent–48 percent once Chance is eliminated from the race. It would be like France letting a first-round plurality winner become president without bothering to hold the second round, an unthinkable situation from the perspective of wanting the will of the national majority to prevail.

The potential consequence of the interstate compact, if successful, became especially vivid in January 2019, when Howard Schultz (the former CEO of Starbucks) announced that he was considering an independent run for the White House in 2020. In making this announcement Schultz immediately caused panic among Democrats, who feared that he would split the anti-Trump vote with their eventual nominee. Although polling at the time showed 56 percent of voters "definitely would NOT vote" for Trump, he could still win re-election with a 44 percent plurality if Schultz siphoned off enough votes to leave the Democratic nominee in second place.[23] While the use of plurality winner-take-all by the states could cause the Electoral College to have this consequence, the proposed compact would replicate the same problem. If Trump were to win a nationwide plurality because the opposition to Trump was divided between the Democrat and Schultz (or other independent), then the proposed compact would award the presidency in 2020 to Trump even if 56 percent of the national electorate strongly opposes his re-election. Simply put, that is a horrific idea and more than enough reason to adamantly oppose adoption of the compact.

It seems that supporters of the multistate compact do not appreciate the implications of what they are advocating. For example, the new group Make Every Vote Count proclaims its concern that the results in 2000 and 2016 demonstrate an increased risk that future elections "are likely to select a President against the will of the majority of voters."[24] Yet the multistate compact that the organization has championed would exacerbate precisely that risk.

To be clear, from the perspective of democratic legitimacy, the compact proposal is pernicious regardless of which major party might be adversely affected in any particular election. In some circumstances a third candidate might pull votes from the Republican nominee, thereby causing the Democrat to win with a plurality. As we have seen, George H. W. Bush believed that this happened to him in 1992. In any event, going forward, no Democrat should gain the White House with only 40 percent of the national popular vote—or perhaps even less—just as no Republican should.[25]

In short, the multistate compact plan is fatally flawed because it would let a mere plurality winner prevail.[26] It would be possible to amend the proposal so that it kicks in only when there is a majority winner of the national popular vote, not merely a plurality winner. While that alteration would fix the proposal's most grievous defect, it would deprive the proposal of much practical significance. As Part Two of this book has demonstrated, the problem with the Electoral College system as it currently operates arises when there is a split among three or more candidates, which prevents any from having a clear majority in a single-round election with simple (unranked) ballots. If a candidate is able to achieve a majority anyway, this problem does not arise.

Advocates of the compact are understandably troubled that swing states play their pivotal role in the existing Electoral College system. They want the votes of Californians on the left to be counted in one big pool just the same as the votes of South Carolinians on the right and, most especially, Wisconsinites in the middle. In the long run, as stated in this book's introduction, it would be preferable to have a single undifferentiated count of all ballots cast nationally, so long as that count produced a majority and not mere plurality winner. But it is not worth moving to an undifferentiated national count if the result of that move is to elect a president with only 40 percent, or perhaps even less, of the national vote. That would make 60 percent of Americans, or even more, equally ineffective in electing their president, whether they live in California, South Carolina, or Wisconsin. By contrast, making pivotal states turn on a majority rather than plurality of their voters is more likely to match the preference of the majority nationwide than letting a national plurality prevail.[27]

The reformers involved in the Make Every Vote Count effort are correct that 2000 and 2016 signal the increased likelihood of future multicandidate splits that will cause problems for the existing Electoral College system. But their solution of letting the plurality winner of the national popular vote prevail is precisely the wrong one, especially given their own professed goal of wanting to effectuate "the will of the majority of voters." Instead, the correct solution is the adoption of state laws that would mandate the appointment of a state's electors in accordance with the majority-rule requirement.

This solution, moreover, does not require adoption by enough states to reach 270 electoral votes or any kind of multistate compact to be effective. Each state can embrace the majority-rule requirement on its own. As the next chapter shows, this reform can have a major impact even if adopted by only a few, or potentially even just one or two, states. There is no need to wait for seven or eight more states to concur in order to accomplish meaningful reform.[28]

Furthermore, if states enact the majority-rule requirement as part of their own laws for the appointment of their presidential electors, this reform would raise no constitutional doubts or risk destabilizing litigation. States would be doing nothing more than what New Hampshire and Massachusetts did in the early years of the Electoral College system: guaranteeing that the appointment of their presidential electors was consistent with the principle of majority rule. Any state that recommitted itself to this principle now would simply be returning to the original Jeffersonian vision of how the Electoral College as redesigned in 1803 was supposed to operate. There would be absolutely nothing unconstitutional or otherwise improper about any state deciding to adopt the majority-rule requirement on its own—and then appointing its electors in a manner consistent with this requirement.

Rather than endeavoring to effectuate the ill-designed multistate compact, reformers should focus their energies on convincing states to commit themselves to the majority-rule requirement.

Keep Plurality Winner-Take-All?

Since there is no perfect electoral system (as social scientists have proved mathematically), some might suggest that we should just stick with the process we currently use, however imperfect it might be. At least we are familiar with the system we have, and thus it is always possible to invoke—thanks to Edmund Burke—a defense of the status quo against the potential unintended consequences of attempting any change. Moreover, some argue that the existing system has the benefit (if one can call it that) of converting a popular-vote plurality into an Electoral College majority, making it seem that the election's winner has more of a mandate than the popular vote alone indicates. In 1992, for example, Clinton won only 43.01 percent of the popular vote nationally, and yet he was able to achieve an Electoral College landslide of 370, 100 more than the 270 necessary for victory.[29]

This argument rests on a kind of deception, or at least a superficiality that masks the true underlying reality. Yes, Clinton won the electoral votes of enough states—32 plus the District of Columbia—to accumulate 370 electoral votes. But did he really win the states that gave him all those electoral votes? The only state (apart from DC) in which he received a majority of the popular vote was his home state of Arkansas. In all the rest he obtained only pluralities.

Did Clinton deserve to get all of Ohio's 21 electoral votes when he received only 40.18 percent of the popular vote in the state? The law gave them to him, but was the law sound in doing so from a democratic perspective? Three-fifths of the state did *not* vote for Clinton, preferring someone else to become president. Why, one might ask, should he get all five-fifths of the state's electoral votes on that basis? Absent knowing whether Ohio really preferred Clinton to Bush in 1992, it makes no sense to give Clinton *all* of Ohio's 21 electoral votes just because Clinton got two-fifths of the state's popular vote. Bush also got two-fifths of the state's popular vote (38.35 percent), and Ross Perot the remaining one-fifth (20.98 percent).

To continue with this example, it would make much more sense, first, to give Clinton 9 of the state's electoral votes (a little more than two-fifths of 21, since he did come out a bit ahead of Bush); then, second, to allot Bush 8 of the state's electoral votes (a little less than two-fifths of 21, 38.10 percent, mirroring almost exactly Bush's share of the popular vote in the state); and, finally, to award Perot the remaining 4 of the state's electoral votes (approximately the same share as his proportion of the state's popular vote). That proportional allocation of electoral votes would much more accurately reflect the popular votes cast in the single round of unranked ballots.[30]

Suppose, using Ohio in 1992 again for illustration, that Bush, not Clinton, would have been the one to win a runoff in the state with Perot removed from the race, as might well have been the case given Ohio's political makeup. Then awarding all of Ohio's 21 electoral votes to Clinton is doubly undemocratic: not only does it deviate from a proportional allocation of electoral votes that would mirror each candidate's share of the popular vote, but it causes winner-take-all to reward the wrong candidate—the one that the majority of the electorate did not prefer, rather than the candidate that the majority of the electorate actually did prefer. This kind of backward outcome is exactly what John Clopton warned against in the 1803 debate on reforming the Electoral College: "When one person is intended for an office and another person actually obtains it, such election, if indeed it can properly be called an election, is not conformable to the will of those by whom it was made."[31]

It is true that there is no perfect electoral system. But, as social scientists who explore the mathematics of voting observe, this truth does not negate the important point that some systems are inferior to others, particularly for the specific purpose of presidential rather than legislative elections.[32] While there are many different forms of majority voting, each with somewhat different attributes—like the difference between instant runoff voting versus Condorcet voting using the same ranked-choice ballots—plurality voting does not even make a pretense of attempting to identify a majority winner and thus is necessarily inferior to various forms of majority voting, at least when the goal is to elect a single chief executive by determining which of several candidates is the one preferred by the electorate as a whole.

Requiring a majority winner in a presidential election makes more sense than permitting a mere plurality winner when one considers the entire process of winnowing the field of potential presidential candidates from many to several to one. Before the start of any presidential election year there are usually a multitude of potential candidates who have some plausible basis for running. For the 2008 election there were 10 declared Democratic and 12 Republican candidates, plus a smattering of independent and third-party candidates. For 2016, there were 17 Republican candidates at the start, and six Democrats (with Hillary Clinton's frontrunner status suppressing additional Democratic candidates). In addition to the many actual independent and third-party candidates who entered the race—including Gary Johnson, Jill Stein, Evan McMullin, and Darrell Castle—Michael Bloomberg, the billionaire former mayor of New York City, seriously considered an independent bid but ultimately decided against pulling votes away from Hillary Clinton as the Democratic nominee. In early 2019, over 20 names have been mentioned as possibilities for the Democratic nominee to challenge Trump's reelection. A handful of Republicans have been identified as possible challengers to Trump for the GOP nomination. There is also the serious possibility of a major independent run by John Kasich, Howard Schultz, and perhaps others, as well as the perennial candidates of the Libertarian, Green, Constitution, and other minor parties.

If at the beginning of each presidential election year Americans were asked to identify their favorite candidate, the plurality winner of this poll would not mean much. In a field of over 20 candidates, the plurality winner easily could poll at less than 10 percent and perhaps even less than 5 percent. The result would provide no indication of what the rest of the electorate, the vast majority of over 90 percent or 95 percent, thinks of the plurality winner.

To be sure, as the American system of presidential elections has developed, it is expected that the process of party primaries will substantially winnow the field of plausible contenders during the first half of the election year. The Democrats will choose a single nominee from their many candidates, and so too will the Republicans. If the

American system of presidential elections were exclusively limited to the traditional two major parties, then the November election would come down to a straightforward choice between just the two nominees who emerge from the major-party primaries. This would be true no matter how crowded either, or both, of those major-party primaries were. And with the November ballot confined to just two choices in every state, the Electoral College winner necessarily would satisfy the Jeffersonian expectation of being preferred by a majority in the states generating that Electoral College victory.

But the reality of US presidential elections is not a theoretically pure two-party system, even if Americans tend to think of elections in exclusively red-versus-blue, two-party terms. As a practical matter, under existing rules the November ballot will list a variety of options besides the Democratic and Republican nominees. In 2000, Florida's November ballot contained 10 presidential candidates, which is why Palm Beach County used the infamous butterfly format to fit all 10 names on a single page. In 2016, Colorado's November ballot contained 22 (!) presidential candidates. While much of the media covered the race as a two-party choice between Hillary Clinton and Donald Trump, and even though only those two candidates appeared on stage for the presidential debates, the actual set of options presented to voters for their choice was many more than just those two.

As we saw in the previous chapter, it is not constitutionally permissible to reduce the November ballot to only the two major-party nominees unless voters prior to November have had an adequate opportunity to displace one or more of those major-party nominees with an independent or third-party preference. Consequently, even if it were possible to change ballot-access rules to avoid the kind of ballot clutter that Florida voters faced in 2000 or Colorado voters confronted in 2016, states cannot limit the November election to a binary option without adopting some form of runoff mechanism (either a two-round or instant form). It is impossible to maintain a true two-party system, and the expectations of majority rule associated with exclusively two-party competition, in a single-round general election that permits plurality winners.

Even after the party primaries and nominating conventions are complete—and this is the key point that is often overlooked—American presidential elections necessarily will present voters a choice among multiple options: A, B, C, D, E, and so forth, not just A and B. Given this inevitable multiplicity of options, the question arises as to what the best decision procedure is for getting to a single winner. Although there is no perfect procedure, a single vote to identify a plurality winner is distinctly inferior because it does not reveal what the majority of voters think of that plurality winner. Even if the plurality winner receives 49 percent in a multicandidate field, it might be the case that 51 percent despise the plurality winner and would have preferred any, or at least several, of the other available options on the ballot. When the choice is between A, B, C, and D—and when A gets 49 percent, B 48 percent, C 2 percent, and D 1 percent—it cannot be said that the electorate as a whole would prefer A to B if those two were the only options available for consideration. Indeed, the animosity of non-A voters to A might be that they all would prefer any of the other options (B, C, or D) if given that choice. In this situation, one can think of A as the "anti-Condorcet" candidate: opposed by a majority of voters when compared head-to-head with every other candidate on the ballot. To let the anti-Condorcet candidate win seems the ultimate perversion of democracy—in other words, an electoral system in which the most opposed candidate prevails seems like an anti-democracy—yet that is what a plurality-winner rule permits, given that an anti-Condorcet candidate may receive a plurality of unranked votes.

The task then is to develop a constitutionally permissible procedure for narrowing the electorate's options to a binary (either/or) choice. That way we can be sure that the majority of voters do not prefer the loser to the winner. The problem is to pick the optimal procedure for narrowing the field of multiple candidates to just two finalists. The fact that there are several plausible alternatives for such a narrowing process does not justify refusing to choose any narrowing process at all. The particular narrowing method can be the one most suitable for the cultural and historical context of the specific democratic polity in question—or in a federal polity, each subsidiary unit can make its own selection of narrowing method in accordance with its own distinctive culture and history. For the purpose of American presidential elections, adopting a suitable narrowing process would permit the system to generate a final stage of two-party competition, as Americans expect, while also providing a constitutionally adequate preliminary opportunity for other parties and candidates to participate.

In any of these narrowing systems, moreover, voters can be given the right to abstain from making a choice between the two finalists, if these voters genuinely are indifferent between them after their own most preferred candidate has been winnowed out. But one cannot simply assume that voters who preferred a third or fourth option on a multicandidate ballot have no preference between the two most popular options. In some circumstances—like Roosevelt supporters in 1912, or Perot supporters in 1992, or perhaps Kasich supporters in 2020— they might genuinely think their most preferred candidate has a plausible shot at prevailing and, therefore, that they should not settle for their second choice when they only get one vote.[33] In other situations, when media pundits incessantly tell them that one of the major-party candidates is a shoo-in for victory, they might reasonably think that they should cast their ballot for a third-party or independent option, their true preference, since the major-party candidate they consider less objectionable has a lock on winning anyway. (It is easy to imagine that in 2016 some voters for Jill Stein or Gary Johnson might have acted differently if the media had not pervasively predicted that Trump had little chance of actually winning.)

Now, returning to the crucial point with which we began this section, if one argues that even with plurality winner-take-all at the state level in the appointment of presidential electors there is still an element of majority rule in the system because a candidate must win an Electoral College majority, the response is that this Electoral College majority is meaningless insofar as it is based on a series of plurality winner-take-all outcomes at the state level. If a candidate wins all of Florida's 29 electoral votes, and all of Pennsylvania's 20 electoral votes, and all of Michigan's 16 electoral votes, and so forth, based solely on 35 percent to 45 percent popular-vote pluralities in those states—when that same candidate would have *lost* runoffs in all those states—then an Electoral College majority that the candidate accumulates does not signify any genuine form of majority support. One cannot say that at least a majority of states preferred this candidate because in fact the opposite is true: since by hypothesis we know that the candidate's opponent would have won runoffs in these states, a majority of states actually preferred the opponent, just like a majority of voters in those states. There is no sense in which plurality winner-take-all at the state level translates into a genuine majority at the federal level.

Moreover, the American presidency is too important to let presidential elections be decided by arbitrary adherence to plurality winner-take-all. There are other issues about which a Burkean prudence in favor of maintaining the status quo, rather than rocking the boat, makes sense. But the method of electing US presidents is not one of those issues. As Part Two details, the entire course of history can change because plurality winner-take-all elects a president whom the voters in the responsible states actually did not want—preferring instead the other main candidate in the race. The flow of history should not turn on such a fluke. Yet it easily could again.

Burkean avoidance of change is not appropriate in this particular context. Instead, states should immediately move to embrace the majority-rule requirement for the appointment of their presidential electors. As observed earlier, this move does not dictate which form of majority rule each state should choose. This flexibility tracks the social science truth that there is no single perfect method. Each state can pick for itself whichever method of majority rule best suits its own particular policies and circumstances. While recognizing that no one form of majority rule must prevail in all states, the majority-rule requirement appropriately renders off-limits plurality winner-take-all, which is inferior to any of the acceptable ways of complying with the majority-rule requirement.

Presently, there is a mismatch between the election system that Americans think they have and the election system that Americans actually have. Like the Jeffersonians who adopted the Electoral College of 1803, Americans today think they have a two-party system for electing presidents. In truth, however, they have a system that permits more than two parties but was never actually designed for multiparty competition. To realign expectations with reality, it is necessary for states to adopt the majority-rule requirement for the appointment of electors. That way, the Electoral College can function properly to permit Americans to make a majority choice between the two main candidates, thereby conforming to both historical and contemporary expectations of how the system is supposed to work, while at the same time accommodating the inevitable reality of multiparty participation.[34]

Litigation to Eliminate Plurality Winner-Take-All?

Because the plurality winner-take-all approach is incompatible with the majoritarian premises and intent of the Electoral College redesign in 1803, one could ask whether the courts could strike down this approach as unconstitutional, rather than waiting for states to adopt new laws to comply with the majority-rule requirement. That is, perhaps lawsuits could seek judicial decrees ordering states to appoint their electors in a manner consistent with the majority-rule requirement. These lawsuits in effect would be asking courts to rule as if the majority-rule requirement were already implicitly part of the Jeffersonian Electoral College adopted in the Constitution by the Twelfth Amendment.

The argument is not absurd. But in my judgment it would be an exercise of judicial overreach. To be sure, plurality winner-take-all is inconsistent with the purposes and premises of the Jeffersonian Electoral College for the reasons elaborated previously. But it remains true that the text of the Constitution does not render it impermissible for a state to adopt plurality winner-take-all. Not every state law that is inconsistent with the spirit of the Constitution is unconstitutional.[35] Sometimes conformity to the Constitution's text suffices to inoculate from litigation a state law that is out of step with the Constitution's spirit.[36] The long history of plurality winner-take-all since the Jacksonian era, combined with the unqualified textual discretion of state legislatures to adopt whatever method of appointing presidential electors that they choose, indicates that it would be better to change the existing system by means of new state laws pursuant to this explicit textual authorization, rather than have unelected judges impose this reform by court decree.

Litigation currently in federal court argues that plurality winner-take-all violates not only the Electoral College as redesigned by the Twelfth Amendment, but also the subsequent adoption of the Equal Protection Clause in the Fourteenth Amendment.[37] This argument also seems to call for judicial overreach. The claim is that plurality winner-take-all violates the idea of one-person-one-vote that previous Supreme

Court decisions have found to be guaranteed by the equal protection clause. But those previous cases concern legislative apportionment and other denial of voting rights. Giving everyone an equal ballot and then declaring the winner based on a mere plurality outcome—while undesirable for the reasons we have considered—does not violate the equal voting rights of all entitled to cast these ballots. It does not, for example, violate equal protection to have plurality winner-take-all for gubernatorial or US Senate elections, whether or not doing so is sound from the standpoint of democracy.[38]

The plaintiffs in the pending cases attempt an argument that presidential elections are different because they are multistep processes in which, first, the citizens vote for electors and, then, the electors vote for president. But this argument seems mistaken in terms of the equal voting rights protected by the Constitution's equal protection clause. The only voting that the citizens themselves do is to pick the electors. The citizens do not vote for president at all; they are not participants in both steps of the two-step process. As long as citizens have equal voting rights in the balloting that chooses the electors, the requirement of equal protection is satisfied. Since plurality winner-take-all to pick electors operates the same way as it does to pick a governor or US senator, it seems just as consistent with equal protection to use plurality winner-take-all for the one as the other.

While plurality winner-take-all is undesirable, and also inconsistent with the purposes and premises of the Jeffersonian Electoral College, it does not seem unconstitutional in a way that should render it subject to judicial invalidation.[39] Rather than pursuing litigation, the reform effort should work to convince states to embrace the majority-rule requirement legislatively. They should do so both because it is inherently a good idea from the perspective of democracy and because it would bring state law into congruence with the majoritarian commitment underlying the Jeffersonian Electoral College that remains operative today.

9

A Feasible Reform

THE ELECTORAL COLLEGE reform that this book proposes—the adoption by individual states of the majority-rule requirement (as defined at the outset of Chapter 7)—has an overriding advantage compared to a constitutional amendment or multistate compact. It can take effect immediately in each state that adopts it, without waiting for any action in any other state. Moreover, its adoption in just a few key states, without more, could prevent the kinds of misfirings of the 1803 Electoral College that we have seen on at least three occasions, and that seem increasingly more likely today. Each state currently has all the constitutional authority it needs to adopt a new state law that fully accords with the majority-rule requirement. Just as Maine and Nebraska have exercised their existing authority to adopt districting systems for the appointment of their electors, so too is every other state in the Union entitled to adopt for itself a method of appointing its electors consistent with the majority-rule requirement.

Maine and Nebraska each acted independently and unilaterally, as entitled under the Constitution, so that their choices immediately took effect in each of those states even as all others continued to exercise plurality winner-take-all. Similarly, if New Hampshire decided to reinstate the kind of runoff it used previously for the appointment of its presidential electors, it could enact that law immediately and on its own, and the runoff would occur there in the next presidential election (assuming it was necessary to identify a majority winner in the state). Likewise, if Florida decided to use instant runoff voting for the appointment of its presidential electors in 2020, then that would be the voting method employed in Florida for that year's presidential election regardless of the other voting methods employed in other states that year.

Florida's constitutional power to make this independent choice would be no different from its power to permit "no-excuse" absentee voting for presidential elections, whether or not other states also permit no-excuse absentee voting as part of their processes for appointing their electors.[1] The same constitutional power, to invoke another specific example, is what permitted states like California to grant women the right to vote in presidential elections—as part of the popular vote that determined the appointment of the state's electors—before the Nineteenth Amendment guaranteed equal voting rights to all women nationally.[2] Just as each state then could make its own choice to let women vote for presidential electors, even if other states did not, so too can each state today decide to adopt instant runoff voting—or any other method of complying with the majority-rule requirement—regardless of whether other states make this same choice.

The Significance of State-by-State Reform

It would be best if all states adopted new laws that complied with the majority-rule requirement. That would guarantee that all future presidential elections would conform to the original Jeffersonian ideal—and expectation—of electing presidents who have demonstrated the kind of compound majority-of-majorities appropriate for the chief executive of a federal republic. Absent the optimal circumstance of universal adoption by all 50 states, as a general proposition it stands that the more states comply with the majority-rule requirement, the more the Electoral College in practice conforms to its original Jeffersonian intent.

Even so, no one should underestimate the practical significance of only a few states adopting this Electoral College reform. If just Florida had adopted instant runoff voting for the 2000 election, the entire Electoral College outcome would have been different. With instant runoff voting in place, Gore would have won Florida's 25 electoral votes regardless of any recount concerning hanging chads, as we saw in Chapter 5. With those electoral votes from Florida, Gore would have achieved the Electoral College majority necessary to win the presidency. (Perhaps the campaign itself would have proceeded differently if Florida had used instant runoff voting in 2000, with Gore and Bush changing their messages in the hope of wooing second-place votes from the supporters of minor-party candidates. Perhaps, too, these changes in campaign messaging might have altered the first-choice preferences that voters had among the candidates. Even so, we can be reasonably confident that Gore, not Bush, would have won Florida if instant runoff voting had been the electoral method employed in the state.)

To be sure, it would have been better if in 2000 not only Florida, but all the states in which there were just plurality winners of the popular vote that year, used instant runoff voting. But as a practical matter, if just Florida had used instant runoff voting in 2000, the election's outcome would have conformed to Jeffersonian expectations. As we saw in Chapter 5, Florida alone made the difference between correctly identifying the true Jeffersonian candidate preferred by a majority of voters in the states producing the Electoral College majority, rather than incorrectly awarding the presidency to the candidate who was not the true Jeffersonian winner in the election. This point is true because the failure to comply with the majority-rule requirement was not consequential in the other states with mere plurality winners of the popular vote in 2000. But it was consequential in Florida. And because the entire Electoral College outcome hinged on Florida, the effect of giving all of Florida's electoral votes to the plurality winner there, who was not the majority-preferred candidate in the state, meant that the entire Electoral College system failed to identify the true Jeffersonian winner just because of the specific nonmajoritarian outcome in Florida.

We can make a similar point about 2016, although not confined to a single state, and more qualified in its analysis. If just Florida and Michigan had used instant runoff voting in 2016, the outcome of the Electoral College might have been different. Take Florida's 29 electoral votes and Michigan's 16 and move them from Trump's column to Clinton's, and the result is that Trump's total drops from 304 to 259, below the 270 threshold for an Electoral College majority, and Clinton's total rises from 227 to 272, above the 270 threshold. To be absolutely clear: it is not at all obvious that Clinton would have been the winner of the popular vote in Florida and Michigan if instant runoff voting had been used in those states in 2016. As we explored in Chapter 6, Trump might have been the majority-preferred candidate in those states, not just the plurality winner there, and so Trump rather than Clinton might have won those states with the use of instant runoff voting. This observation has extra force with respect to Florida, compared to Michigan, given the analysis that it would have been much easier for Clinton to win runoffs in the three Rust Belt states than in the other Trump-plurality states.

More importantly, as we also saw in Chapter 6, even if the results in those states would have flipped with the use of instant runoff voting, it does not follow automatically that Clinton was the true Jeffersonian candidate in 2016. Before reaching that conclusion, one would need to do a full analysis of all the states with mere plurality victories in 2016, including those states in which Clinton herself was a mere plurality winner (Virginia, Minnesota, Colorado, Nevada, New Mexico, and New Hampshire).[3] Still, the mere chance that the whole election might have turned on the adoption of instant runoff voting in just two states—and that achieving this reform in only those two states might have caused the election to produce a genuinely Jeffersonian winner different from the candidate who prevailed in the absence of this reform—is enough to illustrate the power of accomplishing this reform one state at a time.

Or consider again the three Rust Belt states of Pennsylvania, Wisconsin, and Michigan, with their combined 46 electoral votes. What if just these three states had used instant runoff voting in 2016? We can never really know, for the same reasons that it is unknowable what would have happened if these three states had used regular runoffs (as we explored in Chapter 6). But if they had adopted this reform, and if Clinton had prevailed using this voting method—picking up enough Gary Johnson and Jill Stein supporters to be the majority-preferred candidate over Trump—then the use of instant runoff voting in just those three states would have made the difference in the outcome of the entire election. In this scenario, it would not have mattered if Clinton was not the majority-preferred candidate in Florida; being the majority-preferred candidate in the three Rust Belt states would have been enough for an Electoral College victory.[4] To be sure, for

Clinton to have achieved a genuinely Jeffersonian victory, it still would be necessary to determine that Clinton was the majority-preferred candidate in those states where she won only pluralities. But if she was, then being the instant runoff voting winner in these three Rust Belt states would have made Clinton not only the actual Electoral College winner, but also a genuinely Jeffersonian one.

Simply put, this Electoral College reform is *that* powerful. Using instant runoff voting for the appointment of presidential electors in just two or three states potentially can make the difference between an outcome inconsistent with how the Jeffersonian Electoral College is supposed to work and, instead, an outcome that properly produces an Electoral College majority for a genuinely Jeffersonian winner.

Moreover, while the three-state combination of Pennsylvania, Michigan, and Wisconsin is the most obvious one, the same point about the 2016 election applies to several other three-state combinations:

Pennsylvania, Michigan, North Carolina	(51 EVs)
Pennsylvania, Michigan, Arizona	(47 EVs)
Pennsylvania, Wisconsin, North Carolina	(45 EVs)
Pennsylvania, North Carolina, Arizona	(46 EVs)
Florida, Wisconsin, Arizona	(50 EVs)

If instant runoff voting had been the system used in any of these trios, and if Clinton would have won instant runoff voting there, then she rather than Trump would have been the overall Electoral College winner. Indeed just the two-state combination of Florida and North Carolina (44 EVs), like the two-state combination of Florida and Michigan (45 EVs), would have been enough to swing the election from one column to the other. Considering these possibilities, the significance of adopting this reform in just a few states should be abundantly clear.

What is true for 2000 and 2016 is potentially true for future elections. Adopting instant runoff voting, or another method consistent with the majority-rule requirement, in just a few states—or even only one or two—might determine the outcome in 2020 or 2024, or any other future year. Moreover, achieving this reform could make the difference between electing a president who fails or passes the essentially

Jeffersonian test of being the majority-preferred candidate in the states providing the Electoral College victory.

Given the huge significance of enacting this reform in just a few key states, it should be a high priority of reformers to persuade states likely to be the decisive battlegrounds in future presidential elections to embrace the majority-rule requirement for appointing electors.

Mobilizing Popular Opinion to Achieve State-by-State Reform

Americans believe deeply in the idea of majority rule as an essential element of democracy.[5] Americans also correctly link this idea to the Founding of the Republic and, in particular, to Thomas Jefferson and his invocation of "the consent of the governed" as the necessary foundation for the legitimate exercise of government authority in the Declaration of Independence. Or, as Jefferson expressed it in his first inaugural address, all Americans regardless of party can "unite" to embrace as a "sacred principle" that "the will of the majority is in all cases to prevail."[6]

Jefferson is understandably diminished by his hypocritical acceptance of slavery. Even so, as the author of the Declaration, Jefferson remains the foremost father of American democracy.[7] Americans today tend to base their commitment to self-government on the teachings of the Founders.[8] Consequently, reminding Americans today of the Jeffersonian pedigree of the Electoral College, as redesigned in 1803, should be a powerful point in persuading Americans to return the operation of the Electoral College to its original Jeffersonian conception as a form of majority rule.

You can tell Americans "Democracy Means Majority Rule," and that bumper-sticker message will resonate as a matter of basic political principles. But you can also proclaim "The Founders Wanted Presidents Elected by Majority Rule," and that history-based message will likely resonate even more. Add Jefferson's image to the message, saying "Elections Are Supposed to Give Us the Presidents We Want," and you have the core of a plausible public-relations campaign for getting states to adopt the majority-rule requirement as a way to conform with what Jefferson (along with the other Founders of our constitutional democracy) wanted presidential elections to be.

Accordingly, it ought to be possible to generate popular support for a grassroots campaign based on the premises that (1) the Electoral College as reformed after the election of 1800 was expected to operate according to the fundamental principle of majority rule, (2) Thomas Jefferson's victories in 1800 and 1804 and the general Jeffersonian commitment to majority rule provided the foundation for this fundamental expectation, (3) the subsequent implementation of the Electoral College by the states has deviated from this fundamental expectation in ways that are demonstrably harmful and undemocratic, and therefore (4) states should reform their Electoral College laws so as to restore the original Jeffersonian commitment to majority rule.

One should not naïvely think that a public relations campaign of this nature is easy. Nor is it enough to convince a state's citizenry of the merits of the idea. It is necessary to translate that conviction into legislation. In many states, the perceived short-term interests of one political party will be enough to dissuade incumbent politicians from adopting a reform that the public wants, even if what the public wants is as fundamental as a return to the core concept of majority rule.

In neither the short term nor the long term, however, is a recommitment to majority rule inherently advantageous to one particular political party. As we have seen, plurality winner-take-all can work to the disadvantage of either Republicans or Democrats. In 1992 it arguably deprived George H. W. Bush, a Republican, of a re-election victory that he would have obtained if the Electoral College had operated properly. More recently, in 2000 and 2016, it was the Democrats who were disfavored. The next time, whether in 2020 or thereafter, it could be the Republicans disfavored again. As long as the presence of third-party or independent candidates has the potential to pull more votes away from either the Republican or the Democrat, state legislatures currently controlled by either party—or jointly controlled by both— should be willing, as a matter of self-interested logic, to adopt state laws that operationalize the majority-rule requirement.[9]

But self-interested logic does not always prevail in state legislatures, because incumbent politicians are often blinded by a misperception of what is actually in their self-interest. Consequently, it may be necessary for this reform movement to supplement efforts to persuade state legislatures with ballot measures in those states that permit direct democracy through ballot initiatives. In fact, some of the most critical battleground states in presidential elections—including Florida, Michigan, Arizona, Colorado, and Ohio—permit ballot initiatives.[10] As we saw earlier in this chapter, if just Florida and Michigan had adopted the majority-rule requirement for the appointment of their presidential electors, the result of the election in 2016 might have been different. As a matter of generating popular enthusiasm for this reform, it would make sense to start with ballot initiative campaigns in those two states (being careful, again, to make the campaign bipartisan by emphasizing that in future years the same dynamic could adversely affect either major party).

The Constitutionality of Ballot Initiatives as Reform Method

One remaining issue is whether it is constitutional to use a ballot initiative to specify how a state chooses its presidential electors. The issue arises because the federal Constitution explicitly gives "the Legislature" of each state the power to "direct" the "manner" of appointing electors. (The whole relevant clause provides: "Each state shall appoint, in such manner as the Legislature thereof may direct, a number of electors, equal to the whole number of Senators and Representatives to which the State may be entitled in the Congress.") In the litigation over the result of the 2000 presidential election in Florida, George Bush's team made the argument that the Florida Supreme Court had violated this provision of the federal Constitution insofar as the state court's interpretation of the state's recount statutes was so distorted as to vitiate the state legislature's power to control the appointment of the state's electors. This argument was accepted by three Justices of the US Supreme Court in *Bush v. Gore* (Chief Justice Rehnquist, Justice Scalia, and Justice Thomas), rejected by four (Justices Stevens, Souter, Ginsburg, and Breyer), and left unaddressed by the two remaining Justices (O'Connor and Kennedy), who resolved the case on other grounds—namely, that the state's procedure for handling the hanging chads violated the Equal Protection Clause of the Fourteenth Amendment.[11]

A similar argument was considered, and rejected by a 5–4 decision, in *Arizona State Legislature v. Arizona Independent Redistricting Commission*, a 2015 case concerning the power of a state to use a ballot initiative as the means to give the authority to draw the state congressional districts to an independent commission rather than the state's legislature.[12] The case concerned an analogous provision of the federal Constitution, the one authorizing "the legislature" of each state to determine the "times, places, and manner of holding elections for Senators and Representatives" (unless Congress itself superseded those state laws). The majority opinion of the US Supreme Court in that case interpreted the word "legislature" to encompass the ballot initiative procedure, so that it was just as permissible for a ballot initiative to delegate the drawing of congressional districts to a commission as it would be for a state legislature to make this delegation decision.

If the reasoning of this majority opinion were applied to the context of appointing presidential electors, it would be abundantly clear that a ballot initiative constitutionally could determine the method of appointing a state's electors to the same extent that a law enacted by a state's legislature could. But there is good reason to doubt that its reasoning would be so applied. Chief Justice Roberts wrote a vigorous dissent on behalf of himself and Justices Scalia, Thomas, and Alito, arguing that the Constitution's use of the word "legislature" could refer only to the institutional body commonly associated with that term, and not to the people or electorate of a state even if the state's constitution endowed the electorate with the legislative authority to enact statutes by means of ballot initiatives. With Justice Gorsuch stepping into Justice Scalia's shoes, and Justice Kennedy replaced by Justice Kavanaugh, it is highly likely that Chief Justice Roberts now has five votes on the Court for the analysis he employed in his dissent, and thus the majority opinion in the *Arizona State Legislature* case would no longer represent the prevailing view on the Court.

Even so, it does not mean that there is no role for a ballot initiative to play in establishing ground rules for a state legislature's choice regarding the method for appointing the state's presidential electors. Chief Justice Roberts repeatedly made the point that the problem with the Arizona law was that it entirely excluded the state legislature from the process of congressional districting. "There is a critical difference between allowing a State to *supplement* the legislature's role in the legislative process and permitting the State to *supplant* the legislature altogether," the Chief Justice observed, italicizing his own words for emphasis.[13] The essence of the argument was that the state legislature "may not be cut out of th[e] process." As he summed it up: "Put simply, the state legislature need not be exclusive in congressional districting, but neither may it be excluded." It would be entirely consistent with the Chief Justice's point for a ballot initiative to require a state legislature to choose a method of appointing electors consistent with the majority-rule requirement, as we have defined it, while leaving to the state legislature's discretion which of the many means available it prefers.

Consider this possible way to phrase a new provision of a state's constitution, to be adopted by means of a ballot measure, that would commit the state to the majority-rule requirement in the appointment of its presidential electors:

> The Legislature [of this state] shall have the authority to choose the manner of appointing the state's presidential electors, provided that the manner chosen shall comply with the principle of majority rule and, accordingly, shall not cause all of the state's electors to vote for the same individual unless the individual wins a majority of popular votes cast by citizens of the state who are eligible to participate in elections for statewide offices, including governor and US senator.

This new provision of state constitutional law would not deprive the state legislature of the power to determine the method of appointing electors. On the contrary, the state legislature could decide whether or not to adopt an actual runoff, or instead to use instant runoff voting or some other form of ranked-choice balloting, or rather to adopt a districting system like Maine and Nebraska, or to employ a form of proportional allocation including conditional winner-take-all.[14] All of these options would be open to the state legislature. The only choice off-limits to the state legislature would be winner-take-all in the absence of a popular-vote majority. But narrowing the state legislature's choice in this limited way would hardly come close to "totally displac[ing] the legislature," in the Chief Justice's words.[15] Thus, the federal Constitution would not block a state constitution, by means of a ballot initiative, from including this limited constraint that obligates the state legislature to exercise its authority to select the manner of appointing presidential electors in conformity with the majority-rule requirement.[16]

It would be a great step forward if ballot measures in presidential battleground states, like Florida and Michigan, adopted a constitutional clause embodying the commitment to the majority-rule requirement, in language equivalent to the example set forth here. To be sure, after the adoption of these ballot measures, it would be necessary for the legislatures of those states to enact specific ways of complying with the majority-rule requirement. If a legislature were recalcitrant in fulfilling this obligation under the state's constitution, it might be necessary to bring litigation in state court in order to enforce compliance. Nonetheless, the simple adoption of the majority-rule requirement itself as an essential feature of appointing presidential electors would be a major victory in the effort to restore the Electoral College to its Jeffersonian premises and expectations.

Many might think such a victory enough, at least in the short term. Still, it is conceivable that a ballot initiative campaign in a particular state might wish to go further, to test the limits of the Chief Justice's reasoning in his *Arizona State Legislature* dissent. For example, consider this alternative language that might be used in a ballot initiative:

> The Legislature [of this state] shall choose the procedure for appointing the state's presidential electors, provided that an elector shall win a majority of popular votes pursuant to this procedure.

This language would be more constraining than the initial example insofar as it would preclude the state legislature from using a proportionality system as a means of complying with the majority-rule requirement. It still, however, would give the legislature the choice between employing an actual runoff as part of a two-round system, or instead using ranked-choice ballots in a one-round vote. It even would permit districting as long as the winners of each district received a majority, and not just a plurality, of the popular vote in those districts. This degree of legislative latitude should be enough to satisfy the reasoning of the Chief Justice's dissent in the Arizona case.

But it is possible to conceive of harder examples. Suppose a ballot initiative used this language:

> The Legislature [of this state] shall choose the procedure for appointing the state's presidential electors, provided that an elector

shall win a majority of popular votes as demonstrated through the use of ballots that permit voters to rank their preferences among the candidates listed on the ballot.

This language would still leave the legislature with some latitude. For example, the legislature would need to make the choice of what mathematical method to use to calculate the majority winner of the ranked-choice ballots, whether a form of instant runoff voting or instead Condorcet voting (or even some other innovative method). But this language would preclude the use of an actual runoff as the state legislature's preferred method of complying with the majority-rule principle—a choice that New Hampshire, as we have seen, actually employed in the early days of the Republic. To be sure, even this degree of constitutional constraint would not "wholly exclude" (the Chief Justice's words, again) the state's legislature from the process of choosing the method of appointing the state's electors.[17] But at some point the degree of constraint imposed upon the state legislature's choice by a ballot measure might be too much for Chief Justice Roberts and a majority of the Supreme Court, in light of the federal Constitution's apparent decision that the state's legislature play the primary role in this process.

It would not be advisable to press too hard for ballot measures that, by endeavoring to constrain state legislatures to ranked-choice ballots, might invite constitutional repudiation by the US Supreme Court. Instead, it would be better to aim for the adoption of ballot measures that broadly commit the state to the majority-rule requirement, but leave the legislature ample room to determine the best means of compliance. At the same time, it would be appropriate to seek to convince the legislature to adopt instant runoff voting as the specific method of complying with the majority-rule requirement, especially if one thought the legislature would be most inclined to adopt that specific method. The rapidly increasing interest in using ranked-choice ballots for various types of elections is reason to view this policy choice as sensible. But if legislatures in other states are reluctant to embrace instant runoff voting, and instead are more open to other ways of complying with the majority-rule requirement, then prudence as well as federalism entails encouraging the legislature to adopt whatever form of majoritarian voting is most suitable for that state.[18]

Some might like to see instant runoff voting adopted for presidential elections nationwide. That reform would be desirable, but it would take a constitutional amendment and thus is impractical for the foreseeable future, as we have discussed. Recognizing this impracticality, as a second-best alternative to a constitutional amendment, some reformers might wish to pursue instant runoff voting for presidential elections state-by-state, simply because of its desirability without regard to its relationship to the original Jeffersonian intent underlying the Electoral College of 1803. That policy objective is certainly understandable and, in fact, overlaps to a considerable degree with this book's historical analysis. There is nothing wrong with various reformers having different reasons for wanting states to use instant runoff voting to appoint presidential electors. A history-based motive for returning to majority rule can supplement independent policy reasons for pursuing the same reform.

To be completely clear, however, this book does not advocate instant runoff voting exclusively, for its own sake. Instead, this book offers instant runoff voting as one method for bringing the Electoral College system back into conformity with its original Jeffersonian philosophy. For collateral policy reasons, many might consider instant runoff voting to be the most attractive way to comply with this original Jeffersonian intent. And, as a practical matter, instant runoff voting may prove to be the easiest majority-rule method for most state legislatures to adopt. Even so, from the historical perspective developed in this book, instant runoff voting is only one of several means to achieve a Jeffersonian end, rather than instant runoff voting being an end in itself.

Therefore, the Jeffersonian imperative is to generate support for any Electoral College reform that causes states to embrace the basic principle of majority rule. If the reform effort can build momentum so that states one by one begin to adopt the majority-rule requirement for the appointment of their presidential electors, that would lead to the restoration of the Jeffersonian Electoral College. Having presidents elected on the basis of a federally appropriate compound form of majority rule, even if some states identified majority wins by means of actual runoffs rather than ranked-choice ballots, would be no small accomplishment. It certainly would be a vast improvement over the un-Jeffersonian system of plurality victories that prevails today, which permits the election of minority-rule presidents vehemently opposed by strong majorities.

Conclusion

THE INSTITUTIONAL DEFICIENCIES afflicting American democracy today are not limited to the Electoral College. They include gerrymandering, which distorts the representation of voters in Congress and state legislatures by manipulating the boundaries of voting districts so as to give incumbents, or one political party, an unfair advantage over competitors. They include also the polarizing effect of primary elections, which force candidates to adopt more extreme positions in order to win their party's nomination, a problem that presently afflicts both district and statewide races (like governor or US senator).[1] But the presidency is so powerful an office, dominating so much of American politics, that reinvigorating the institutions of American democracy would be incomplete without repairing the flawed way in which the Electoral College currently operates.

Electoral College reform should also be considered in the context of wider concerns about America's declining civic commitment to democratic norms and values. Soon after the results of the 2016 election stunned pundits, a multitude of books emerged fretting over the fate of democracy in America. With titles like *How Democracies Die*, or *Fascism: A Warning*, or still more pointedly *Can It Happen Here?: Authoritarianism in America*, these texts argued that democracy is more fragile than most realize, even in the United States. While not predicting that America will suffer the same degree of deterioration experienced recently by Hungary, Poland, or Turkey, the books nonetheless sounded the alarm. Jon Meacham's *The Soul of America: The Battle for Our Better Angels*, in particular, was an effort to cast this clarion call not as a deathbed dirge but as a revival anthem.[2]

All of these works rest on an important truth: ultimately, the sustenance of democracy lies in culture, not law. Unless the American people are sufficiently committed to the ethics of democracy—especially respect for opposing views and willingness to let the loyal opposition have its turn at governance when it wins free and fair elections—the legal apparatus of democracy will not be robust enough to maintain a practice of collective self-government. No rule of law can operate as a perpetual bulwark against despotism if the populace truly wants the despot to prevail.

Even so, there is another truth: institutions matter. Rules and structures can create a barrier making it more difficult, even if not impossible, to effectuate a tyranny. Conversely, weaknesses in a society's rules and structures for self-government can make it easier to undermine that society's democracy than if those rules and structures are oak-like in their sturdiness. Consequently, as important as it may be at this moment in history to reinvigorate the nation's cultural commitment to democratic norms, it is imperative to remedy the institutional deficiencies that contribute to the risk that Americans might be tempted to pursue authoritarian alternatives to poorly performing democratic procedures.[3]

Much angst has been generated by the 2016 presidential election. Is Donald Trump's ability to win properly understood as a signal of authoritarian tendencies within the American electorate? Will Donald Trump's performance as president foster such tendencies, thereby creating something of a vicious circle? This book is not the place to address sociological questions of this nature. Instead, what this book can offer is an institutional and historical analysis that can put sociological concerns in a broader perspective.

In this regard, it is worth observing that Donald Trump's presidency might have been an institutional accident—a malfunctioning of electoral machinery—in precisely the same way that James Polk's presidency was. What was accidental about Polk's victory over Henry Clay in 1844, as we saw in Chapter 4, was that an Electoral College redesigned in 1803 for competition between two political parties could not cope four decades later with a third-party candidate being a factor in the race. Between Clay and Polk as the two main candidates, a majority of voters preferred Clay to Polk in enough states for an Electoral College majority. On that basis, Clay should have been elected president according to the majoritarian premises of how the Electoral College system was supposed to operate. But Polk won because the presence of a third candidate prevented the system from recognizing the electorate's majoritarian preference for Clay. That failure was the accident, and something similar may have happened in 2016.

It is too much to say, for reasons we explored in Chapter 6, that Hillary Clinton definitely would have won if the Electoral College had worked as intended. Nor is it correct to say, as many assume, that Clinton was preferred by a *majority* of American voters, just because she won almost 3 million more votes than Trump nationally. She still received less than 50 percent of the votes nationwide, and we do not know that she would have beaten Trump in a nationwide runoff. Even so, the unavoidable fact remains that Trump's 2016 election was the product of minority, not majority, rule because his overall Electoral College victory depended upon his sub–50 percent wins in several pivotal states. It was Jill Stein and especially Gary Johnson who made Trump inevitably a minority-rule winner, unable to claim the special status of democratic legitimacy that flows from being a majority-rule choice.

The 2016 election also illustrates America's inadequate understanding of its presidential election process. Hillary Clinton and Donald Trump were not the only two candidates on the ballot. Yet the predominant perception of the campaign was that it was a two-candidate race, in keeping with the basic two-party structure of American politics. All the talk was red versus blue, him versus her, in the hyperpolarized environment of contemporary politics. They certainly were the only two candidates on the stage for the three general-election debates.

If the 2016 election actually had been a two-candidate race, as most people perceived it, which candidate would have won the Electoral College? We do not know. But that uncertainty is precisely the problem. The possibility that Clinton might have won runoffs in enough states for an Electoral College majority is cause for alarm from a Jeffersonian perspective. The Electoral College may have failed to identify the candidate who was supposed to win according to its own majoritarian criteria. The point is not a partisan one. The Electoral College malfunctions whenever it produces a minority-rule president, whether that malfunction benefits Democrats or Republicans, or any other party in the past, present, or future.

This analysis is important to diagnosing accurately what currently ails America's political system. If the outcome of the 2016 presidential election was an institutional accident because of a defect in the system's mechanisms for achieving majority rule, that diagnosis is quite distinct from concluding that America's political culture has become corrupted by a preference for anti-democratic values among a majority of American voters. Simply put, if a majority of voters in states with a majority of electoral votes wanted Clinton, but the Electoral College gave them Trump, that kind of institutional malfunction is markedly different from a potential concern that a majority of voters favor a president with authoritarian tendencies.

Although consternation over the outcome of the election in 2016 has caused increased awareness of the Electoral College, the concern that the system is not operating properly should not be limited to the last election alone. Instead, as Part Two of this book demonstrated, the risk of the system causing anti-majoritarian outcomes has increased in the last quarter-century to its highest level in history, certainly much higher than in most of the twentieth century and approached only by a couple of comparable periods in the previous one. The potentially decisive role of Ross Perot in 1992, Ralph Nader in 2000, and Gary Johnson in 2016, taken together, should make Americans fearful of the system's incapacity to handle third-party or independent candidates in future elections.

At a time when partisan competition was confined to two parties (Federalists and themselves), the Jeffersonians did not anticipate the need for additional institutional mechanisms to assure that their redesigned Electoral College would always deliver the kind of majoritarian results they envisioned. Yet the same institutional deficiency that caused the accident of Polk's victory in 1844, as well as the accident of Bush's victory in 2000, risks repetition of the same type of accident in 2020 and beyond. Only a repair of this institutional deficiency, by adopting state laws that assure conformity to the principle of majority rule in the appointment of presidential electors, will prevent this kind of anti-majoritarian accident from occurring again.

There is reason to think that the last quarter-century's increased risk of anti-majoritarian outcomes will only intensify for the foreseeable future. In the hyperpolarized political environment that has mushroomed over the last few decades (and shows no signs of abating), campaigns accentuate the negative traits of opposing candidates.[4] Many voters cast ballots against candidates they dislike, rather than in favor of candidates they admire.[5] The vituperations of cable news and social media exacerbate this negativity. In this caustic arena, third-party and independent candidates will attempt to attract the support of disaffected voters who are looking for some less-maligned alternative. Even if these additional candidates have little chance of breaking through and becoming one of the two main alternatives under active consideration by the electorate, they are likely to play an ever-greater role in determining which of the two main candidates has a sub–50 percent plurality.[6]

This problem could occur as soon as the 2020 election. Indeed, Howard Schultz's contemplated independent candidacy exemplifies the increasing likelihood of disruptive bids attempting to capitalize on disaffection caused by polarization. Schultz defended his possible entry into the race in precisely these terms: "Polarization and divisiveness among Republicans and Democrats are spoiling the potential of our country, making it possible for a new choice to emerge."[7]

Whatever the assessment of 2016, next time it could be clear that a majority of voters—both nationally and in all the decisive swing states—want to repudiate Trump and deny him a second term. Yet the anti-Trump majority, perhaps as much as 60 percent of the electorate, might split its opposition between his Democratic opponent and one or more other candidates, thereby causing Trump to win re-election with as little as 40 percent of the popular vote, or even less (these sub–50 percent pluralities occurring, again, both nationally and in the key swing states). Anyone anxious about the future of American democracy should focus on this potential frustration of majority rule, which would give Trump a second term that the majority of American voters do not want him to have. Equally alarming would be the victory of a Democratic nominee with only 40 percent, or less, of the popular vote because the opposition to the Democrat was split.

It is not enough to hope that Howard Schultz and others—including John Kasich, as considered in the introduction—ultimately decide to refrain from running as independents. It is necessary to adopt the institutional reform that will protect majority rule whenever such individuals go forward with their independent bids. Majority rule should not be at the mercy of personal whim, especially not in the context of presidential elections, when so much power rides on how the system tallies the preferences expressed by the electorate's ballots.

One must hope that there never comes a time when an authoritarian-leaning populist, either on the Right or the Left, has the support of a majority of American voters, and not mere pluralities. If this should ever happen, then institutionally that populist candidate is entitled to win the presidency, and America must rely upon other structural mechanisms that are part of the Constitution—including separation of powers, federalism, the Bill of Rights and its enforcement by an independent judiciary—to protect the ongoing operation of democracy from lasting damage caused by a duly elected president's authoritarian tendencies. It would be wrong, however, to deny the presidency to a populist candidate whom the majority of voters truly want to win. To do so would be an anti-majoritarian defeat of democracy, just as it would be any time a truly majority-preferred candidate is denied victory. Democracy should not undermine itself in an effort to save itself.

Instead, American democracy should become more genuinely democratic, to avoid self-inflicted wounds caused by the accidental election of presidents lacking the majority support of the electorate. The Jacksonian features of the Electoral College system that permit anti-majoritarian results should be removed, thereby allowing the system to perform in the federally majoritarian way that its Jeffersonian architects intended. If an authoritarian-leaning populist is to win the Electoral College, that result should be because the populist actually achieved the kind of compound majority-of-majorities that the Jeffersonians sought and expected. It should not be because the populist obtained only pluralities in the decisive states and blocked the Electoral College victory of an opponent who was actually preferred over the populist by a majority of voters in those decisive states. That kind of accidentally undemocratic result, contrary to the original Jeffersonian intent of our Electoral College, is exactly what institutional reform should endeavor to forestall as its most urgent priority.

To accomplish this reform objective, it is not necessary to undertake the seemingly impossible task of a constitutional amendment. Nor is it necessary, or even efficacious, to pursue the challenging project of a multistate compact, which still would permit a plurality rather than majority winner to prevail (as explained in Chapter 8). Instead, it is necessary only to convince key swing states to adopt the majority-rule requirement, preventing these states from awarding all their electoral votes to a candidate who did not receive popular-vote majorities in those states.

Among the many specific ways for a state to comply with this majority-rule requirement, the method known as instant runoff voting is likely to be the most promising—at least in the short run.[8] Instant runoff voting is currently catching on, gaining greater attention and acceptance and thus building momentum, especially with its recent statewide adoption in Maine.[9] It should be possible, therefore, to persuade states individually to employ instant runoff voting to determine which candidate receives their Electoral College votes. States already possess full constitutional power to make this move, in the same way that Maine and Nebraska previously chose to use districting methods—rather than plurality winner-take-all—to determine their Electoral College votes.

But an advantage of the Jeffersonian Electoral College's inherently federal structure is that it permits each state to choose its particular method for securing majoritarian choice. If a state is not enamored with instant runoff voting, it can employ an actual runoff or instead use conditional winner-take-all or another proportional method of allocating its electoral votes. Maybe some states would find preferable a preliminary Labor Day vote, as described in Chapter 7, that causes the November ballot to be confined to the top two finalists. An ambitious state could even experiment with the kind of Condorcet voting favored by some, including the Nobel laureates Eric Maskin and Amartya Sen.[10]

The important point is simply that swing states in particular should take the initiative of using one of the many methods consistent with the majority-rule requirement. As Chapter 9 explains, in several key swing states—including Florida and Michigan—citizens can adopt the majority-rule requirement itself by means of a ballot initiative, leaving to the state legislature the task of choosing the particular means of implementation. If only Florida and Michigan had done so before 2016, the result of the election might (although not necessarily would) have been different. To recognize this is to understand the power of this institutional reform on a state-by-state basis.

A restoration of the federally majoritarian vision for the Jeffersonian Electoral College would be a great institutional improvement in the functioning of American democracy. Assuming that major reform is achieved, perhaps sometime afterward it might become necessary to consider the prospects for further Electoral College reform. For example, if there occurred an election in which the federally majoritarian winner—the candidate preferred by a majority of voters in the states that generate an Electoral College majority—was not the candidate preferred by a majority of the entire American electorate nationwide, then the impetus might develop to jettison the Jeffersonian commitment to a federalism-based version of majority rule. Even then, the move to a nationwide version of majority rule would raise difficult questions. Not only would there remain the procedural challenge of a constitutional amendment, but there would be the conceptual question of how best to identify the nationwide majority: instant runoff voting, an actual runoff, the alternative approach of Condorcet voting, and so forth. Confronting this question inevitably will remind Americans that the federalism built into the structure of the Jeffersonian Electoral College has the advantage of letting states choose for themselves among these alternative conceptions of how best to secure majority rule. Thus, for now the reform priority should be simply to bring the Jeffersonian Electoral College back into compliance with the principle of majority rule, as it was intended to be.

Restoration of the Jeffersonian Electoral College would also help return the nation to a democratically appropriate form of two-party competition. Since the foundational rivalry between Federalists and Jeffersonians, two-party competition has been a defining feature of American politics. Even more importantly, two-party competition has been the essential core of how Americans have understood their own system of self-government.

Yet as we have explored, the reality conflicts with that conception, and the consequence has been a kind of national self-delusion about the nature of the political system. Americans think they have a two-party system, but they do not. They have neither the benefits of a true two-party system that routinely guarantees majority rule nor the advantages of a true multiparty system that genuinely enables a variety of partisan perspectives to shape the formation of government policy. Instead, America has the worst of both worlds: a defective attempt to operationalize two-party competition, and an embryonic form of a multiparty system that is so stunted in its development as to be essentially stillborn.

Adoption by states of the majority-rule requirement for the casting of their Electoral College votes would cure this malady. It would enable third-party and independent candidates to participate without risk of inappropriately determining which of the candidates prevail in contravention of the preferences of the majority in each state. An open system would give previously minor parties and newly insurgent movements a real chance to break through and to challenge the two main parties for preeminence. But after this fair opportunity had occurred, then the system could focus on the electorate's preference between the two preeminent contenders (whether or not these candidates were the nominees of the two previously dominant parties).

Once the electorate's choice has come down to the two leading alternatives, democracy entails that the majority-preferred option, and not the minority-preferred option, prevail. This "fundamental principle" is what the Jeffersonians themselves recognized in 1803 and endeavored to implement in their reform of the Electoral College. As George Campbell expressed it, "the will of the majority must . . . prevail and control the will of the minority."[11]

Our task then—invoking the words of James Holland, Campbell's fellow Jeffersonian—is to rehabilitate this "first principle of our Government," so that defective procedures never again "defeat the will of the majority" in an "election of the Chief Magistrate."[12]

NOTES

Unless otherwise indicated, all numbers relating to the results of presidential elections—whether (a) concerning electoral votes or popular votes, or (b) reported as absolute numbers or percentages, or (c) contained within the text of this book, or its tables, or these notes—are derived from either *Dave Leip's Atlas of U.S. Elections*, available at https://uselectionatlas.org/, or CQ Press, *Presidential Elections*, 1789–2004 (Washington, DC, 2005). Where noted, additional election data is sourced to the website *A New Nation Votes*, https://elections.lib.tufts.edu.

Introduction

1. Kasich "hinted in December that he could run as an independent candidate in 2020." Tal Axelrod, "Kasich Fundraising off CNN Job amid 2020 speculation," *The Hill*, January 17, 2019. Howard Schultz, the former head of Starbucks, whipped up a media frenzy in early 2019 when he announced that he was exploring the possibility of an independent run for the White House. The immediate reaction to his announcement, as well as Schultz's response to that reaction, recognized the possibility that his presence in the race could cause Trump's re-election when otherwise the Democratic nominee would win. See Michael Scherer and Tracy Jan, "Howard Schultz' Challenge to Democrats: Nominate a Centrist for President and I'll Abandon My Independent Campaign," *Washington Post*, February 14, 2019.

2. President Trump's approval ratings, at 41.7 percent in mid-February of 2019, hovered around 40 percent for most of his presidency up to this

point. See "How Popular Is Donald Trump?," FiveThirtyEight, https://projects.fivethirtyeight.com/trump-approval-ratings/.

3. Writing in October 2017, when President Trump's approval rating was about 38 percent, the Democratic political consultant Doug Sosnik wrote:

> In order to maintain and nurture his base, Trump will continue to embrace conflict, which will probably solidify his historically low approval ratings. Trump cannot win a two-person race this way. But, he can prevail in a field with strong independent candidates on the ballot. (Doug Sosnik, "Trump Is on Track to Win Reelection," *Washington Post*, October 6, 2017)

4. See D. Roderick Kiewiet, "Approval Voting: The Case of the 1968 Election," *Polity* 12, no. 1 (1979), 170 (Nixon would have beaten Humphrey if just the two of them had been on the ballot). See also Steven J. Brams, *The Presidential Election Game* (New Haven, CT: Yale University Press, 1978), 222–29.

5. For a review of what happened in 2000, see chapter 11 of Edward B. Foley, *Ballot Battles: The History of Disputed Elections in the United States* (New York: Oxford University Press, 2016). For a similar account, which includes some illuminating commentary from participants that was unavailable for the *Ballot Battles* chapter, see Foley, "*Bush v. Gore*: The Court Stops the Recount," in *Election Law Stories*, ed. Joshua A. Douglas and Eugene D. Mazo (St. Paul, MN: Foundation Press, 2016), 541–76.

6. William Poundstone, *Gaming the Vote: Why Elections Aren't Fair (and What We Can Do about It)* (New York: Hill & Wang, 2008), 90; Robert W. Bennett, *Taming the Electoral College* (Stanford, CA: Stanford University Press, 2006), 127. Michael C. Herron and Jeffrey B. Lewis, "Did Ralph Nader Spoil Al Gore's Presidential Bid?: A Ballot-Level Study of Green and Reform Party Voters in the 2000 Presidential Election," *Quarterly Journal of Political Science* 2, no. 3 (August 2007), 222. See also Brian F. Schaffner, *Politics, Parties, and Elections in America*, 7th ed. (Boston: Cengage Learning, 2012), 37; Barry C. Burden, "Minor Parties in the 2000 Presidential Election," in *Models of Voting in Presidential Elections: The 2000 U.S. Election*, ed. Herbert F. Weisberg and Clyde Wilcox (Stanford, CA: Stanford University Press, 2004), 206–27.

7. This book uses the years 1787 and 1803 to refer to the initial and subsequent Electoral College, respectively, because those were the years in which their provisions were formulated and deliberated by their architects. To be sure, neither version of the Electoral College became law until these provisions were ratified by the states. Thus one could refer to the initial Electoral College of 1788 and the subsequent Electoral College of 1804. Since the focus of this book is the ideas the architects had when designing the Electoral College, the former dates are better suited to this purpose.

8. For an earlier recognition of this crucial federalism point, see Samuel Issacharoff, "Law, Rules, and Presidential Selection," *Political Science Quarterly* 120, no. 1 (Spring 2005), 166: "As a result, there is not a single representative institution created by our constitutional framework in which the will of the representative majority is not filtered through the states, at least to some degree." See also Bennett, *Taming the Electoral College*, 55 (discussing federalism justification for aggregating state-specific results into an overall national total).

9. See Iain McLean, "Electoral Systems," in *The Routledge Handbook of Elections, Voting Behavior, and Public Opinion*, ed. Justin Fisher, Edward Fieldhouse, Mark N. Franklin, Rachel Gibson, Marta Cantijoch, and Christopher Wlezien (New York: Routledge, 2018), 213.

10. The definitive work on this history will be Alexander Keyssar, *Why Do We Still Have the Electoral College?* (Cambridge, MA: Harvard University Press, forthcoming).

Chapter 1

1. Jack Rakove, in particular, has written extensively on the Electoral College adopted in the 1787 Convention. See Jack N. Rakove, "Presidential Selection: Electoral Fallacies," *Political Science Quarterly* 119 (2004), 21. In addition to Keyssar's forthcoming book, *Why Do We Still Have the Electoral College?*, which contains its own account of the system's creation, the two most helpful books for understanding the origins and development of the Electoral College are Richard P. McCormick, *The Presidential Game: The Origins of American Presidential Politics* (New York: Oxford University Press, 1982), and James W. Ceaser, *Presidential Selection: Theory and Development* (Princeton, NJ: Princeton University Press, 1979).

2. See Bruce Ackerman, *The Failure of the Founding Fathers: Jefferson, Marshall, and the Rise of Presidential Democracy* (Cambridge, MA: The Belknap Press of Harvard University Press, 2005), 5–6: "In 1787 the Convention delegates could reasonably suppose that their electoral college had been engineered to select a statesman who transcended petty factionalism as president."

3. Joshua D. Hawley, "The Transformative Twelfth Amendment," *Wm. & Mary Law Review* 55 (2014), 1538; Jeremy D. Bailey, *Thomas Jefferson and Executive Power* (New York: Cambridge University Press, 2007), 195; Lucius Wilmerding Jr., *The Electoral College* (New Brunswick, NJ: Rutgers University Press, 1958), 40.

4. Rakove, "Presidential Selection," 29; Ceaser, *Presidential Selection*, 96; McCormick, *The Presidential Game*, 21–22; Ackerman, *Failure of the Founding Fathers*, 28.

5. The Convention delegates anticipated the possibility that a state might fail to appoint any presidential electors, and indeed in the very first election

New York failed to do so because of a deadlock in the state legislature. The majority requirement applied to the number of electors actually appointed by the states, not the whole number of electors entitled to be appointed by all the states. See McCormick, *The Presidential Game*, 29–30.

6. To illustrate with an example, suppose the total number of electors is 138 (as was true for the elections of 1796 and 1800). Then 70 is the minimum majority of electors, and to win the candidate with the largest number of votes must have at least this many. In other words, the winning candidate must receive votes from a majority of the electors, with it not mattering whether those votes are first-choice or second-choice votes. It would not suffice for a candidate to receive votes from exactly half the electors (69), even if the next highest number of votes (again, either first-choice or second-choice) was far smaller, say 30 or even 20.

7. Rakove, "Presidential Selection," 29; McCormick, *The Presidential Game*, 25–26; Ceaser, *Presidential Selection*, 83–84. There was an ambiguity in the original Constitution insofar as the text stated, "if no person have a majority, then from the five highest on the list" the House shall elect the president. What if there were a tie for fifth place? Or indeed a tie for any of the first five places? Did the text contemplate sending the House more than five names in this situation?

8. Max Farrand, *The Records of the Federal Convention of 1787* (New Haven, CT: Yale University Press, 1966), 514. On the perceived aristocratic nature of the Senate, see Norman R. Williams, "Why the National Popular Vote Compact Is Unconstitutional," *BYU Law Review* (2012), 1523, 1558.

9. Farrand, *Records of the Federal Convention of 1787*, 525.

10. Ibid,. 526–27.

11. Ibid., 535–36.

12. Ibid., 29.

13. McCormick, *The Presidential Game*, 22–23; Ceaser, *Presidential Selection*, 43; Hawley, "Transformative Twelfth Amendment," 1511–13.

14. Madison to Henry Lee, January 14, 1825.

15. In private correspondence in the 1820s, Madison set forth his ideas concerning compound majoritarianism appropriate for a federal system, particularly as it applied to presidential elections. In these letters, Madison made clear that he did not favor electing presidents based on a plurality, rather than majority, of votes. He wanted a winning candidate to be "the real choice of a majority of his Constituents," but he also acknowledged that given the role of the states in the federal system— what he called "our complex system of polity"—it was necessary that the "federal will" be not a simple majority of the nationwide popular vote, but instead a majority of "the Presidential Electors, representing, in a certain proportion both the nation & the States." Recognizing that no candidate might win a majority of Electoral College votes, as indeed happened in 1824, Madison balked at letting a candidate become president based on

a mere plurality of Electoral College votes, since that plurality might not adequately capture "the Major will of the nation," which the "mode of electing the Executive Magistrate" must aim to achieve as effectively as possible. Rather, Madison proposed to reform the runoff procedure to be employed in the absence of an Electoral College majority. Instead of "State equality" (as the existing runoff procedure requires), Madison preferred a "joint vote of the Houses of Congress," being closer to the "republican principle of numerical equality."

Moreover, and crucially, in order to guarantee that this runoff congressional vote result in a majority winner, and not a mere plurality, Madison would limit the runoff to only two rather than three candidates. Madison recognized that this change might eliminate a third-place candidate who, as the Marquis de Condorcet had explained, actually was the one genuinely preferred to all others by a majority of votes: "It might be a question, whether the *three* instead of the *two* highest names, might not be put within the choice of Congress; inasmuch as it not unfrequently happens, that the Candidate third on the list of votes, would in a question with either of the two first, outvote him, & consequently be the real preference of the Voters." Ultimately, however, Madison thought it wiser—more conducive to achieving a majoritarian result that avoided a factional winner—to limit the runoff to two, rather than three, finalists: "But this advantage of opening a wider door and a better chance to merit, may be outweighed by an increased difficulty in obtaining a prompt & quiet decision by Congress, with three candidates before them, supported by three parties, no one of them making a majority of the whole." Thus throughout his analysis, Madison made clear that his goal was a method of electing presidents most capable of reflecting "the will of the Majority of voters" in a way consistent with the "complex system of polity" necessitated by the federal nature of the United States. See Madison to Henry Lee, January 14, 1825; Madison to George Hay, August 23, 1823; Madison to Robert Taylor, January 30, 1826. See generally, Donald O. Dewey, "Madison's Views on Electoral Reform," *Political Research Quarterly* 15 (1962), 140.

16.   See David F. Epstein, *The Political Theory of The Federalist* (Chicago: University of Chicago Press, 1984), 61–67; Alan Brinkley, Nelson W. Polsby, and Kathleen M. Sullivan, *New Federalist Papers: Essays in Defense of the Constitution* (New York: Twentieth Century Fund, 1997), 8. Some of the most significant of the *Federalist Papers*, including No. 10, have even been "translated" into contemporary vernacular, much as the King James Version of the Bible has been updated in new translations. See S. Adam Seagrave, *The Accessible Federalist: A Modern Translation of 16 Key Federalist Papers* (Indianapolis: Hackett Publishing, 2017), 4–8. See also Cass Sunstein, "Interest Groups in American Public Law," *Stanford Law Review* 38 (1986), 29 (urging a revival of Madisonian theory).

17. The vision of a president above party drew on the earlier British idea of a "Patriot King." See Bailey, *Thomas Jefferson and Executive Power*, 3; Hawley, "Transformative Twelfth Amendment," 1511–14.

Chapter 2

1. This first election carried over into 1789; but in keeping with the quadrennial nature of presidential elections, it makes sense to date the first one in 1788, with the second four years later, and so forth. A vast collection of documents concerning this first election is contained in Merrill Jensen and Robert A. Robert, eds., *The Documentary History of the First Federal Elections, 1788–1790*, 4 vols. (Madison: University of Wisconsin Press, 1976).

2. CQ Press, *Presidential Elections*, 180. See also McCormick, *The Presidential Game*; Tadahisa Kuroda, *The Origins of the Twelfth Amendment: The Electoral College in the Early Republic, 1787–1804*, Contributions in Political Science, no. 344 (Westport, CT: Greenwood Press, 1994).

3. McCormick, *The Presidential Game*, 27–31; Kuroda, *Origins of the Twelfth Amendment*, 28–38.

4. McCormick, *The Presidential Game*, 27–31; Kuroda, *Origins of the Twelfth Amendment*, 28–38.

5. In these two states, the Electoral College districts were not the same as districts for congressional elections. (Delaware, being the least populous state, had only one representative in Congress.) CQ Press, *Presidential Elections*, 190; 1788 Va. Acts, ch. I; Del. Laws 5 (1788); see also McCormick, *The Presidential Game*, 28–31; Kuroda, *Origins of the Twelfth Amendment*, 28–38.

6. 1788 Mass. Acts 258; McCormick, *The Presidential Game*, 29; Kuroda, *Origins of the Twelfth Amendment*, 30–31.

7. Ronald M. Peters Jr., *The Massachusetts Constitution of 1780: A Social Compact* (Amherst: University of Massachusetts Press, 1974); Charles Stewart, "Elections under Majority Voting in the Antebellum Period" (unpublished manuscript, May 10, 2018). See also Marc W. Kruman, *Between Authority & Liberty: State Constitution Making in Revolutionary America* (Chapel Hill: University of North Carolina Press, 1997), 160; Willi Paul Adams, *The First American Constitutions: Republican Ideology and the Making of the State Constitutions in the Revolutionary Era* (Lanham, MD: Rowman and Littlefield Publishers, 2001), 26.

8. The exact language of the Massachusetts constitution regarding gubernatorial elections provided:

> In case of an election by a majority of all the votes returned, the choice shall be by them declared and published: But if no person shall have a majority of votes, the House of Representatives shall, by ballot, elect two out of four persons who had the highest number of votes, if so many shall have been voted for; but, if otherwise, out

of the number voted for; and make return to the Senate of the two persons so elected; on which, the Senate shall proceed, by ballot, to elect one, who shall be declared Governor. (Peters, *The Massachusetts Constitution of 1780*, 210 [reprinting text of constitution as appendix])

9. There were no separately designated positions. Instead, it was akin to some contemporary school board or city council elections, where multiple seats are filled at the same time from votes cast for multiple candidates.

10. 1788 N.H. Laws, ch. 4:

> The person having the majority of Votes shall . . . be duly appointed & declared elected[.] And in case it Shall so happen that the whole or any part of the number of electors are not chosen by the people then the General Court shall take a number of names out of the Candidates who have the highest number of Votes equal to double the number of electors wanting from which the Senate and House shall in such way and manner as may be by them agreed on proceed to appoint the Electors wanting.

11. Kuroda, *Origins of the Twelfth Amendment*, 29.

12. 1788 Pa. Laws 144; 1788 Md. Laws, ch. X, § VI.

13. Owen S. Ireland, "The People's Triumph: The Federalist Majority in Pennsylvania, 1787–1788," *Pennsylvania History: A Journal of Mid-Atlantic Studies* 56, no. 2 (April 1989), 93–113, 93–94; Norman K. Risjord, *Chesapeake Politics, 1781–1800* (New York: Columbia University Press, 1978), 281–82, 284, 330–33.

14. Kuroda, *Origins of the Twelfth Amendment*, 33, 37; McCormick, *The Presidential Game*, 35.

15. Richard Hofstadter, *The Idea of a Party System: The Rise of Legitimate Opposition in the United States, 1780–1840*, 4th ed. (Berkeley: University of California Press, 1975); Gordon S. Wood, *Empire of Liberty: A History of the Early Republic, 1789–1815*, The Oxford History of the United States (New York: Oxford University Press, 2009).

16. McCormick, *The Presidential Game*, 44–45.

17. CQ Press, *Presidential Elections*, 190; *The Connecticut Gazette*, November 8, 1792, [3]; 1788 S.C. Acts 3; *The Augusta Chronicle and Gazette of the State*, November 24, 1792, [3]; 1788 N.J. Laws 481.

18. *The Providence Gazette and Country Journal*, December 8, 1792, [3]; 1791 Vt. Acts & Laws 43; 1792 N.Y. Laws 378. Neal R. Peirce and Lawrence D. Longley, *The People's President: The Electoral College in American History and the Direct Vote Alternative* (New Haven, CT: Yale University Press, 1981), 248.

19. Del. Laws 1054 (1792); Kuroda, *Origins of the Twelfth Amendment*, 55.

20. McCormick, *The Presidential Game*, 46–48; Kuroda, *Origins of the Twelfth Amendment*, 54–55; CQ Press, *Presidential Elections*, 190; 1792 Va. Acts 537; 1792 Ky. Acts 16; 1791 Pa. Laws 241–42; 1792 Md. Laws, ch.

V;1792 Va. Acts 537; 1792 Ky. Acts 16; 1791 Pa. Laws 241–42; 1792 Md. Laws, ch. V.

21. The state also reduced the number of districts to four, appointing multiple electors in each of these larger districts (1792 Mass. Acts 25).

22. "The Legislature," *The Salem Gazette*, November 20, 1792, [2].

23. 1792 N.H. Laws 399:

> And the secretary shall, on the first day of November next, lay the [votes] before the supreme executive magistrate and council, to be by them examined. And in case there shall appear to be any or the full number, who have a majority of votes, the person or persons having such majority shall be appointed and declared electors. But in case there shall not be any, or the whole number having such majority, the supreme executive magistrate in the presence of the council shall cause to be made out, a list of the persons having the highest number of votes equal to double the number of electors wanted . . . and the names of the persons contained in the list so made, shall be transmitted to the selectmen of the several towns, parishes, and plantations and places aforesaid respectively, who shall warn a meeting to be holden on the twelfth day of November next.

24. *The New Hampshire Gazette*, November 28, 1792, [3].

25. See Jeffrey L. Pasley, *The First Presidential Contest: 1796 and the Founding of American Democracy* (Lawrence: University Press of Kansas, 2013).

26. Pasley, *The First Presidential Contest*, 346, 348. (Kuroda incorrectly states that Georgia used a districting system in 1796. Kuroda, *Origins of the Twelfth Amendment*, 67.)

27. CQ Press, *Presidential Elections*, 190; 1795 Md. Laws, ch. LXIII; 1792 N.C. Sess. Laws, ch. XVI; see also McCormick, *The Presidential Game*, 53; Kuroda, *Origins of the Twelfth Amendment*, 67.

28. 1796 Tenn. Pub. Acts 109; see also CQ Press, *Presidential Elections*, 190; McCormick, *The Presidential Game*, 56; Kuroda, *Origins of the Twelfth Amendment*, 68.

29. 1796 N.H. Laws 545.

30. "Federal Representatives," *The Federal Mirror*, October 4, 1796, [3].

31. "Pennsylvania Electoral College 1796," *A New Nation Votes: American Election Returns, 1787–1825*, https://elections.lib.tufts.edu/catalog/cv43nz221; "Georgia Electoral College 1796," *A New Nation Votes: American Election Returns, 1787–1825*, https://elections.lib.tufts.edu/catalog/j9602101m.

32. "Massachusetts' Legislature," *Polar Star and Boston Daily Advertiser*, November 22, 1796, [3].

33. CQ Press, *Presidential Elections*, 196; ,McCormick, *The Presidential Game*, 56; Pasley, *The First Presidential Contest*, 406.

34. For background, see Wood, *Empire of Liberty*. The 1800 election, given its drama and importance, has spawned a vast literature. One especially good work is James Roger Sharp, *The Deadlocked Election of 1800: Jefferson, Burr, and the Union in the Balance* (Lawrence: University Press of Kansas, 2010). See also Edward J. Larson, *A Magnificent Catastrophe: The Tumultuous Election of 1800, America's First Presidential Campaign* (New York: Free Press, 2007); Susan Dunn, *Jefferson's Second Revolution: The Election Crisis of 1800 and the Triumph of Republicanism* (Boston: Houghton Mifflin Harcourt, 2004); John Ferling, *Adams vs. Jefferson: The Tumultuous Election of 1800* (New York: Oxford University Press, 2004).

35. McCormick, *The Presidential Game*, 61, 67; Kuroda, *Origins of the Twelfth Amendment*, 89–90, 94–95.

36. 1798 R.I. Pub. Laws 139; Kuroda, *Origins of the Twelfth Amendment*, 94.

37. McCormick, *The Presidential Game*, 71; Kuroda, *Origins of the Twelfth Amendment*, 73–74, 95.

38. CQ Press, *Presidential Elections*, 180; Peirce and Longley, *The People's President*, 38.

39. CQ Press, *Presidential Elections*, 197.

40. Sharp, *The Deadlocked Election of 1800*, 126.

41. See Ackerman, *Failure of the Founding Fathers*, 36–45.

42. See Sharp, *The Deadlocked Election of 1800*, 56–58; Ackerman, *Failure of the Founding Fathers*, 3, 107.

43. Ackerman, *Failure of the Founding Fathers*, 102, 108. For evidence that Burr actively plotted to have the House break the tie in his favor, see Thomas N. Baker, "'An Attack Well Directed': Aaron Burr Intrigues for the Presidency," *Journal of the Early Republic* 31, no. 4 (Winter 2011), 553. I am grateful to Larry Lessig for drawing my attention to this account.

44. Ackerman, *Failure of the Founding Fathers*, 99–101; Ron Chernow, *Alexander Hamilton* (New York: Penguin Press, 2004), 631–35. Hamilton, although less influential than previously, still had followers in Federalist circles, and he worked to persuade James Bayard of Delaware eventually to support Jefferson over Burr. Bayard, in turn, played a crucial role in resolving the electoral stalemate in the House of Representatives. The details of the 1800 election are endlessly fascinating, and this book's summary can serve only as a teaser for those who would like to learn more.

Chapter 3

1. See Charles William Hill, *The Political Theory of John Taylor of Caroline* (London: Associated University Press, 1977), 9–17.

2. Madison to George Hay, August 23, 1823.

3. Kuroda, *Origins of the Twelfth Amendment*, 127–52.

4. Kuroda, *Origins of the Twelfth Amendment*, 30; Bailey, *Thomas Jefferson and Executive Power*, 195–211; Hawley, "The Transformative Twelfth Amendment," 1510.

5. Kuroda, *Origins of the Twelfth Amendment*, 127, 133; James Horn, Jan Ellen Lewis, and Peter S. Onuf, *The Revolution of 1800: Democracy, Race, and the New Republic* (Charlottesville: University of Virginia Press, 2002).

6. Hawley, "The Transformative Twelfth Amendment," 1501; Bailey, *Thomas Jefferson and Executive Power*, 201; Kuroda, *Origins of the Twelfth Amendment*, 124–26.

7. Dumas Malone, *Jefferson the President: First Term, 1801–1805* (Boston: Little, Brown, 1970), 395.

8. Ibid.

9. Hawley, "The Transformative Twelfth Amendment," 1545; Bailey, *Thomas Jefferson and Executive Power*, 199–200.

10. See Harlow Giles Unger, *John Marshall: The Chief Justice Who Saved the Nation* (Boston: Da Capo Press, 2014); Alf J. Mapp Jr., *Thomas Jefferson: Passionate Pilgrim* (Lanham, MD: Rowman and Littlefield, 2009), 74.

11. Hawley, "The Transformative Twelfth Amendment," 1512; Bailey, *Thomas Jefferson and Executive Power*, 201; Ceaser, *Presidential Selection*, 102; see also Greg Weiner, *Madison's Metronome: The Constitution, Majority Rule, and the Tempo of American Politics* (Lawrence: University Press of Kansas, 2012).

12. Hawley, "The Transformative Twelfth Amendment," 1542; Bailey, *Thomas Jefferson and Executive Power*, 207. Ackerman appropriately recognizes that in the aftermath of the 1800 election, Jefferson claimed a mandate as a majoritarian winner of the presidency. But Ackerman goes too far in claiming that "the revolution of 1800" established a "plebicitarian presidency" in which the will of the national majority regardless of federalism was entitled to prevail. See Ackerman, *Failure of the Founding Fathers*, 5. Instead, as Hawley has observed, Ackerman overlooks the sophistication of the constitutional theory underlying the Twelfth Amendment as crafted by the Jeffersonians. See "The Transformative Twelfth Amendment," 1504–5. That sophistication includes a commitment to federalism and thus the developing of the correspondingly complex idea of a compound majority-of-majorities.

13. Ceaser, *Presidential Selection*, 58–59, 80: "The electoral system was thus carefully designed to help promote what could be regarded as a legitimate national majority." See also Kuroda, *Origins of the Twelfth Amendment*, 15: "The framers were not numerical majoritarians who only counted heads but complex majoritarians concerned with a heterogeneous people, composed of factions and organized into states." Cf. Judith Best, "Presidential Selection: Complex Problems and Simple Solutions," *Political Science Quarterly* 119 (2004), 39 (using the unfortunate term

"concurrent majorities," given its association with John Calhoun, to describe the fundamentally Madisonian idea that the Electoral College was designed to achieve a complex form of majority rule that, through federalism and the separation of powers, "seeks majority rule with minority consent").

14. See Alexander Keyssar, *The Right to Vote: The Contested History of Democracy in the United States* (New York: Basic Books, 2000), 15–25.

15. Garry Wills, among others, has argued that Jefferson won the presidency in 1800 only because the original Constitution's infamous three-fifths clause gave the slave states extra electoral votes (based on their extra seats in the House of Representatives). See Garry Wills, *"Negro President": Jefferson and the Slave Power* (New York: Houghton Mifflin, 2005). This point, however, does not negate the significance of the Jeffersonian claim to be the majority party for the purpose of the Electoral College redesign in 1803. The Jeffersonians were claiming that they were the majority party in the states that provided their Electoral College votes for Jefferson. They were not attempting to defend the number of electoral votes those states were allocated in the federal system. Thus the Electoral College was redesigned in 1803 to be a majoritarian institution, as the Jeffersonians conceived it, and its majoritarian nature remains relevant today—long since purged of its connection with the pernicious three-fifths clause—even if the way in which the Jeffersonians conceived of their status as the majority party was flawed from our modern perspective.

Furthermore, it is important to emphasize that the Jeffersonians of 1803, in their Electoral College redesign, were looking forward to Jefferson's re-election of 1804 at least as much as they were looking backward to his victory in 1800. Their conception of themselves as the majority party, to be vindicated as such by the redesigned Electoral College in 1804, was based in part on the strength of their midterm victories in 1802 and their still-increasing popularity after the Louisiana Purchase. Finally, the actual voting in 1804 vindicated the Jeffersonians on this crucial point. Jefferson's re-election victory and his status as a majoritarian winner in no way depended upon the odious three-fifths clause.

16. Ackerman, *Failure of the Founding Fathers*, 148.

17. Kuroda, *Origins of the Twelfth Amendment*, 113.

18. 13 Annals of Cong. 423.

19. See Keyssar, *Why Do We Still Have the Electoral College?*

20. "Clopton, John (1756–1816)," *Biographical Directory of the United States Congress*, http://bioguide.congress.gov/scripts/biodisplay.pl?index=C000531.

21. 13 Annals of Cong. 490.

22. 13 Annals of Cong. 491.

23. 13 Annals of Cong. 491.
24. 13 Annals of Cong. 492.
25. 13 Annals of Cong. 493.
26. 13 Annals of Cong. 534.
27. See Unger, *John Marshall*, 214; Mapp, *Thomas Jefferson: Passionate Pilgrim*, 74. See also Wood, *Empire of Liberty*, 370.
28. Charles Francis Adams (ed.), *Memoirs of John Quincy Adams*, vol. 1 (Philadelphia: J. B. Lippincott & Co., 1874), 276.
29. 13 Annals of Cong. 164.
30. 13 Annals of Cong. 164.
31. 13 Annals of Cong. 180.
32. 13 Annals of Cong. 181.
33. 13 Annals of Cong. 182.
34. 13 Annals of Cong. 182.
35. 13 Annals of Cong. 183.
36. 13 Annals of Cong. 183.
37. "Wright, Robert (1752–1826)," *Biographical Directory of the United States Congress*, http://bioguide.congress.gov/scripts/biodisplay. pl?index=W000768.
38. 13 Annals of Cong., 200.
39. 13 Annals of Cong., 153.
40. See Kuroda, *Origins of the Twelfth Amendment*, 127–36.
41. 13 Annals of Cong., 90.
42. 13 Annals of Cong., 90.
43. 13 Annals of Cong., 91–92.
44. 13 Annals of Cong., 95.
45. 13 Annals of Cong., 97.
46. Kuroda, *Origins of the Twelfth Amendment*, 130.
47. There was discussion then, as there has been since, on whether the specific language employed by the Senate for this purpose was as clear as intended (see Kuroda, *Origins of the Twelfth Amendment*, 133–43). This language, which remains in the Twelfth Amendment today, provides: "If no person have such majority, then from the persons having *the highest numbers on the list not exceeding three* on the list of those voted for as President, the House of Representatives shall choose immediately, by ballot, a President." Although this verbal formulation could be construed in such a way that "not exceeding three" modifies "persons," rather than "numbers," this construction raises a feasibility problem whereas the alternative construction does not. If there is a tie for third place in the Electoral College (and no majority), then *on this construction* the Twelfth Amendment does not provide any indication of what to do in the event of this tie: only three "persons" should go to the House as candidates, but which of those tied for third place should be the single third candidate for the House to consider? Alternatively, if

"not exceeding three" modifies "numbers" rather than persons, there is no such technical difficulty. If there are candidates receiving different numbers of vote totals in the Electoral College, either there will be fewer than three different vote totals (just a first and second place, although there may be ties for either of these two places), or three vote totals (including ties for any of these three places), or more than three vote totals (including, again, ties for any of these three places). But even if there are more than three distinct vote totals, the third highest vote total is a unique—and thus identifiable—position. Thus, *on this construction*, the Twelfth Amendment commands that the cutoff, for determining which candidates are eligible for consideration by the House, are those candidates who receive either the first, second, or third largest number of votes; no candidates receiving the fourth largest number of votes, or any candidates lower down in order, are eligible for consideration by the House. Given that this construction eliminates any technical difficulty, it surely is the preferred construction.

48. 13 Annals of Cong., 103.

49. Senator Samuel Smith of Maryland, for example, offered these observations:

> The provision admitting the choice by the House of Representatives, was itself intended only for an extreme case, where great inconvenience might result from sending a defective election back to the people, as is customary in Massachusetts, where, if the majority is deficient, a new election is required. Our object in the amendment is or should be to make the election more certain by the people.

Likewise James Jackson of Georgia "wished to prevent the choice from devolving upon the House of Representatives; he wished it to be out of their power, if it should devolve upon them, to elect any man not evidently intended by the people; the smaller number would render this more certain." 13 Annals of Cong., 113.

50. 13 Annals of Cong., 103. See Hawley, "The Transformative 12th Amendment," 1550; Bailey, *Thomas Jefferson and Executive Power*, 208.

51. Kuroda, *Origins of the Twelfth Amendment*, 145.

52. 13 Annals of Cong., 736.

53. "Campbell, George Washington (1769–1848)," *Biographical Directory*, http://bioguide.congress.gov/scripts/biodisplay.pl?index=C000083.

54. 13 Annals of Cong., 719.

55. 13 Annals of Cong., 719.

56. 13 Annals of Cong., 720. As printed in the Annals, the passage reads "designed [*sic*] by the majority," but it is evident from the content, including the use of the word "designate" in the immediately preceding sentence, that "designed" here is a typographical error, and "designated" is what Clopton said and what was intended to be printed.

57. Campbell spoke of the consequence being that "the minority would not have the man of their choice, but one from whom they expect some favor, in consequence of having contributed to his elevation" (13 Annals of Cong., 720)—a clear reference to how both Republicans and Federalists viewed Burr after 1800.
58. 13 Annals of Cong., 720.
59. 13 Annals of Cong., 721.
60. 13 Annals of Cong., 719.

Chapter 4

1. Tashida Kuroda, *The Origins of the Twelfth Amendment* (Westport, CT: Greenwood Press, 1994), 164.
2. 1820 Conn. Acts 454 (replacing legislative appointment with popular vote); 1791 Vt. Acts 43; 1813 N.Y. Laws 246; 1800 Del. Laws 143; 1792 S.C. Acts 3; 1804 Ga. Laws 3; 1803 Tenn. Pub. Acts 66. For more on state methods of appointing electors in the contentious 1800 election, see "The Election of 1800–1801," The Lehrman Institute, accessed February 25, 2019, https://lehrmaninstitute.org/history/1800.html#state.
3. 1804 N.J. Laws 310; 1807 N.J. Laws 40; 1801 Pa. Laws 32; 1798 R.I. Pub. Laws 136; 1803 Va. Acts 72; 1803 Ohio Laws 88.
4. Prior to government-printed ballots, "voters got their ballots either from a partisan, at the polls, or at home, by cutting them out of the newspaper." Jill Lepore, "Rock, Paper, Scissors," *The New Yorker*, October 13, 2008. See also Ruth C. Silva, "State Law on the Nomination, Election, and Instruction of Presidential Electors," *American Political Science Review* 42, no. 3 (June 1948), 525–26.
5. "Massachusetts 1804 Electoral College," *A New Nation Votes*.
6. The exact language of the statute provided for declaring, as winning candidates to perform the role of electors, "who may be elected by a majority of votes; and in case the full number of nineteen shall not appear to have been chosen, the deficiencies shall be supplied from the several districts respectively, where they may happen, or at large, in the case that there shall be no deficiency in any one district, by joint ballot of the Senate and House of Representatives." 1804 Mass. Acts 19.
7. 1804 N.H. Laws 39; "New Hampshire 1804 Electoral College," *A New Nation Votes*.
8. "Electoral Votes for President and Vice President, 1789–1821," National Archives and Records Administration, https://www.archives.gov/federal-register/electoral-college/votes/1789_1821.html.
9. "1812 President of the United States, Electoral College," *A New Nation Votes*.
10. "1816 President of the United States, Electoral College," *A New Nation Votes*.

11.   See Peirce and Longley, *The People's President*, 248. For specific statutes, see:

Alabama: 1820 Ala. Laws 19
Connecticut: 1820 Conn. Acts 454
Delaware: 1800 Del. Laws 143
Georgia: 1804 Ga. Laws 3
Illinois: 1819 Ill. Laws 101
Indiana: 1816 Ind. Acts 251; 1820 Ind. Acts 131
Kentucky: 1803 Ky. Acts 100; 1807 Ky. Acts 5; 1811 Ky. Acts 225; 1815 Ky. Acts 557; 1819 Ky. Acts 953
Louisiana: 1812 La. Acts 1; 1820 La. Acts 82
Maine: 1820 Me. Laws 31
Massachusetts: 1804 Mass. Acts 19; 1812 Mass. Acts 94; 1816 Mass. Acts 233; 1820 Mass. Acts 245
Maryland: 1802 Md. Laws 35
Missouri: 1820 Mo. Laws 5
Mississippi: 1820 Miss. Laws 100
New Hampshire: 1804 N.H. Laws 39; 1808 N.H. Laws 29; 1820 N.H. Laws 263
New Jersey: 1804 N.J. Laws 310; 1807 N.J. Laws 40; 1812 N.J. Laws 3
North Carolina: 1803 N.C. Sess. Laws 212; 1815 N.C. Sess. Laws 7
Ohio: 1803 Ohio Laws 88; 1807 Ohio Laws 121; 1823 Ohio Acts 29 (enacted February 1820)
Pennsylvania: 1801 Pa. Laws 32
Rhode Island: 1798 R.I. Pub. Laws 136
South Carolina: 1792 S.C. Acts 3
Tennessee: 1803 Tenn. Pub. Acts 66; 1807 Tenn. Pub. Acts 124; 1812 Tenn. Pub. Acts 6; 1815 Tenn. Pub. Acts 33
Vermont: 1791 Vt. Acts 43
Virginia: 1803 Va. Acts 72

12.   The 1812 version of the Massachusetts districting system appeared to permit plurality winners, although the relevant statutory language is ambiguous (see 1812 Mass. Acts 94). Conversely, in 1820 the statute seemed to require election "by a majority of votes," although this statute also was ambiguous regarding the consequence if the plurality winner in a district lacked a majority of votes (see 1820 Mass. Acts 245). As it was, in neither year did the outcome require these ambiguities to be resolved. "1812 President of the United States"; "1820 President of the United States," *A New Nation Votes*.

13.   1804 N.H. Laws 39; 1808 N.H. Laws 29; 1812 N.H. Laws 46; 1816 N.H. Laws 57; 1820 N.H. Laws 263; *A New Nation Votes* (for New Hampshire Electoral College 1808, 1812, 1816, 1820).

14. For an excellent account of this election, see Donald Ratcliffe, *The One-Party Presidential Contest: Adams, Jackson, and 1824's Five-Horse Race* (Lawrence: University Press of Kansas, 2015).

15. Although the Jeffersonians in 1803 anticipated only two presidential contenders, given the competition between themselves and the Federalists, their experience with this two-party competition was not so extensive that they wanted to eliminate the special runoff procedure in the event that more than two candidates unexpectedly occurred in a given year.

16. James Klotter, *Henry Clay: The Man Who Would Be President* (New York: Oxford University Press, 2018).

17. Also, it is worth remembering that when casting their popular votes in those states employing this method of appointing electors, the voters were not employing ballots that contained the names of the presidential candidates—as is true in today's practice—but instead recognized that they were voting for the named electors; and given the fluidity of factional politics in 1824, voters understood that the electors they cast ballots for might end up choosing a different presidential candidate when actually exercising their official Electoral College power. Thus, to say that there was a definitive national popular vote for Jackson—in contrast to Adams or Clay or Crawford, when all four purported to be candidates of the single Republican Party—is something of an anachronism. Indeed, it is easier to speak of a nationally prevailing popular vote for Jefferson in 1804, given the stark two-party politics that then existed, than it is to speak of a nationally prevailing popular vote for Jackson in 1824, given the four-way intraparty factionalism that occurred that year. Ratcliffe, *The One-Party Presidential Contest*, Appendix; Donald Ratcliffe, "Popular Preferences in the Presidential Election of 1824," *Journal of the Early Republic* 34, no. 1 (Spring 2014), 45–77.

18. Ratcliffe "Popular Preferences," 254.

19. Lynn Hudson Parsons, *The Birth of Modern Politics: Andrew Jackson, John Quincy Adams, and the Election of 1828* (New York: Oxford University Press, 2009).

20. In 1824, the 10 states that used plurality winner-take-all to appoint their electors were Alabama, Connecticut, Indiana, Mississippi, New Jersey, North Carolina, Ohio, Pennsylvania, Rhode Island, and Virginia. In 1828, the 15 states that had adopted this system included the same 10 plus Illinois, Kentucky, Louisiana, Missouri, and Vermont. See CQ Press, *Presidential Elections*, 181; Pierce and LongleyPeirce, *The People's President*, 310–11; Lisa Thomason, "Jacksonian Democracy and the Electoral College: Politics and Reform in the Method of Selecting Presidential Electors, 1824–1833" (PhD diss., University of North Texas, 2001).

    Georgia, as discussed in the text at page 66, adopted a majority requirement. To examine the actual laws operative for each of these states in 1828, see 1827 Ala. Laws 86; 1828 Conn. Acts 179; 1828 Ind. Act 61; 1824 La. Acts 64; 1828 Miss. Laws 7; 1813 N.J. Laws 60; 1815 N.C. Sess. Laws 7; 1807 Ohio Laws 121; 1801 Pa. Laws 32; 1798 R.I. Pub. Laws 136; 1822 Va. Acts 42; 1824 Ga. Laws 58; 1827 Ill. Laws 188; 1824 Vt. Acts 4.

21. Madison to George Hay, August 23, 1823. Madison's proposal for ranked choice ballots differed from the initial Electoral College system of 1787, in which the two votes of each elector were unranked and of equal weight (as described in Chapter 1). For additional details on Madison's views, see note 15 to Chapter 1.

22. For a thorough discussion of the various congressional proposals and deliberations, see Keyssar, *Why Do We Still Have the Electoral College?*, chapter 3.

23. Helpful discussions of New York politics in 1824 can be found in Craig Hanyan and Mary L. Hanyan, *De Witt Clinton and the Rise of the People's Men* (Montreal: McGill-Queen's University Press, 1996); Daniel Walker Howe, *What Hath God Wrought: The Transformation of America, 1815–1848* (New York: Oxford University Press, 2007); Donald B. Cole, *Martin Van Buren and the American Political System* (Princeton, NJ: Princeton University Press, 2014); Lee Benson, *The Concept of Jacksonian Democracy: New York as a Test Case* (Princeton, NJ: Princeton University Press, 1965); Dixon Ryan Fox, *The Decline of Aristocracy in the Politics of New York* (New York: Longman, Green & Co., 1919). Always valuable, even if it needs to be supplemented with newer accounts, is Jazeb Hammond, *The History of Political Parties in the State of New York* (Syracuse, NY: Hall, Mills & Co., 1852).

24. The description of the committee report, including quotations, is from *Journal of the Assembly of the State of New-York at Their Fourth-Seventh Session* (Albany, NY: Leake and Crowell, 1824), 146–47.

25. Hammond, *The History of Political Parties*, 146.

26. *Journal of the Senate of the State of New-York at Their Fourth-Seventh Session*, 253–54.

27. 1825 N.Y. Laws 53.

28. 1829 N.Y. Laws 231.

29. Thomason, 86. 1824 La. Acts 64; 1827 Ill. Laws 188; 1827 Ky. Acts 165; 1824 Vt. Acts 4; 1824 Mo. Laws 354. *Journal of the General Assembly of the State of Vermont*, 12–15, 1824–1825.

30. The text of the new Georgia law explicitly provided that the state's electors would be "those persons who may have received a number of votes amounting to a majority of the persons who shall have voted for electors." The statute continued that if "none of persons voted for having received a majority," then "the General Assembly shall proceed by a joint ballot to the election of electors for President and Vice President of the United States." The statute also provided that if some received a majority, but not

the full number of electors to which Georgia was entitled, then the state's legislature by a joint ballot would supply the rest. See 1824 Ga. Laws 58.

In 1860, Georgia needed to invoke this legislative runoff provision. John Breckinridge (the Southern Democrat) received 48.89 percent of the vote in Georgia, with Stephen Douglas (the regular Democrat) and John Bell (the Constitutional Unionist) splitting the rest. The state's legislature proceeded to exercise its statutory authority to appoint the Breckinridge electors. Georgia did not abandon its majority-rule requirement for presidential elections until 1964, a move that enabled George Wallace to win the state's electoral votes in 1968 with only 42.83 percent of the popular vote.

31. There is no doubt that Jackson was the majority-preferred candidate in South Carolina, which retained legislative appointment of electors.

32. "December 8, 1829: First Annual Message to Congress," UVA Miller Center, https://millercenter.org/the-presidency/presidential-speeches/december-8-1829-first-annual-message-congress.

33. Keyssar, *Why Do We Still Have the Electoral College?*, chapter 3.

34. 1823 Ala. Laws 86; 1827 Ala. Laws 86 (extends 1823 law); 1832 Ala. Laws 3 (1823 law not limited to five electors); 1828 Conn. Acts 179; 1829 Del. Laws 432; 1824 Ga. Laws 49; 1827 Ill. Laws 188; 1831 Ind. Acts 58; 1831 Ky. Acts 46; 1824 La. Acts 58; 1832 Me. Laws 39; 1831 Miss. Laws 380; 1824 Mo. Laws 354; 1807 N.J. Laws 40; 1813 N.J. Laws 60 (restoring 1807 N.J. law after repeal); 1829 N.Y. Laws 234; 1815 N.C. Sess. Laws 7; 1830 Ohio Laws 41; 1801 Pa. Laws 32; 1798 R.I. Pub. Laws 136; 1832 Tenn. Pub. Acts 18; 1824 Vt. Acts 4; 1831 Va. Acts 28.

35. CQ Press, *Presidential Elections*, 181.

36. 1831 Md. Laws 449; 1833 Md. Laws 306.

37. When Massachusetts switched from a district-based system to a statewide popular vote in 1824, it failed to include specific statutory language requiring a majority vote (1824 Mass. Acts 40). For the 1828 election, it added such language, expressly providing that "each person who shall have received a majority of votes" shall be a duly appointed presidential elector for the state (1828 Mass. Acts 3). But the 1828 statute, like the one from 1820, failed to specify the consequence if an elector position remained unfilled for lack of the requisite majority vote. By 1832, the operative statutory language remedied this omission, explicitly instructing: "if, upon the examination of the votes as aforesaid, it shall appear that a majority of the whole number of electors have not been chosen, in the manner herein before provided, it shall be the duty of the Governor, by proclamation, to call the General Court together forthwith, and the General Court, by joint ballot of the senators and representatives assembled in one room, shall choose as many electors as shall be necessary to complete the number of electors to which this Commonwealth may then be entitled" (1832 Mass. Acts 485). In this way, by 1832 Massachusetts

had reverted to the requirement of a legislative runoff that it first adopted forty years earlier, in 1792. New Hampshire, on the other hand, never deviated during this Jacksonian period from its express requirement to use a legislative runoff if a popular vote majority was lacking. 1824 N.H. Laws 4; 1828 N.H. Laws 282 (also in force in 1832).

38. John Niven, *Martin Van Buren: The Romantic Age of American Politics* (New York: Oxford University Press, 1983); Cole, *Martin Van Buren and the American Political System*, 256–81; Michael F. Holt, *The Rise and Fall of the American Whig Party* (New York: Oxford University Press, 1999).

39. See Robert W. Merry, *A Country of Vast Designs: James K. Polk, the Mexican War, and the Conquest of the American Continent* (New York: Simon & Schuster, 2010), 128; see also Charles Grier Sellers, *James K. Polk*, Volume II: *Continent* (Princeton, NJ: Princeton University Press, 2015), 214; John Bicknell, *America 1844: Religious Fervor, Westward Expansion, and the Presidential Election That Transformed the Nation* (Chicago: Chicago Review Press, 2015); Robert Remini, *Henry Clay: Statesman for the Union* (New York: Norton, 1991), 662; Sean Wilentz, "The Bombshell of 1844," in *America at the Ballot Box*, ed. Gareth Davies and Julian E. Zelizer (Philadelphia: University of Pennsylvania Press, 2015), 36–58.

40. Howe, *What Hath God Wrought*, 688.

41. Polk also won Michigan with less than 50 percent of the popular vote, but its five electoral votes—unlike New York's 36—would not have made a difference in which candidate reached an Electoral College majority.

42. Holt, *Rise and Fall*, 195.

43. Amy S. Greenberg, *A Wicked War: Polk, Clay, Lincoln, and the 1846 U.S. Invasion of Mexico* (New York: Knopf, 2012), 60. See also Poundstone, *Gaming the Vote*, 60–61.

44. David S. Heidler and Jeanne T. Heidler, *Henry Clay: The Essential American* (New York: Random House, 2010), 392.

45. Melba Porter Hay and Carol Reardon, eds., *The Papers of Henry Clay* (Lexington: University Press of Kentucky, 1991), 10:167.

46. Harlow Giles Unger, *Henry Clay: America's Greatest Statesman* (Boston: Da Capo Press, 2015), 234.

47. Lincoln to Williamson Durley, Springfield, October 3, 1845, in *Collected Works of Abraham Lincoln*, Volume 1 (Ann Arbor: University of Michigan Digital Library Production Services, 2001).

48. Hammond, *The History of Political Parties*, 3:480.

49. This point is emphasized in Vernon Volpe, "The Liberty Party and Polk's Election, 1844," *Historian* 53, no. 4 (Summer 1991), 691–710. Volpe, however, overcorrects for the prior mistake of assuming that all Birney voters would have supported Clay as a second choice. Indeed, Volpe (at 708–9) himself ultimately acknowledges that Clay could have won over some of Birney's voters: "If New York's antislavery voters were at

all responsible, then Clay must bear the burden of blame" for how he handled the Texas issue in the campaign. Thus Volpe does not undermine what he calls "the truism that had some 5,000 New York Liberty voters cast their ballots for Clay, he would have been president."

50.   Horace Greeley, *Recollections of a Busy Life* (Port Washington, NY: Kennikat Press, 1971), 65. Greeley says that if Clay had not made a campaign mistake, he would have had enough Birney votes to become president. That observation suggests that these Birney voters were sufficiently persuadable that in a two-person race, or runoff, between Clay and Polk, they would have been willing, even if reluctantly, to vote for the candidate whom they perceived as the lesser of two evils.

51.   Klotter, *Henry Clay*, 323.

52.   Wilentz, "Bombshell of 1844," 36. In his monumental *The Rise of American Democracy* (at 574) Wilentz had written that Birney voters "could claim that they had decided a presidential election." Wilentz, like Holt, acknowledged that multiple factors caused Clay's defeat, including Whig dalliance with anti-Catholicism. Still, neither Wilentz nor Holt contradicted the analysis of historians earlier or since that the Liberty Party was decisive. As one recent study of the election explains: "Had [Clay] taken a firmer stand against annexation and not waffled multiple times, he might have disarmed the Liberty Party and hung onto New York, even with the massive Catholic turnout against him." Bicknell, *America 1844*, 229–30.

53.   "Letter from Hon. John P. Kennedy," *New York Tribune*, November 29, 1844; "Prediction and Fulfillment—The Recent Election," *New York Herald*, November 21, 1844.

54.   See 1832 Mass. Acts 485 (in effect for 1844 election); 1828 N.H. Laws 282 (in effect for 1844 election). See also "Political Intelligence," *New York Herald* (September 7, 1848), p. 3: "a *majority* is required in Massachusetts and New Hampshire" whereas "a *plurality* elects" in other states.

55.   John Stilwell Jenkins, *History of Political Parties in the State of New York* (Auburn, NY: Alden & Markham, 1846), 467–68.

56.   Keyssar, *Why Do We Still Have the Electoral College?*

57.   Holt, *Rise and Fall*, 198–99; Foley, *Ballot Battles*, 400–401.

58.   Klotter, *Henry Clay* at 325, quoting Mark W. Summers, *The Plundering Generation* (New York: Oxford University Press, 1988).

59.   The best evidence of the lingering effect of the 1824 debate in 1844 was an essay Horace Greeley wrote for his paper's readers to remind them of this history. See "Silas Wright and the Rights of the People—The Struggle of 1824," *New York Daily Tribune* (September 9, 1844). Greeley, an ardent Whig, was adamantly opposed to the Democratic candidate for governor that year, Silas Wright. To attack Wright, Greeley resurrected Wright's role in 1824 as a proponent of the idea "a *majority*, and not a *plurality*, of votes should be requisite to a choice" of the state's presidential electors.

NOTES TO PAGES 71–75

Greeley saw Wright's support of this idea as a ruse for keeping the state legislature's control over the appointment of electors, since it was apparent that no candidate in 1824 would be capable of a popular-vote majority— and, as we recall, there was insufficient time remaining that year for a popular-vote runoff. Greeley wanted his readers to see Wright as betraying the values of "Republicanism" and "Popular Rights" that as a Democrat Wright claimed to profess.

When Greeley wrote this essay, he was clearly aware of the possibility that Birney and the Liberty Party might cause a three-way split in New York's popular vote for the presidency, thereby preventing any candidate from achieving a majority. At the time, however, he was still confident that Clay would prevail over Polk, even if only with a plurality. See Mitchell Snay, *Horace Greeley and the Politics of Reform in Nineteenth-Century America* (Lanham, MD: Rowman and Littlefield, 2011), 89. Heading into the 1844 vote, Greeley as an ardent Clay supporter saw no reason to abandon New York's plurality method of appointing electors in favor of requiring a popular-vote majority (even assuming that a popular-vote runoff would have been feasible that year).

Other circumstances in 1844 contributed to Greeley's animosity toward abandoning New York's plurality system of appointing electors, despite the risk that Birney's presence might cause Polk to win. Earlier that year, Maine had switched from a plurality to majority requirement for the appointment of that state's electors. (Compare 1840 Me. Laws 188, with 1844 Me. Laws 334.) There, the state's legislature was under Democratic control, and Greeley saw the move as a partisan ploy to permit the legislature to award the state's electoral votes to Polk if Clay came up short of a popular majority in the state. See "Maine—Ominous," *New-York Daily Tribune,* March 8, 1844.

Greeley, however, was not altogether wedded to plurality voting and hostile to majority-rule requirements. On the contrary, when the issue arose at New York's constitutional convention in 1846 of making the state's governor elected on the basis of a majority rather than plurality popular vote, Greeley told his readers: "the *principle* is one that I am Yankee enough to venerate and maintain" (reflecting the fact, well known at the time, that New England states required majority votes for the election of their governors). Recognizing full well that the consequence of the proposal was that the state's "Legislature" would "select one of the highest candidates" "if no one candidate has a majority," Greeley nonetheless explicitly affirmed: "If I had a seat on that floor I would have been anxious to represent a constituency who were ready for Majority Governors." See "Plurality Governors," *New-York Daily Tribune,* July 17, 1846.

Despite this professed belief in the majority-rule principle, there is no evidence that Greeley endeavored to apply it to the context of presidential elections or to explore the feasibility of a popular-vote runoff, or some other mechanism for assuring majority votes, in advance of the 1848 election—when, again, the possibility of a third-party candidacy might threaten to fracture the electorate. As a general matter, Greeley was thoroughly committed to the idea of a two-party system, and his focus after 1844 remained on eliminating the political significance of third parties, rather than pursuing institutional reforms that might counteract the significance that they otherwise inevitably would threaten to have.

60. Thurlow Weed explicitly made the point: "The result of the last presidential election . . . will open the eyes of the people to the reckless designs" of third-party efforts like Birney's. The short-term pain, he thought, would "cure the evil" long-term. A third party "will not again have power," he predicted. Thurlow Weed, *Life of Thurlow Weed Including His Autobiography and a Memoir* (Boston: Houghton Mifflin and Company, 1884), 126.

61. Silbey has observed that despite the obvious rise of third parties in the 1840s, the dominant attitude remained "the loyalty to the two-party system" and thus an unwillingness, or perhaps even incapacity, to reimagine an institutional arrangements suitable to the ongoing presence of significant third-party participation. Joel Silbey, *Party over Section: The Rough and Ready Presidential Election of 1848* (Lawrence: University Press of Kansas, 2009), 82. One newspaper in 1844 acknowledged that most of the public was confused over the distinction between majority and plurality elections: "People talk about majorities for this man or that, when it is probable that in half the northern states no man will get a majority at all. A plurality elects the electors in most of the States, and when people speak of majorities they mean over the principal opposing candidate and not over all." "Election! 'To the Polls!'" *Burlington Free Press*, November 1, 1844.

62. Clay, in particular, wrote letter after letter conveying the sentiment that it was "useless and unavailing to lament to the irrevocable event." Instead, "the Whigs, or some of them, in Congress would do well to have an early consultation and adopt some system of future action." In this way they can "seek to discern the means by which the Country may be saved from the impending dangers." Hay and Reardon, *Papers of Henry Clay*, 10:160.

63. Greenberg, *A Wicked War*, 274 (in 1879, Grant told a journalist, "I do not think there was ever a more wicked war than that waged by the United States on Mexico"). See also Ron Chernow, *Grant* (New York: Penguin, 2017), 38: "In his *Memoirs*, Grant blasted the Texas scheme as an imperialist adventure, pure and simple, designed to add slave states to the Union."

64. "The consequences of the election of 1844 went far beyond Texas annexation, important as that was," wrote Howe. "Almost surely there would have been no Mexican War, no Wilmot Proviso, and therefore less reason for the status of slavery in the territories to have inflamed sectional

passions." More provocatively, Howe continues: "some historians have carefully examined the likely consequences of a Clay victory in 1844 and concluded that it would probably have avoided the Civil War of the 1860s." Howe, *What Hath God Wrought*, 689–90. More guarded is Wilentz's assessment: "If Polk's opponent, Henry Clay, had won, the Civil War at the very least could have been forestalled," or "so the argument goes." Wilentz, "Bombshell of 1844," 36.

65.   Biographies of Clay, old and new, make this point. "Had a third of Birney's votes (or approximately five thousand) gone to Clay," one historian observes, "the Texas question would have been handled in a more conciliatory manner and the Mexican War might never have occurred." More speculatively, "there might never have been a Civil War." Remini, *Henry Clay*, 668. "Many historians argue . . . that had Clay won in 1844, there would have been no conflict with Mexico, and possibly no Civil War." Klotter, *Henry Clay*, 379. "A Clay victory . . . certainly would have altered the landscape in which [the 'irrepressible'] conflict was adjudicated through the 1850s." There likely would have been "no Bleeding Kansas" and thus "no prelude to civil war on the frontier." Bicknell, *America 1884*, 251.

66.   Weed, *Life of Thurlow Weed*, 124, 126.

67.   Holt, *Rise and Fall*, 368–70. For an excellent biography of Van Buren, which carefully details why the former leader of the Democrats (and a major progenitor of America's two-party system) would run as a third-party candidate over the issue of slavery, see Niven, *Martin Van Buren*, 586. For a comprehensive discussion of this important election, see Silbey, *Party over Section*.

68.   See Poundstone, *Gaming the Vote*, 62–63.

69.   "Electoral Vote of Massachusetts," *Weekly National Intelligencer*, December 2, 1848, [1]. In 1851, Massachusetts abandoned its requirement that electors receive a majority of the popular vote in order to avoid a legislative runoff, joining instead the prevailing practice of permitting the appointment of electors by a mere plurality of the popular vote (see 1851 Mass. 579–80). New Hampshire likewise moved to permitting plurality winners, rather than requiring majority winners, for the appointment of its electors in 1852. (New Hampshire adopted this change in December of 1848, but it did not become operative until the next presidential election. See 1848 N.H. Laws 684.) Ironically, the apparent aim of this move was to "weaken third party organizations" by encouraging voters to "unite themselves to one or the other of the two strongest parties." See "Election by Plurality," *Portsmouth Journal*, December 16, 1848, [2]. Insofar as the goal was to foster a two-party system unaffected by third parties, this legislative change did not anticipate that if it failed to eliminate third parties entirely, then they might affect which major party would be the plurality winner.

70. If Van Buren would have won a runoff against Taylor in New York, with Van Buren receiving New York's electoral votes on that basis, the consequence would have been to send the election to the House of Representatives (as in 1824) under the Twelfth Amendment's special procedure when no candidate receives a majority of Electoral College votes. That outcome would also have been consistent with the Jeffersonian design of the Twelfth Amendment. Thus, there was no risk of 1848 being a repeat of what had happened in 1844: the wrong candidate, from a Jeffersonian perspective, receiving an Electoral College majority. Unlike Polk, Cass had no chance of winning New York's electoral votes—being the third-place finisher behind Van Buren there—and thus Cass had no chance for achieving an Electoral College majority in the same un-Jeffersonian way that Polk did.

71. Howe, *What Hath God Wrought*, 833. Joel Silbey reaches the same conclusion, although by a somewhat different route. He observes that even if one were to remove New York from Taylor's column "because of the extraordinary fragmenting of the Democrats" there, one must put Ohio and Indiana back in the Whig column. These states, "with almost as many electoral votes as New York, a total of thirty-five between them, went to Cass largely because of Whig, not Democratic, defections to Free Soil." Thus, Silbey sees it as a wash: "If these three are considered together as the critical states, they successfully cancelled out each other's determinative influence in the final results." Silbey, *Party over Section*, 144–45. See also Holt, *Rise and Fall*, 374 ("had there been no Free Soil ticket in 1848, and had New York gone Democratic and Ohio Whig, . . . Taylor still would have won the electoral vote, 150–40").

72. David Herbert Donald, *Lincoln* (New York: Simon & Schuster, 1995), 257; James M. McPherson, *Battle Cry of Freedom: The Civil War Era* (New York: Oxford University Press, 1988), 229; David M. Potter, *The Impending Crisis, 1848–1861* (New York: Harper & Row, 1976), 489. See also William J. Cooper, *We Have the War upon Us: The Onset of the Civil War, November 1860–April 1861* (New York: Knopf, 2012); Douglas R. Egerton, *Year of Meteors: Stephen Douglas, Abraham Lincoln, and the Election That Brought on the Civil War* (New York: Bloomsbury Press, 2010).

73. See Egerton, *Year of Meteors*, 335–38.

74. Poundstone, *Gaming the Vote*, 64–65; McLean, "Electoral Systems," 218.

75. See Foley, *Ballot Battles*, chapter 5.

76. Michael Holt, *By One Vote: The Disputed Presidential Election of 1876* (Lawrence: University Press of Kansas, 2008), 32.

77. For a lively account of this election, see Mark Wahlgreen Summers, *Rum, Romanism, and Rebellion* (Chapel Hill: University of North Carolina Press, 2000).

78. The numbers in the text are the ones reported by CQ Press. Leip has slightly different numbers: 563,154 for Cleveland, and 562,005 for Blaine, making a margin of 1,149. For more granular analysis of the returns in New York, see Summers, *Rum, Romanism, and Rebellion*, 289–97.

79. Poundstone, *Gaming the Vote*, 68–69. See also Richard R. John, "Markets, Morality, and the Media: The Election of 1884," in *America at the Ballot Box: Elections and Political History*, ed. Gareth Davies and Julian E. Zelizer (Philadelphia: University of Pennsylvania Press, 2015), 83 ("any vote for Butler is a vote for Blaine"). Leip has Butler's total at 17,004.

80. John, "Election of 1884," 87:

> If any single individual tipped the scales, it was almost certainly the Prohibition Party candidate, John St. John. Had Republican Party leaders prevailed upon St. John to take himself out of the running in New York, Blaine would have obtained many if not most of St. John's twenty-five thousand votes—far more than Blaine needed to win New York and the election.

More succinctly, "St. John unquestionably was a spoiler." Poundstone, *Gaming the Vote*, 68. See also Summers, *Rum, Romanism, and Rebellion*, 295 (one Republican bluntly saying he wished St. John had been paid to stay out of the race). Leip has St. John's total at 25,006.

81. "Party Divisions of the House of Representatives, 1789 to Present," https://history.house.gov/Institution/Party-Divisions/Party-Divisions/; "Party Divison," https://www.senate.gov/history/partydiv.htm.

82. See Summers, *Rum, Romanism, and Rebellion*, 292–94; William Gorham Rice and Francis Lynde Stetson, "Was New York's Vote Stolen?," *North American Review* 199, no. 698 (January 1914), 90.

83. Charles W. Calhoun, *Minority Victory: Gilded Age Politics and the Front Porch Campaign of 1888* (Lawrence: University Press of Kansas, 2008).

84. See Calhoun, *Minority Victory*, 170: "The GOP labored mightily to curtail losses to the Prohibitionists."

85. Poundstone, *Gaming the Vote*, 70.

86. See Richard White, *The Republic for Which It Stands* (New York: Oxford University Press, 2017); Mark Wahlgren Summers, *Party Games: Getting, Keeping, and Using Power in Gilded Age Politics* (Chapel Hill: University of North Carolina Press, 2004); H. Wayne Morse, *From Hayes to McKinley: National Party Politics, 1877–1896* (Syracuse, NY: Syracuse University Press, 1969).

Chapter 5

1. For an especially dramatic account of the Roosevelt-Taft friendship and the rift between them in 1912, see Doris Kearns Goodwin, *The Bully Pulpit: Theodore Roosevelt, William Howard Taft, and the Golden Age of Journalism* (New York: Simon & Schuster, 2013). See also Geoffrey

Cowan, *Let the People Rule: Theodore Roosevelt and the Birth of the Presidential Primary* (New York: Norton, 2016); Lewis L. Gould, *Four Hats in the Ring: The 1912 Election and the Birth of Modern American Politics* (Lawrence: University Press of Kansas, 2008); James Chace, *1912: Wilson, Roosevelt, Taft, and Debs—The Election That Changed the Country* (New York: Simon & Schuster, 2004).

2. The hypothesis underlying this specific scenario is that Republicans would have come out of their convention united behind Roosevelt as their candidate, with Taft having graciously acquiesced in Roosevelt's nomination. The circumstances clearly would have been different if Taft had continued to seek re-election after having been denied the GOP nomination, but had been barred from the ballot all across the county (as he actually was in a couple of states). See John Milton Cooper Jr., *Woodrow Wilson: A Biography* (New York: Random House, 2009), 175–76. In this alternative situation, disgruntled Taft supporters might have actually cast some ballots for Wilson, or declined to vote for Roosevelt, out of retribution for what they perceived as a stolen nomination even if Wilson was less ideologically compatible than Roosevelt. (I am grateful to Anthony Gaughan for suggesting this clarification.) For a previous analysis, including discussion of specific states, see Edward B. Foley, "Third-Party and Independent Presidential Candidates: The Need for A Runoff Mechanism," *Fordham Law Review* 85, no. 993 (December 2016), 1003:

> Roosevelt would have won Colorado, Connecticut, Delaware, Idaho, Illinois, Indiana, Iowa, Kansas, Maine, Massachusetts, Montana, Nebraska, New Hampshire, New Jersey, New Mexico, New York, North Dakota, Ohio, Oregon, Rhode Island, West Virginia, Wisconsin, and Wyoming—for a combined 252 Electoral College votes—all of which Wilson actually won due to the Republican fissure between Roosevelt and Taft. Add these 252 Electoral College votes to those of Michigan, Minnesota, Pennsylvania, South Dakota, and Washington, which Roosevelt actually won, as well as those of Utah and Vermont, which Taft won, and Roosevelt would have won 329 Electoral College votes, far more than the 266 necessary for a majority.

3. Here, the possibility that some Taft supporters would have balked at supporting Roosevelt as their second choice, because of lingering bitterness over the feud at the GOP convention, cannot be ignored. Still, it is more probable that Taft supporters would have sided with Roosevelt, even if somewhat reluctantly, rather than the Democrat. See Poundstone, *Gaming the Vote*, 72.

4. See Poundstone, *Gaming the Vote*, 72–73.

5. The following table provides the details of the 23–22–3 partisan divide among state delegations in the House of Representatives in February 1913,

when the House would have had to elect the president if no candidate had received a majority of electoral votes:

Party Control of State Delegations in House of Representatives

#	Democrat	Evenly Split	Republican
1.	Alabama	Maine	California
2.	Arizona	Nebraska	Wyoming
3.	Arkansas	New Mexico	Connecticut
4.	Colorado		Delaware
5.	Florida		Idaho
6.	Georgia		Illinois
7.	Indiana		Iowa
8.	Kentucky		Kansas
9.	Louisiana		Massachusetts
10.	Maryland		Michigan
11.	Mississippi		Minnesota
12.	Missouri		Montana
13.	New Jersey		Nevada
14.	New York		New Hampshire
15.	North Carolina		North Dakota
16.	Ohio		Oregon
17.	Oklahoma		Pennsylvania
18.	Rhode Island		South Dakota
19.	South Carolina		Utah
20.	Tennessee		Vermont
21.	Texas		Washington
22.	Virginia		Wisconsin
23.	West Virginia		

"House Elections, 1910," Maps, CQ Press, accessed February 22, 2019, http://library.cqpress.com/elections/map.php?state=&type=house&year=1910. Arizona and New Mexico had representatives who were seated after these two states joined the union. One of the two representatives from Rhode Island died in November 1912, leaving this seat vacant.

6.   One possibility, often under consideration, was that the contingent runoff should be a majority vote of the House and Senate sitting jointly as a single body. See Keyssar, *Why Do We Still Have the Electoral College?*

7.   See, e.g., Robert H. Ferrell, *Woodrow Wilson and World War I* (New York: Harper & Row, 1986), 156: "One comes, at last, to the central question about Woodrow Wilson and World War I: why the President of the United States almost perversely insisted upon losing the fight, to use his word, for the League of Nations and thereby became the Great Architect of World War II?" Other historians, to be sure, dispute this analysis. See Margaret MacMillan, *Paris 1919: Six Months That Changed the*

World (New York: Random House, 2002), 493–94. (I am grateful, again, to Anthony Gaughan for illuminating details of this historical debate.) See also John Lukacs, "The Election of Theodore Roosevelt, 1912: Brokering an Earlier End to World War I," in *What If? 2: Eminent Historians Imagine What Might Have Been*, ed. Robert Cowley (New York: Berkley Books, 2001), 181; Jeff Nilsson, "Teddy Roosevelt and World War I: An Alternative History," *Saturday Evening Post*, April 17, 2014.

8. Runoffs in states where Hughes had only a plurality might have added to Wilson's genuinely Jeffersonian win. For example, Hughes won Minnesota's 12 electoral votes with only 46.35 percent of the popular vote, and there Wilson (with 46.25 percent) and Benson (5.19 percent) combined for a majority (51.54 percent).

9. In a two-person race with just Dewey, Truman also would have been the majority-preferred candidate in the other two states where he won only a plurality: Tennessee and Virginia. There, Truman's share of the vote was much smaller than it otherwise would have been because of Strom Thurmond's candidacy as a Dixiecrat. If confined to a choice between only Truman and Dewey, Dixiecrat voters clearly would have preferred the Democrat, despite his support for racial equality and civil rights. These Dixiecrats might have been reluctant Truman voters, but they certainly would not have voted for Dewey, since the Republican Party also supported civil rights and had not yet embarked on its southern strategy. Even if all the Dixiecrat voters had refused to vote for Truman, and just stayed home, in a two-person race Truman would have received the majority of votes in Virginia and Tennessee. See Andrew E. Busch, *Truman's Triumphs: The 1948 Election and the Making of Postwar America* (Lawrence: University Press of Kansas, 2012), 158.

10. See Foley, "America in the Middle of Its Century: A Tarnished Ideal," in *Ballot Battles*, chapter 8.

11. Even in the North, Wallace voters preferred Nixon, because he was significantly less supportive of civil rights than Humphrey, who had made that issue his crusade. Brams, *The Presidential Election Game*, 220–29. See Kiewiet, "Approval Voting," 170; Paul R. Abramson, John H. Aldrich, Phil Paolino, and David R. Rohde, "Third-Party and Independent Candidates in American Politics," *Political Science Quarterly* 110, no. 3 (Autumn 1995), 358. Peirce and Longley, *The People's President*, 74 ("Independent analysts think Wallace hurt Nixon much more than Humphrey."). See generally Michael A. Cohen, *American Maelstrom: The 1968 Election and the Politics of Division* (New York: Oxford University Press, 2016).

12. What is true about Illinois that year is also true of other states. Michigan is another state where Reagan would have won a runoff against Carter. His plurality there was 48.99 percent. Anderson's share of the popular vote was 7.04 percent. Reagan needed only 14.3 percent of Anderson's votes, or about three in twenty, to reach a majority in Michigan. Achieving this,

as he would have, would have added 21 electoral votes based on being the majority-preferred candidate in the state. These 21 would have been an alternative to the 29 from Illinois as a way of reaching 270 based on states where Reagan was the majority-preferred candidate.

The same point, moreover, can be made about Pennsylvania's 27 electoral votes, given Reagan's plurality there of 49.59 percent and Anderson's share being 6.42 percent. Reagan would have needed only 6.4 percent of Anderson's votes in Pennsylvania to win a runoff—and thus be the majority winner—in the state.

There was also a Libertarian candidate on the ballot in 1980. But his presence ultimately does not affect the analysis. At most, if it were thought that Carter would have won more Libertarian votes in a runoff, then Reagan's share of Anderson's votes would need to increase correspondingly. But it is also possible that Reagan might have picked up more Libertarian votes than Carter, thus requiring Reagan to pick up even fewer Anderson votes.

13. Clinton won another 14 states with less than 45 percent of the popular vote: Colorado (40.13 percent), Connecticut (42.21 percent), Delaware (43.51 percent), Georgia (43.47 percent), Iowa (43.29 percent), Kentucky (44.55 percent), Michigan (43.77 percent), Minnesota (43.48 percent), Missouri (44.07 percent), New Jersey (42.95 percent), Ohio (40.18 percent), Oregon (42.48 percent), Washington (43.40 percent), and Wisconsin (41.13 percent).

14. Jon Meacham, *Destiny and Power: The American Odyssey of George Herbert Walker Bush* (New York: Random House, 2015), 521. See also Kyle Balluck, "Perot Cost Father Reelection, Says Bush," *The Hill* (November 9, 2014); Ronald B. Rapaport and Walter J. Stone, *Three's a Crowd: The Dynamics of Third Parties, Ross Perot, & Republican Resurgence* (Ann Arbor: University of Michigan Press, 2011), 147; J. David Gillespie, *Challengers to Duopoly: Why Third Parties Matter in American Two-Party Politics* (Columbia: University of South Carolina Press, 2012), 8 ("Many Republicans blamed Perot for spoiling Bush's 1992 reelection bid by siphoning away millions of votes"); Poundstone, *Gaming the Vote*, 74.

15. Perot suspended his campaign in July but returned to the race in October (Meacham, *Destiny and Power*, 514–18).

16. "Ross Perot reduced rather than increased Bill Clinton's margin of victory over George Bush." Dean Lacey and Barry C. Burden, "The Vote-Stealing and Turnout Effects of Ross Perot in the 1992 U.S. Presidential Election," *American Journal of Political Science* 43, no. 1 (1999), 233, 252.

17. In the intervening election (1996) Perot ran again, this time as the nominee of the Reform Party. He did not do as well as in 1992. Although he again caused Clinton to win many states with pluralities, not majorities, there is even more reason to believe that Clinton would have won runoffs that year against Bob Dole, his Republican challenger, than

against Bush, the Republican incumbent four years earlier. For example, in 1996 Clinton won 48.02 percent of the popular vote in Florida, Dole only 42.32 percent. Perot's share there was 9.12 percent. Clinton would have needed little more than a fifth of Perot's supporters in Florida to reach a majority in the state. Thus there is little reason to view Clinton's victory in 1996, unlike his earlier one in 1992, as less authentically Jeffersonian than Reagan's in 1980—with Perot in 1996 more like John Anderson in being quite clearly inconsequential.

18. See Foley, *Ballot Battles*, 279–306.

19. See Poundstone, *Gaming the Vote*, 90; Michael C. Herron and Jeffrey B. Lewis, "Did Ralph Nader Spoil Al Gore's Presidential Bid: A Ballot-Level Study of Green and Reform Party Voters in the 2000 Presidential Election," *Quarterly Journal of Political Science* 2, no. 3 (2007), 222. See also Schaffner, *Politics, Parties and Elections in America*, 37; Barry Burden, "Minor Parties in the 2000 Presidential Election," in *Models of Voting in Presidential Elections: The 2000 U.S. Election,* ed. Herbert F. Weisberg and Clyde Wilcox (Stanford, CA: Stanford University Press, 2004). See also Bennett, *Taming the Electoral College,* 142: "If it is true that Nader voters overwhelmingly favored Gore over Bush as their second choices, then an 'instant run-off' system in Florida, for instance, would have resulted in a Gore victory in 2000."

20. If the Florida legislature had awarded the state's electoral votes to Bush regardless of the popular vote in the state, then one could argue that Bush's Electoral College victory would have been sufficiently Jeffersonian insofar as the authors of the 1803 redesign clearly contemplated that state legislatures might appoint electors directly. But that did not happen. Instead, Florida purported to award its electoral votes to the more popular candidate in the race. But this Florida failed to do. Gore undeniably was more popular than Bush, based on the votes cast in the election. Thus, the failure to award Florida's electoral votes to Gore had the consequence of subverting the Jeffersonian operation of the Electoral College in 2000. Bush prevailed without having the support of the majority of voters in the states that gave him his Electoral College victory, and even worse, Gore had majority support in enough states for an Electoral College victory and yet was not awarded the presidency. Hence, the major malfunction of the system in 2000.

21. For an early and sober analysis of Bush's presidency by leading historians, see Julian E. Zelizer, *The Presidency of George W. Bush: A First Historical Assessment* (Princeton, NJ: Princeton University Press, 2010). See also Jean Edward Smith, *Bush* (New York: Simon & Schuster, 2016).

Chapter 6

1. Evan McMullin, a former CIA officer from Utah, ran in the 2016 election on behalf of the "Never Trump" group of Republicans after Trump secured

their party's nomination—and after more prominent anti-Trumpers, like Mitt Romney, declined to do so. Although receiving only 0.53 percent of the vote nationally (half of Jill Stein's 1.06 percent and less than a sixth of Gary Johnson's 5.27 percent), McMullin got a whopping 21.31 percent in his home state, almost as much as Clinton's 27.17 percent. Representing a splinter group from the Republican Party, McMullin was the first choice of at least some voters who reluctantly would have supported Trump over Clinton in a two-person race. Consequently, it is very hard to imagine Clinton, rather than Trump, prevailing in Utah if there had been a runoff between the two of them in the state.

2.   "2016 Electoral College Results," *National Archives and Records Administration*, accessed February 12, 2019, https://www.archives.gov/federal-register/electoral-college/votes/2000_2005.html#2016.

3.   The five faithless electors who abandoned Clinton in the Electoral College would have been decisive if, as hypothesized, she won runoffs in the three Rust Belt states but Trump won a runoff in New Hampshire. The Electoral College tally in that scenario, with no faithless electors, would have been 274 for Clinton and 268 for Trump. In that circumstance, it is doubtful that the five electors would have been faithless—and if they had, chaos would have ensued. Litigation would have endeavored to force these electors to remain faithful, thereby preventing the election from going to the House in the absence of an Electoral College majority. In any event, from a Jeffersonian perspective, Clinton still would have been the genuinely Jeffersonian candidate in the race, since she would have been the majority-preferred candidate in enough states for an Electoral College majority. The Jeffersonians, if true to their own principles, would not have approved of faithless electors blocking the election of a candidate who, like Jefferson himself, had demonstrated the right kind of compound majority-of-majorities for a federal republic.

4.   The Federal Election Commission's official results list Clinton's national plurality as 48.18 percent. "Official 2016 Presidential General Election Results," *Federal Election Commission*, January 30, 2017, https://transition.fec.gov/pubrec/fe2016/2016presgeresults.pdf. David Leip has Clinton's national plurality as 48.02 percent. Leip, *2016 Presidential General Election Results*.

5.   The website *Vox* commissioned an analysis that purported to show that Clinton would have beaten Trump if instant runoff voting had been the system used for the election. Dylan Matthews, "Would a Different Style of Voting Have Changed the 2016 Election? We Tested 5 Alternatives," *Vox*, November 25, 2016, https://www.vox.com/policy-and-politics/2016/11/25/13733322/instant-runoff-ranked-voting-2016. But this analysis needs to be considered very cautiously. For one thing, it is based on a public opinion survey, not actual voting data. For another, it is a generic national analysis, not focused state-by-state, which obviously is what matters

for Electoral College purposes. There are also substantially more voters who ranked independent candidate Evan McMullin first in the *Vox* survey sample, 2.9 percent, than in any of the swing states where Trump won by a plurality. The same is true for Jill Stein, 2.8 percent, and Gary Johnson, 5.8 percent, making for a much higher percentage of first-choice preferences in the survey for candidates other than Clinton or Trump than occurred in the actual election. Still, the exercise is illustrative of the fact that instant runoff voting *might* have made a difference to the outcome of the 2016 election: Hillary Clinton *might* have beaten Trump if IRV had been used in all the states where Trump won only pluralities. See also Todd Donovan (ed.), *Changing How America Votes* (Lanham, MD: Rowman & Littlefield Publishers, 2017), 6, 80 (contemplating whether "enough Johnson or Stein voters" might have "ranked Clinton over Trump to make a difference").

Chapter 7

1. The Jeffersonians also thought that one way states could conform to majoritarian principles was by having their legislatures directly appoint electors whose partisan preferences would align with the majority of the popular electorate in the states. The majority-rule requirement, in the specific way it is articulated in this chapter, would not permit states to return to the method of direct legislative appointment of presidential electors. This particular constraint reflects the overwhelming judgment of history that the citizens of a state, rather than its legislature, should exercise the power to appoint a state's electors.

2. Article V of the Constitution also permits amendments by means of a new constitutional convention, but that alternative procedure has never been used. Congress can propose that the states ratify an amendment by means of state conventions rather than state legislatures, but in either case three-fourths of the states are necessary for ratification.

3. 1792 N.H. Laws 399. See also note 69 to Chapter 4.

4. 3 U.S.C. § 1, 2; Thomas Berry, "A Presidential-Election Runoff Would Be Legal for States to Adopt," *The National Review*, April 14, 2016.

5. See Foley, *Ballot Battles*, chapter 11.

6. Federal law also requires that military and overseas voters receive their absentee ballots 45 days in advance of an election. See 52 U.S.C. § 20302(a)(7). In the case of a runoff, a state could send both the initial and runoff ballots at the same time, instructing military and overseas voters to select on their runoff ballots only between the two candidates who, as a result of the initial election, advance to the runoff.

7. David M. Farrell, *Electoral Systems: A Comparative Introduction* (New York: Palgrave, 2001), 50; Chenwei Zhang, "Towards a More Perfect Election: Improving the Top-Two Primary for Congressional and State Races," *Ohio State Law Journal* 73, no. 615 (2012).

8. In 2016, both major parties held their nominating conventions in July. The Democrats have selected July 13–16 as the dates for their convention in 2020. The Republican convention is scheduled for much later: August 24–27. A convention this close to Labor Day would make it difficult, if not impossible, for the printed ballots to contain the name of the officially nominated candidate.

    That logistical matter could be resolved in one of two ways. The party could move its convention earlier, for example, to late July instead of late August. Or the Labor Day ballot could simply say "Republican nominee" where the name of the candidate otherwise would be. Virtually all voters would know the name of the Republican nominee when casting their Labor Day ballots, especially if the nominee were the incumbent president (as is expected). Moreover, it would be entirely legal for the ballot to display simply "Republican nominee" in this situation. After all, voters do not actually vote for the presidential candidate, but instead the party's slate of electors who prior to the convention have pledged to support the party's nominee, whomever it turns out to be. See *Ray v. Blair*, 343 U.S. 214 (1952) (upholding the constitutionality of state laws requiring would-be electors for each party to pledge to cast their electoral votes for their party's presidential nominee, although not deciding what would happen if a faithless elector broke that pledge).

    Ultimately, it would be the party's choice between these two alternatives. The party could not force a state to abandon its Labor Day vote. Under the Constitution, the state would be entirely entitled to hold this preliminary Labor Day vote if it wished, as a way to winnow the field of presidential candidates to just two finalists for the November ballot. The party then would need to decide how it wished to participate in the state's chosen method for appointing its electors.

9. The National Association of Secretaries of State published a guide to the ballot access requirements for presidential candidates in all 50 states: "Summary: State Laws Regarding Presidential Ballot Access for the General Election," *National Association of Secretaries of State*, October 2016, https://www.nass.org/sites/default/files/surveys/2017-08/research-ballot-access-president-Oct16.pdf.

10. The existing system of primaries and caucuses leading up to the two major parties' nominating conventions has, in recent years, started with the Iowa caucuses in January (or early February), followed by the New Hampshire primary, and soon thereafter a Super Tuesday of multiple primaries. For the 2016 calendar, see "2016 Party Nomination Overview," *270towin*, https://www.270towin.com/2016-election-calendar/.

11. States could employ so-called sore-loser laws to prevent individuals who attempted to win a major party's nomination, and who thus participated in the party's primaries, from subsequently appearing as an independent candidate on the Labor Day ballot. *Storer v. Brown*, 415 U.S. 724 (1974).

12.   *Anderson v. Celebrezze*, 460 U.S. 780 (1983).

13.   *Williams v. Rhodes*, 393 U.S. 23, 32 (1968).

14.   Several readers of an earlier draft of this book suggested that states
      should avoid the problem of minor-party and independent candidates
      affecting the result between the two major-party candidates by sharply
      limiting the access of minor-party and independent candidates to the
      November general election ballot. If as a practical matter only the two
      major-party candidates are able to qualify for the November general
      election ballot, then the winner of the popular vote necessarily will
      receive a majority rather than a mere plurality. This suggestion, however,
      is inconsistent with existing case law, which is unlikely to be overruled
      even by a more conservative Court in the aftermath of Justice Kennedy's
      retirement. Moreover, to the extent that a state's ballot access rules are
      only moderately strict, thereby enabling more popular minor-party and
      independent candidates to make it on the ballot (like John Anderson
      in 1980, or Ross Perot in 1992 and 1996), while weeding out fringe
      candidates with hardly any support, these ballot access rules would
      fail to solve the problem of a third or fourth candidate affecting the
      result between the top two vote-getters. As we saw in Part Two, a high-
      profile third-party candidate like Teddy Roosevelt in 1912 can affect
      the outcome of the election just as easily as a lower-profile candidate,
      like Ralph Nader in 2000. Only an electoral system that actually
      guarantees that the winner will be a candidate with a majority, and not
      just a plurality, of votes can avoid this problem. Limiting ballot access is
      not an adequate solution. Nor is it fair to third-party and independent
      candidates who want a realistic chance of convincing voters that, in a
      given year, voters should choose an alternative other than the nominees
      of the two major parties.

15.   The Supreme Court has frequently quoted its statement in *Storer
      v. Brown*, 415 U.S. 724 (1974), that a "two-stage process . . . functions
      to winnow out" the field of candidates, so that the second stage can
      produce a winner that reflects a genuinely democratic choice of the
      voters. The Court most recently invoked this statement in upholding
      Washington state's version of the so-called top-two primary system,
      which is the exact functional equivalent of a two-round system that
      entails an initial election followed by a runoff between the top two
      finalists. *Washington State Grange v. Washington State Republican Party*,
      552 U.S. 442 (2008).

16.   Stephen G. Wright, "Voter Turnout in Runoff Elections," *Journal of
      Politics* 51, no. 385 (1989). See also Robert G. Boatright (ed.), *Routledge
      Handbook of Primary Elections* (New York: Routledge, 2018) (while top-
      two primaries have recently shown higher turnout rates than traditional
      partisan primaries, these increased rates still lag considerably behind
      general election turnout rates).

17. The organization Fair Vote has a lot of useful information on instant runoff voting and how it works. http://www.fairvote.org/. See also Donovan (ed.), *Changing How America Votes*, chapters 6 and especially 8.

18. Jason McDaniel, "Ranked Choice Voting Likely Means Lower Turnout, More Errors," *Cato Unbound: A Journal of Debate* (December 13, 2016), https://www.cato-unbound.org/2016/12/13/jason-mcdaniel/ranked-choice-voting-likely-means-lower-turnout-more-errors; see also Craig M. Burnett and Vladimir Kogan, "Ballot (and Voter) 'Exhaustion' under Instant Runoff Voting: An Examination of Four Ranked-Choice Elections," *Journal of Electoral Studies* 37, no. 41 (2015).

19. "How to Mark a Ballot," *Ranked Choice Voting*, rankedchoicevoting.org.

20. Like Boyton, others have used cartoon animals to illustrate the simplicity of casting a ranked-choice ballot: "Vote Different Santa Fe," https://d3el53auod7w62.cloudfront.net/wp-content/uploads/2018/01/09/rankedchoiceanimals-630x606.jpg.

21. "Ranked Choice Voting's Midterm Report," *FairVote*, July 11, 2018, http://www.fairvote.org/ranked_choice_voting_s_midterm_report. See also Editorial, "Ranked Choice Is the Right Choice," *Washington Post*, January 25, 2019.

22. Interestingly, in the 1820s James Madison proposed a version of ranked choice voting by the presidential electors themselves. See Keyssar, *Why Do We Still Have the Electoral College?* Although different in details from the use of ranked choice voting to appoint the electors, Madison's proposal demonstrates that using ranked-choice ballots as a way to identify majority support for a candidate in a race with more than two contestants is consistent with Madison's overall conception of "complex" majoritarianism for a federal system (see note 15 to Chapter 1).

23. See, e.g., W. D. Wallis, *The Mathematics of Elections and Voting* (New York: Springer, 2014), 7, 10. One mathematical alternative, known as the Coombs method, is to eliminate the candidate with the most last-place votes, rather than the candidate with the fewest first-place votes, and to apply this method sequentially until a majority winner is identified.

24. This method is sometimes called a "contingent vote" and is used to elect the president in Sri Lanka. A variation, known as the "supplementary vote" in which voters are limited to ranking only their top two choices, is used in London mayoral elections. "Supplementary Vote," *Electoral Reform Society*, https://www.electoral-reform.org.uk/voting-systems/types-of-voting-system/supplementary-vote/; see also Farrell, *Electoral Systems*, 55; "Sri Lanka Presidential Election Demonstrates Value of Ease of Ranking Candidates," *FairVote*, January 9, 2015; Michael Levy, "Alternative Vote," *Encyclopaedia Britannica*.

25. In a system that permits voters to rank fewer candidates than the total number of candidates on the ballot, it is theoretically possible (although very unlikely) that the winning candidate, after all lesser-ranked

opponents are eliminated, has fewer than a majority of all ballots cast in the election while still having more ballots than the candidate mathematically identified as the runner-up. One can choose to handle this theoretical point in a variety of ways: either ignoring it as likely irrelevant as a practical matter, or deeming it consistent with the principle of majority rule insofar as the system aims at achieving a majority winner even if it theoretically might fail to do so on a rare occasion, or requiring voters to rank all (or enough) candidates to avoid even this theoretical possibility. See also *Dudum v. Arntz*, 640 F.3d 1098, 1110 (9th Cir. 2011) (analyzing this point in detail in an opinion that upholds the constitutionality of instant runoff voting, limited to ranking only three candidates, against a Fourteenth Amendment challenge).

26. Eric Maskin and Amartya Sen, "A Better Electoral System in Maine," *New York Times*, June 10, 2018; Eric Maskin and Amartya Sen, "How Majority Rule Might Have Stopped Donald Trump," *New York Times*, April 28, 2016; Eric Maskin and Amartya Sen, "The Rules of the Game: A New Electoral System," *New York Review of Books*, January 19, 2017. See also Amartya Sen, *Collective Choice and Social Welfare: Expanded Edition* (Cambridge, MA: Harvard University Press, 2018); Wallis, *The Mathematics of Elections and Voting*, chapter 3; Iain McLean and Fiona Hewitt (eds.), *Condorcet: Foundations of Social Choice and Political Theory* (Northampton, MA: Edward Elgar, 1994).

27. See Michael C. Munger, *Choosing in Groups* (New York: Cambridge University Press, 2015), 50; also William V. Gerlain and Dominique Lepelley, *Elections, Voting Rules, and Paradoxical Outcomes* (Cham, Switzerland: Springer, 2017), 12.

28. See Alec Slatky, "Why the Condorcet Criterion Is Less Important Than It Seems," *FairVote*, August 10, 2010.

29. See Keyssar, *Why Do We Still Have the Electoral College?*, on history of Electoral College districting proposals.

30. In theory, the use of plurality voting in district elections could replicate the problem of plurality voting in statewide elections. In practice, however, plurality voting in district elections is unlikely to cause the severe anti-majoritarian consequences of statewide plurality winner-take-all. The reason is that if district-based plurality voting causes one major party to do better in some districts than it would under majority rule, then the opposing major party is likely to do better than it otherwise would in other districts. These windfalls would tend to cancel each other out, causing the ratio of wins for each major party to be roughly similar to what it would be under majority rule. If it turned out that plurality-based voting in districts skewed this ratio sharply in favor of one party, then it would be necessary to consider whether a district-based system with plurality voting should be deemed inconsistent with a modern-day Jeffersonian commitment to majority rule.

NOTES TO PAGES 132–135   215

31. See Peirce and Longley, *The People's President*, 144. Keyssar's forthcoming book also discusses the history of the effort to amend the Constitution to require states to use this kind of proportional system for the casting of their electoral votes.

32. One possible rounding formula is the "largest remainder" method: "How Proportional Representation Elections Work," *FairVote*. It would also be possible, at least in theory, to use ranked-choice ballots for the purposes of allocating a state's electoral votes proportionally between the top two finalists based on the ballot rankings (rather than conducting the last round of the instant runoff process in order to produce a single winner in the state, who receives all of the state's electoral votes). While this idea has some normatively attractive properties, including giving representation in the Electoral College process to the runner-up candidate in a state, my impression is that this idea would not be attractive for a state to adopt, at least not in the near future. First, by refusing to use the ranked-choice ballots to identify a single winner in the state, a state's use of this method would reduce the state's relative clout among other states within the Electoral College; consequently, for a state that took the trouble to use ranked-choice ballots, there would be great pressure to use them "all the way," so to speak, to a single winner. Second, and conversely, for any state that wanted a proportional allocation of its electoral votes, and thus was willing to abandon winner-take-all, it would be much more straightforward for the state simply to use conventional nonranked ballots combined with an aggressive rounding formula that essentially eliminated all but the top two vote-getters from receiving a proportional share. The practical difference would be that the proportional share between these two candidates would not be adjusted based on the rankings of voters who preferred other candidates, but this marginal benefit does not seem worth the marginal cost for a state that fundamentally prefers a proportional system to a majority-based version of winner-take-all.

33. To comply with the majority-rule requirement, in the situation where the leading candidate had only a plurality of popular votes, the proportionality formula would need to make sure that at least one other candidate received at least one of the state's electoral votes. Thus, for example, in a state with only three electoral votes, the plurality winner could receive two electoral votes at most, with the remaining electoral vote going to the candidate receiving the next highest number of popular votes.

Chapter 8

1. "Gallup Polls," The Electoral College, *FairVote*, accessed February 15, 2019, http://archive.fairvote.org/electoral_college/Gallup_Polls.pdf.

2. "Gallup Polls."

3. Lydia Saad, "Americans Would Swap Electoral College for Popular Vote," Gallup, October 24, 2011, https://news.gallup.com/poll/150245/americans-swap-electoral-college-popular-vote.aspx. See also Keyssar, *Why Do We Still Have the Electoral College?*, chapters 6 and 7 (discussing the history of Gallup polling on the Electoral College).
4. "Americans Have Long Questioned Electoral College," News, Gallup, November 16, 2000, https://news.gallup.com/poll/2305/americans-long-questioned-electoral-college.aspx.
5. Keyssar, *Why Do We Still Have the Electoral College?*
6. See Judith Best, *The Choice of the People? Debating the Electoral College* (Lanham, MD: Rowman & Littlefield, 1996); Best, "Presidential Selection," 39–59. See also Jean-Francois Laslier, "And the Loser Is . . . Plurality Voting," in Dan S. Felsenthal and Moshé Machover, eds., *Electoral Systems: Paradoxes, Assumptions, and Procedures*, Studies in Choice and Welfare (New York: Springer, 2011), 327–51; Matthew Soberg Shugart, "Elections: The American Process of Selecting a President: A Comparative Perspective," *Presidential Studies Quarterly* 34, no. 3 (September 2004), 632–55. Many op-ed writers have noted the problem with electing a president based only on a slim plurality. See, e.g., William M. Daley, "Dump the Electoral College? Bad Idea, Says Al Gore's Former Campaign Chairman," *Washington Post*, December 4, 2016; Allen Guelzo and James Hulme, "In Defense of the Electoral College," *Washington Post*, November 15, 2016.
7. According to data compiled by the Institute for Democracy and Electoral Assistance, of the countries that elect presidents the vast majority (86) use a version of a two-round system. "Electoral System for the President," Electoral System Design Database, The International Institute for Democracy and Electoral Assistance, accessed February 16, 2019, https://www.idea.int/data-tools/question-view/130359. See also Rachel Lewis, Rob Richie, and Jack Santucci, "Majority Rule in International Presidential Elections: The Dominant Role of Runoffs around the World," *FairVote*, June 6, 2006, 4. See also Farrell, *Electoral Systems*, 45 ("Two-round systems are common in many of those countries with directly elected presidents"). France used its two-round system for its most recent presidential election in which the centrist candidate, Emmanuel Macron, defeated the right-wing nationalist, Marine Le Pen, with two-thirds of the second-round vote. See Gregor Aisch, Matthew Bloch, K.K. Rebecca Lai, and Benoît Morenne, "How France Voted," *New York Times*, May 7, 2017.
8. Manuel Álvarez-Rivera, *Presidential and Legislative Elections in France*, 1974, http://electionresources.org/fr/president.php?election=1974.
9. Manuel Álvarez-Rivera, *Presidential and Legislative Elections in France*, 1981, http://electionresources.org/fr/president.php?election=1981.
10. Manuel Álvarez-Rivera, *Presidential and Legislative Elections in France*, 1995, http://electionresources.org/fr/president.php?election=1995.

11. See McLean, "Electoral Systems," in Fisher et al., eds., *The Routledge Handbook of Elections, Voting Behavior and Public Opinion*, chapter 17; Eric Maskin and Amartya Sen, *The Arrow Impossibility Theorem*, Kenneth J. Arrow Lecture Series (New York: Columbia University Press, 2014); Jonathan K. Hodge and Richard E. Klima, *The Mathematics of Voting and Elections: A Hands-On Approach*, Mathematical World 22 (Providence, RI: American Mathematical Society, 2005).

12. Jon Henley, "Le Pen Vote Shocks France," *Guardian*, April 22, 2002; "Macron and Le Pen Advance to the Second Round of the French Election," *Economist*, April 23, 2017.

13. See, e.g., Douglas J. Amy, *Behind the Ballot Box: A Citizen's Guide to Voting Systems* (Westport, CT: Praeger, 2000).

14. Steven J. Brams and Peter C. Fishburn, *Approval Voting*, 2nd ed. (New York: Springer, 2007).

15. Michel Balinski and Rida Laraki, *Majority Judgment: Measuring, Ranking, and Electing* (Cambridge, MA: MIT Press, 2011).

16. There is an organization devoted to the effort of adopting the National Popular Vote plan: https://www.nationalpopularvote.com.

17. See Robert W. Bennett, "Popular Election of the President without a Constitutional Amendment," *Green Bag* 4, no. 3, 241 (Spring 2001). For Bennett's extended analysis of his original idea, see Bennett, *Taming the Electoral College*, especially chapter 9. See also "National Popular Vote," Elections and Campaigns, National Conference of State Legislatures, May 31, 2019, http://www.ncsl.org/research/elections-and-campaigns/national-popular-vote.aspx.

18. Making Every Vote Count, accessed February 16, 2019, https://www.makingeveryvotecount.com/; Mark Pazniokas and Clarice Silber, "Connecticut Commits to National Popular Vote for President," *Connecticut Mirror*, May 5, 2018; Reid Wilson, "Colorado Governor Will Sign Bill Aimed at Bypassing Electoral College," *The Hill*, February 25, 2019.

19. See Norman R. Williams, "Why the National Popular Vote Compact Is Unconstitutional," *BYU Law Review* 2012, no. 5 (December 1, 2012), 1523–79. See also Derek T. Muller, "The Compact Clause and the National Popular Vote Interstate Compact," *Election Law Journal: Rules, Politics, and Policy* 6, no. 4 (November 2007), 372–93; Derek T. Muller, "More Thoughts on the Compact Clause and the National Popular Vote: A Response to Professor Hendricks," *Election Law Journal: Rules, Politics, and Policy* 7, no. 3 (September 2008), 227–32.

20. See Foley, *Ballot Battles*, chapter 5.

21. Nate Silver, "Why a Plan to Circumvent the Electoral College Is Probably Doomed," *FiveThirtyEight*, April 17, 2014, https://fivethirtyeight.com/features/why-a-plan-to-circumvent-the-electoral-college-is-probably-doomed/.

22. Ibid.
23. "Washington Post–ABC News Poll," *Washington Post*, February 8, 2019, https://www.washingtonpost.com/politics/polling/democrats-undecided-2020-candidates-trump-looks/2019/02/08/e862c28e-23b4-11e9-b5b4-1d18dfb7b084_page.html.
24. Vinod Bakthavachalam and Jake Fuentes, "The Impact of Close Races on Electoral College and Popular Vote Conflicts in US Presidential Elections," http://election.princeton.edu/wp-content/uploads/2017/10/bakthavachalam_fuentes17_MEVC_popular-electoral-split-model-8oct2017.pdf.
25. It would be possible to jettison the idea of a multistate compact, and instead have each state decide on its own to award all of its electoral votes to the winner of the national popular vote, rather than to the winner of the popular vote in that specific state. But that alternative is just as bad insofar as it permits an Electoral College victory based on a plurality, rather than majority, of the national popular vote.
26. Andrew Rudalevige, "The Electoral College Has Serious Problems. So Do Any Alternatives," *Washington Post* (Monkey Cage), November 15, 2016, https://www.washingtonpost.com/news/monkey-cage/wp/2016/11/15/should-the-u-s-keep-or-get-rid-of-the-electoral-college/; Gail Dryden and Barbara Klein, "National Popular Vote Compact Study, Opposing Arguments" (Chapel Hill: League of Women Voters, 2008), http://lwvodc.org/files/npvargument_con.pdf.
27. To be technical, if Wisconsin is the median state, then the median Wisconsin voter is more likely to be closer to the median national voter than is a 40th-percentile voter nationwide, who may control the national outcome in a plurality voting system if the remaining 60 percent of the voters nationwide are fractured among two or more alternatives. For some discussion of the relevant concepts underlying this point, see Stephen Ansolabhere and William Leblanc, "A Spatial Model of the Relationship between Seats and Votes," *Mathematical and Computer Modeling* 48 (2008), 1409, 1417–18.

   There remains the concern that the Electoral College suppresses turnout in those deeply blue or red states, like California or South Carolina, that are unlikely to be pivotal. This phenomenon, of course, is no different than voters living in deeply blue or red congressional districts, who believe their votes will not matter either for the outcome of their district, or for control of Congress itself, which will turn on the results in competitive districts. This phenomenon, therefore, is inherent in the Electoral College being a multimember body, rather than one unified national electorate. Unless it is replaced by a constitutional amendment, the turnout consequences of the Electoral College having this multimember character must be accepted as they are for any multimember representative assembly. On the civic responsibility of voters to exercise the franchise for the good of the community, regardless of their self-interested calculation of whether or how voting affects their personal well-being, see Edward B. Foley, "Voters as Fiduciaries," *University of Chicago Legal Forum* 6 (2015)), 153.

28.   The economists Sen and Maskin suggest that the National Popular Vote Interstate Compact proposal could be modified to incorporate ranked-choice voting:

> The compact is worded to elect the plurality winner. But if that were changed to electing the "national ranked-choice voting winner," that system would work as well for presidential races as it does at lower levels. (Eric Maskin and Amartya Sen, "A Better Electoral System in Maine," *New York Times*, June 10, 2018)

But this suggestion rests on a fundamental misunderstanding of how voting works in America. Unless *all 50* states one-by-one agree to adopt ranked-choice ballots for their presidential popular vote, it would be impossible to generate ranked-choice ballots for the entire national electorate. It would *not* suffice for the states that join the interstate compact to use ranked-choice ballots. Suppose, for example, that enough states to reach 270 adopt the compact, including an agreement to use ranked-choice ballots, but that Texas is not one of those states. In that situation, with Texas using conventional ballots that do not permit voters to rank preferences among candidates, there is no way for the compact to award their 270 electoral votes to the winner of the national popular vote—which necessarily must include the votes from Texas—based on a ranking of preferences.

Since the whole reason for pursuing the idea of an interstate compact was to avoid the necessity (and difficulty) of a constitutional amendment, an interstate compact that requires unanimous buy-in from all fifty states—as this suggestion would—is entirely self-defeating. It would be easier (although still hugely difficult) to adopt a constitutional amendment, which would require only three-fourths of the states, thereby forcing the remainder of states to comply with a constitutional amendment whether or not they supported it. Moreover, if the goal is to adopt ranked-choice ballots on a state-by-state basis (as this suggestion necessarily would entail), then the focus should be not to secure adoption in whatever states amount to 270 electoral votes, but instead to target pivotal states whose electoral votes, whatever their absolute number, might tip the Electoral College balance.

29.   See Sanford Levinson and John McGinnis, "Should We Dispense with the Electoral College?," *University of Pennsylvania Law Review PENNumbra* 156 (2007), 10–37; Akhil Reed Amar, "A Constitutional Accident Waiting to Happen," *Constitutional Commentary* 12 (1995), 143–46. For an important earlier version of this Burkean argument against

eliminating the Electoral College, see Alexander M. Bickel, *Reform and Continuity: The Electoral College, the Convention, and the Party System*, rev. ed. (New York: Harper & Row, 1971).

30. Winner-take-all is democratically legitimate when it is based on a majority, rather than plurality, of the popular vote. After all, many democratic elections must be winner-take-all: a statewide race for governor, for example, or US senator. There is no way to divvy up proportionally the votes cast for multiple candidates who are seeking to win a single seat, like the governorship of a state (or each statewide race for US senator). Therefore, to settle these inherently winner-take-all elections by majority rule is perfectly fair—as France, for example, does with its winner-take-all presidential elections. Consequently, given that the US presidency is ultimately a single chief executive position, like a governor or mayor, it is not unreasonable for a state legislature to decide that all of the state's electoral votes should be cast for the single presidential candidate whom that state's electorate prefers. But that legislative decision to adopt winner-take-all is reasonable if, but only if, the candidate who receives all of the state's electoral votes is actually the candidate preferred by a majority of the state's electorate.

31. 13 Annals of Cong., 491.

32. Iain McLean introduces his summary of the topic with this first sentence: "In general, there is no best electoral system, but some are worse than others." McLean, *Electoral Systems*, 207. In comparing plurality winner-take-all with the kind of two-round system that France uses for presidential elections, McLean sees the latter as clearly superior to the former, which he includes among "the very worst rules which purport to be democratic" (214). Although mere plurality winners might be appropriate for legislative elections, he continues, they are "highly problematic for elections to a single post" (214).

33. For a discussion of how a "rational voter" who most prefers a third-party candidate might strategically calculate how to cast a ballot in a simple plurality system, see Bennett, *Taming the Electoral College*, 70–71 (and sources relied upon therein).

34. There is some risk that requiring candidates to win a majority of a state's popular vote in order to receive all of a state's electoral votes would increase the possibility of a genuine three-way split in the Electoral College itself, causing no candidate to receive a majority of electoral votes, as might have occurred in 1912 (as explained in Chapter 5). But this small risk needs to be balanced against eliminating the more frequent problem of a third-party candidate distorting which of the two major-party candidates wins the Electoral College, as occurred in 1844, 1884, and 2000, and may have occurred in additional years (like 1992 and 2016). Moreover, if another presidential election actually were to go to the

House of Representatives as in 1824, the public's antipathy for a one-state-one-vote runoff procedure in the modern era might finally be the impetus for a constitutional amendment to jettison the Electoral College in favor of a national two-round system of the kind France has.

35. I would argue, for example, that some efforts by state laws and state officials to suffuse government proceedings with religiosity are inconsistent with the spirit of the constitutional prohibition against state establishment of a religion. But as the Supreme Court has long held, some practices of this nature are beyond the reach of judicial invalidation. See *Marsh v. Chambers*, 463 U.S. 783 (1983); see also *Town of Greece v. Galloway*, 134 S.Ct. 1811 (2014).

36. Capital punishment may seem "cruel and unusual," but it is harder to argue that it is always unconstitutional insofar as the Constitution explicitly authorizes it (permitting "life" to be taken with "due process"). Likewise, in the field of voting rights, one might think that the disenfranchisement of convicted felons—especially after their release from incarceration upon completion of their sentences—would be inconsistent with the constitutional principle of "one person, one vote" applicable to adult citizens generally. The same provision of the Constitution that is the source of the "one person, one vote" principle (the Fourteenth Amendment) also contains an explicit authorization that the states may deny the right to vote for "participation in rebellion, or other crime" without suffering adverse consequences. See *Richardson v. Ramirez*, 418 U.S. 24 (1974).

37. Professor Lawrence Lessig has been working with David Boies, among others, to pursue litigation along these lines: https://equalvotes.us/.

38. "We are aware of no successful challenge to plurality voting generally." *Dudum v. Arntz*, 640 F.3d 1098, 1111 n. 19 (9th Cir. 2011), citing *Edelstein v. City & Cnty. of S.F.*, 29 Cal.4th 164, 183, 126 Cal.Rptr.2d 727, 56 P.3d 1029 (Cal.2002) ("Plurality rule is not anathema to the federal or state Constitutions").

39. For more on this point, see Katherine Florey, "Losing Bargain: Why Winner-Take-All Vote Assignment Is the Electoral College's Least Defensible Feature," *Case Western Reserve Law Review* 68, no. 2 (2017), 317–96.

Chapter 9

1. Currently, states vary in their absentee voting rules. According to the National Conference of State Legislatures, 20 states require a statutorily authorized excuse in order to cast an absentee ballot, while 27 states do not, and three other states have moved to all-mail voting. "Absentee and Early Voting," Research, National Conference of State Legislatures, updated January 25, 2019, http://www.ncsl.org/research/elections-and-campaigns/absentee-and-early-voting.aspx.

2. See Eleanor Flexner and Ellen Fitzpatrick, *A Century of Struggle: The Woman's Rights Movement in the United States* (Cambridge, MA: Harvard University Press, 1996), 253; see also Jo Freeman, "The Rise of Political Women in the Election of 1912," https://www.jofreeman.com/polhistory/1912.htm.

3. Clinton also won Maine's at-large electoral votes with a plurality (see Table 6.3).

4. Caroline J. Tolbert and Kellen Gracey, "Changing How America Votes for President," in Donovan (ed.), *Changing How America Votes*, at 79–80.

5. Hong Min Park and Steven S. Smith, "Public Attitudes about Majority Rule and Minority Rights in Legislatures: A Survey Experiment," *American Panel Survey*, http://taps.wustl.edu/files/taps/imce/park_smith_nov_2013-1.pdf.

6. "First Inaugural Address," The Papers of Thomas Jefferson, Princeton University, 2006, https://jeffersonpapers.princeton.edu/selected-documents/first-inaugural-address-0.

7. For a fresh and nuanced account of Jefferson, see John B. Boles, *Jefferson: Architect of American Liberty* (New York: Basic Books, 2017).

8. Americans "hold in enormous reverence the main actors and episodes in their country's political history. Sometimes their reverence borders on ancestor worship": Anthony King, *The Founding Fathers v. the People* (Cambridge, MA: Harvard University Press, 2012), 130. "Recent crises have increased reverence for the founding fathers; this is nothing new": Richard B. Bernstein, *The Founding Fathers: A Very Short Introduction* (New York: Oxford University Press, 2015), 5. See also R. B. Bernstein, *The Founding Fathers Reconsidered* (New York: Oxford University Press, 2009) (offering a more realistic view of the Founders in light of the hagiographic lens through which most Americans traditionally have viewed them).

9. Historically, states have found it advantageous to award all their electoral votes to a single candidate, rather than dividing their electoral votes proportionally or by district. In this way, each state can maximize its clout in determining the election of the president. But while this self-interest on the part of states is a reason for winner-take-all, it does not specifically require *plurality* winner-take-all. Instead, each state can maximize its clout by giving all of its electoral votes to the majority, rather than plurality, winner of the popular vote. Thus, a state might be disinclined to choose a proportional or districting system as a way to comply with the majority-rule requirement—although Maine and Nebraska obviously have overcome this disincentive. In any event, notwithstanding the state-by-state competition to maximize Electoral College clout, there should be no disincentive to adopt instant runoff voting, or an actual runoff, as the means for determining which candidate wins all of the state's electoral votes.

10. "Initiative and Referendum States," National Conference of State Legislatures, http://www.ncsl.org/research/elections-and-campaigns/chart-of-the-initiative-states.aspx.

11. See Foley, *Ballot Battles*, chapter 11.

12. *Arizona State Legislature v. Arizona Independent Redistricting Commission*, 135 S.Ct. 2652 (2015).

13. Ibid. at 2687 (Roberts, C.J., dissenting). Unless otherwise noted, subsequent quotations from this opinion appear at the same page.

14. Derek Muller has determined that in 2016 Hillary Clinton would have prevailed if all states had used a proportional system to allocate their electoral votes, while Donald Trump would have won if all states had employed conditional winner-take-all. Muller, "Five Fictional Electoral College Outcomes from the 2016 Presidential Election," *Excess of Democracy* (blog), February 24, 2017, http://excessofdemocracy.com/blog/2017/2/five-fictional-electoral-college-outcomes-from-the-2016-presidential-election.

15. *Arizona State Legislature*, 135 S.Ct. at 2691.

16. In this respect, this new provision of the state constitution would be no different than a state constitutional provision requiring a secret ballot in any popular vote that determines the appointment of presidential electors. This limited constraint would still leave the state legislature with wide latitude in determining the nature of the popular vote to be used to appoint electors, including whether the popular vote would be statewide or in a districting system. But the constitutional provision would commit the state to the fundamental principle of the secret ballot insofar as popular voting is employed to appoint electors. A state is entitled to consider the principle of majority rule to be fundamental just as the principle of the secret ballot is so considered.

17. *Arizona State Legislature*, 135 S.Ct. at 2678.

18. My own preference is for the various forms of achieving majority rule consistent with winner-take-all (instant runoff voting, Condorcet voting, a two-round system), rather than the various forms of proportional allocation of electoral votes. The reason is that a state legislature controlled by one particular party might move to a form of proportional allocation, including a districting system, in order to undercut an opposing party's electoral strength—particularly if there is a fear that the opposing party might prevail in the popular vote statewide in the next presidential election. A version of this partisan ploy occurred in Michigan in 1892 (the so-called Miner law). See Keyssar, *Why Do We Still Have the Electoral College?* Similar partisan maneuvers have been threatened in various states, including Pennsylvania and Colorado, in recent years. See Kathy Kiely, "Colo. Initiative Could Make 2004 a Repeat of 2000: Presidential Race Could Face Chaos," *USA TODAY*, September 27,

2004; Associated Press, "Republicans Want to Change Laws on Electoral College Votes, After Presidential Losses," *Fox News*, January 19, 2013.

The advantage of instant runoff voting or other winner-take-all systems consistent with majority rule is that they are not susceptible to the same kind of partisan manipulation, since (for reasons already stated in the text) no party has an inherent advantage in winner-take-all being based on either a plurality or majority vote. If in an effort to comply with the majority-rule requirement partisan manipulation of the various proportionality options became a problem, it might become necessary to modify the reform so as to limit states to the winner-take-all methods of complying with majority rule. For now, however, I would not pursue the reform in this more limited way. The use of districting by Maine and Nebraska, while not as desirable, is not understood as an effort at partisan manipulation. If other states chose to emulate those two on a nonpartisan basis, this impulse to abandon plurality winner-take-all should not be condemned, but instead harnessed as part of the broader effort toward demand for compliance with the majority-rule requirement. At this initial stage of the reform effort, the majority-rule "tent" should be as broad as possible, with a presumption in favor of flexibility for states, so that the reform movement can gather momentum and maximize recruitment of supporters.

Conclusion

1. For an excellent and careful assessment of the current institutional conditions of American democracy, see Bruce E. Cain, *Democracy More or Less: America's Political Reform Quandary* (New York: Cambridge University Press, 2015). See also Benjamin I. Page and Martin Gilens, *Democracy in America?: What Has Gone Wrong and What We Can Do about It* (Chicago: University of Chicago Press, 2018). In 2014, the Bipartisan Policy Center's Commission on Political Reform delivered a report specifying achievable institutional adjustments to improve the operation of American democracy: "Governing in a Polarized America: A Bipartisan Blueprint to Strengthen Our Democracy," https://bipartisanpolicy.org/library/governing-polarized-america-bipartisan-blueprint-strengthen-our-democracy/.

2. Steven Levitsky and Daniel Ziblatt, *How Democracies Die* (New York: Crown, 2018); Madeleine Albright, *Fascism: A Warning* (New York: Harper, 2018); Cass R. Sunstein, *Can It Happen Here?: Authoritarianism in America* (New York: HarperCollins, 2018); Jon Meacham, *The Soul of America: The Battle for Our Better Angels* (New York: Random House, 2018).

3. For a prescient statement of this basic point about the need to focus on repairing the institutions of American democracy, see Richard H. Pildes, "Romanticizing Democracy, Political Fragmentation, and the Decline

of American Government," *Yale Law Journal* 124, no. 3 (December 2014), 804.

4. Gregory Wallace, "Negative Ads Dominate in Campaign's Final Days," *CNN*, November 8, 2016, https://www.cnn.com/2016/11/08/politics/negative-ads-hillary-clinton-donald-trump/index.html.

5. Abigail Geiger, "For Many Voters, It's Not Which Presidential Candidate They're For but Which They're Against," *Pew Research Center*, September 2, 2016, https://www.pewresearch.org/fact-tank/2016/09/02/for-many-voters-its-not-which-presidential-candidate-theyre-for-but-which-theyre-against/.

6. Matthew Dean Hindman and Bernard Tamas, "The U.S. Has More Third-Party Candidates Than It's Seen in a Century. Why?," *Washington Post* (Monkey Cage), August 31, 2016.

7. Howard Schultz, "A Third-Party Centrist Candidate Like Me Could Win the Presidency in 2020," *USA Today*, January 29, 2019; but see also Kevin Kruse and Julian Zelizer, "Historians: Howard Schultz Could Reelect Trump," *CNN Opinion*, January 29, 2019.

8. Steven Hill, *10 Steps to Repair American Democracy* (New York: Routledge, 2015), 97.

9. The subtitle of one recent article was "Momentum Is Building for a New Way of Settling Candidate-Packed Elections." Matt Vasilogambros, "Maine Tried a New Way of Voting. Will Other States Follow?" *Stateline* (Pew), June 26, 2018, https://www.huffpost.com/entry/maine-tried-a-new-way-of-voting-will-other-states_b_5b324003e4b0afb641b00903.

10. Maskin and Sen, "The Rules of the Game"; Maskin and Sen, "A Better Electoral System in Maine"; Maskin and Sen, "How Majority Rule Might Have Stopped Donald Trump."

11. 13 Annals of Cong. 719.

12. 13 Annals of Cong. 736.

INDEX

For the benefit of digital users, indexed terms that span two pages (e.g., 52–53) may, on occasion, appear on only one of those pages.